Web Pages That Suck

Learn Good Design by Looking at Bad Design

Web Pages That Suck

Learn Good Design by
Looking at Bad Design

Vincent Flanders

Michael Willis

SYBEX

San Francisco • Paris • Düsseldorf • Soest

Associate Publisher: Amy Romanoff

Contracts and Licensing Manager: Kristine Plachy

Acquisitions & Developmental Editor: Suzanne Rotondo

Editor: Lee Ann Pickrell

Technical Editor: Ann Navarro

Book Designers: Design Site, Tracy Dean, Sergie Loobkoff

Desktop Publisher: Design Site, Berkeley, CA.

Photographer: Hislop Photography, Bakersfield, CA. 93309

Production Coordinator: Eryn Osterhaus

Indexer: Ted Laux

Companion CD: Molly Sharp, Kate Kaminski, and John D. Wright

Cover Designer: Design Site, Jack Myers

SYBEX Inc., 1154 Marina Village Parkway, Alameda, CA 94501.

Library of Congress Card Number: 97-81077

ISBN: 0-7821-2187-X

Printed in Canada

10 9 8 7 6 5 4 3 2 1

After the 90-day period, you can obtain replacement media of identical format by sending us the defective disk, proof of purchase, and a check or money order for $10, payable to SYBEX.

Disclaimer

SYBEX makes no warranty or representation, either expressed or implied, with respect to the Software or its contents, quality, performance, merchantability, or fitness for a particular purpose. In no event will SYBEX, its distributors, or dealers be liable to you or any other party for direct, indirect, special, incidental, consequential, or other damages arising out of the use of or inability to use the Software or its contents even if advised of the possibility of such damage. In the event that the Software includes an online update feature, SYBEX further disclaims any obligation to provide this feature for any specific duration other than the initial posting.

The exclusion of implied warranties is not permitted by some states. Therefore, the above exclusion may not apply to you. This warranty provides you with specific legal rights; there may be other rights that you may have that vary from state to state. The pricing of the book with the Software by SYBEX reflects the allocation of risk and limitations on liability contained in this agreement of Terms and Conditions.

Shareware Distribution

This Software may contain various programs that are distributed as shareware. Copyright laws apply to both shareware and ordinary commercial software, and the copyright Owner(s) retains all rights. If you try a shareware program and continue using it, you are expected to register it. Individual programs differ on details of trial periods, registration, and payment. Please observe the requirements stated in appropriate files.

Copy Protection

The Software in whole or in part may or may not be copy-protected or encrypted. However, in all cases, reselling or redistributing these files without authorization is expressly forbidden except as specifically provided for by the Owner(s) therein.

To our families

VINCENT FLANDERS SAYS THANKS

I've got a lot of people to thank for making WebPagesThatSuck.com a success and for making this book possible. Indulge me.

The Biggest Thanks

Rob McCarthy—the coolest guy in America, who also happens to run the best company in America. Without him, I would never have had the opportunity of a lifetime.

My wife, Elizabeth, and my daughter, Michaela. Without them, there is no meaning.

Thanks for Making the Site a Success

Yahoo! If it wasn't for them, you wouldn't be holding this book.

Elizabeth Gardner, Vern Evans, and *Internet World* magazine (formerly *WebWeek* magazine). Elizabeth wrote a profile of WebPagesThatSuck.com and Vern took the great photos.

Brian Nelson of CNN's *Computer Connection* for a great profile and Cheryl Corrigan who told Brian about me.

PC Magazine for saying my site was one of the 100 most important sites on the Internet.

Everyone who wrote about the site.

Last, and by no means least, all the people who found the site valuable. Without the people…

Book Thank You's

Michael Willis. A great designer, a great talent, a great guy. It's a testimony to his patience that we're still friends after writing this book.

Brian Gill and Rick Ranucci from Studio B Productions, Inc. and John Reedy. They fought long and hard for a contract that would make me slightly happy. Much thanks to Mark L. Levine for writing *Negotiating a Book Contract*. Every author or prospective author needs a copy of this book. Trust me on this one.

Scott Hislop from Hislop Photography for the great photos and his flexibility.

Bill Nelson of Nelson Media for the great promotional video.

Lee Ann Pickrell from Sybex. It's a shame the world is losing such a great editor to management. She'll always remember the last book she edited.

Suzanne Rotondo from Sybex for having the foresight to see that my Web site would make a great book and for her marketing expertise.

Amy Romanoff from Sybex for all her marketing efforts in getting this book on the shelves.

Tracy Dean and the folks from Design Site for all the hours spent in putting together a book that's killer, not killed.

Ann Navarro for checking the book for technical accuracy.

Eryn Osterhaus for dotting the (*i*)s, crossing the (*t*)s, and for making sure the tenses were correct.

The Folks at Lightspeed Net and Lightspeed Software

Fun folks, all.

Brad White, Chris Payne, Ampy Buchholz, Robert Mann, Jason Lee, Margo Dickey, Michele Hatfield, Jennifer Blackwood, Chandra Terry, Dave Waterman, Geoff McAvoy, Jeff Jennings, Merleen Johnson, Evette Ogden, Joel Heinrichs, Bill Anthony, Madeline Trino, Rob Jones, Tom Ellenburg, Tom Punt, Bryan Burgin, Denise Wright, Brett Campbell, Brian Friesen, Steve Cabalka, Cynthia Massey, Glenn Nitayangkul, Grant Goldberg, Jim Murkland, Philip Linscott, Wing Mar, Brandi Evans, Danny Quebral, Deanne Hodges, Eric Schwocho, Janice Karns, Juan Morentin, Nick Acquaviva, Roy Byers, Scott Moses, Steve Hefner, Barbara Foster, Todd Barlow, Noel Stone, Bev Butler, Bret Trubey, Raina Kochevar, Ferrell Ramey, Vinita Ramnani, Michael Bennett, Lori Hansen, Tom Bailey, Karl Hamel, Bob Covey, Jack Johnson, Kim Bummerts, Jason Forsythe, James Tackett, Ryan Bond, Jennifer Jones, Frank Kruz, Robert Craighead, and anyone I may have left out.

Personal Thanks

Paula Minahan for giving me my first writing job.

Perriann Hodges for dedicating her book to me.

MICHAEL WILLIS SAYS THANKS

I wish to thank Vincent for giving me the incredible opportunity to help him with this book; my wife, Nancy, and kids, Bentley and Sophia, for overlooking many late nights; Chris "Weblord" Payne; Bentley Mooney for the encouragement; John Byrum, who owes me big for not making him a Weasel; my dive buddy, Brad Wheelan; my mom and dad, without them I wouldn't be here…literally; my sister Lisa and her husband Joe for their prayers; Suzanne Rotondo, Amy Romanoff, Lee Ann Pickrell, and Eryn Osterhaus from Sybex for their patience and hard work; Ann Navarro for making sure the book was technically accurate; Tracy Dean—one fab designer and now a friend as well; Bill Nelson for helping me with a video for the book; Scott Hislop, who shot the photos for this book; Paul Zehner for teaching me what LOL means; Jan Garone for her encouragement; Lightspeed Net for their support; Mary Tabor because someday she'll have to thank me in her book; my high-priced lawyer, F. Bentley Mooney Sr., for his good advice; and finally my crew, Jim Bennett and Shawna Grissom, for being the best help I've ever had!

109 FIXING YOUR TEXT PROBLEMS

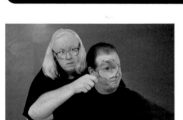

233 OTHER WAYS TO MARKET YOUR SITE

246 APPENDIX: ABOUT THE CD

WHY YOU NEED TO BUY THIS BOOK

There are two problems with most of the current crop of Web design books on the market.

The first problem is the books are boring as heck and operate on the following principle: "I'm going to show the little people how to make a cool page—I'll even give them the code and show them my magic Photoshop tricks, but they'll never be able to make a page that looks as good as mine." (Insane laughter of the designer/author fades.) What these designers neglect to mention is they often spend hours tweaking the pages, going through revision after revision. What you see is the final version.

If there are two people who aren't boring, it's me, Vincent Flanders, and my co-author, Michael Willis. Let's face it, anyone who will pose in an Elvis costume that's cut down to the navel can't be boring. If you're one of the millions of visitors to the original WebPagesThatSuck.com site (`http://www.webpagesthatsuck.com`), you'll know humor played an important part in its success. WebPagesThatSuck.com is about education and entertainment or, as we call it,

"edutainment." People learn best when they're enjoying the process and humor is a great tool toward this end. We're using humor in this book for the very same reason.

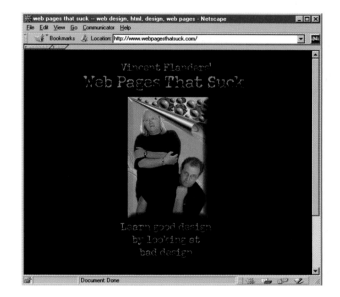

The original WebPagesThatSuck.com site

The second problem with most of the current crop of Web design books is the majority of Web book authors think the most important part of a Web site is design. The truth is, the most important part is actually using design to make money.

Design books get wrapped up in the concept of design-for-design's sake, forgetting what the goals of a Web site are—to build an image and/or to get visitors to write the owners of the site a check with lots of zeros in front of the decimal point.

Personal pages are the exception to this rule. However, it's still important to have a good looking home page because it's the world's first impression of who you are. The tips in this book are also extremely applicable to personal pages.

THE BACKGROUND OF THE ORIGINAL WEBPAGESTHATSUCK.COM SITE

WebPagesThatSuck.com is an award-winning site that teaches good design by looking at bad design. It has won some of the most important awards on the Internet and has made headlines elsewhere.

PC Magazine: The Top 100 Web Sites on the Internet

Yahoo!: Pick of the Week

c|net: Best of the Web

Original Cool Site of the Day

Profiled in *WebWeek* (now called *Internet World*)

Profiled on CNN's *Computer Connection* show

And there are many others.

Winning awards and being a favorite site weren't the original goals; I just wanted to get out of teaching a class in Web design. I was teaching HTML coding at Lightspeed Net in Bakersfield, California, and someone suggested I teach a class in Web design. Realizing I'd be stuck forever teaching the class, I decided it would be easier to put together a Web site on the topic. In my HTML classes, I would take time to show people sites with significant "deficiencies" and explain what the precise shortcomings were for each site. It became such a popular part of my class that I decided to "teach good design by showing bad design." Thus, WebPagesThatSuck.com was born.

I never expected such a positive response. Yahoo! was the first to notice my site, and when they made it the "Pick of the Week," well... the visitors haven't stopped coming. Later in the book, I'll talk about how important it is to get your site listed in Yahoo! Without Yahoo!, WebPagesThatSuck.com would have been a bad gas smell in the history of the Internet.

Both Michael and I had a great time writing this book. We hope you find it enjoyable and educational, too.

SPECIAL NOTE

In the book, we talk a lot about how important it is for Web sites to update their content. It's also important for them to periodically redesign their sites. I suspect by the time this book is printed some of the sites won't look the same. I hope they look better than they did when Michael and I visited.

ABOUT THE AUTHORS

Vincent Flanders most recently worked as Webmaster for Lightspeed Net, an Internet Service Provider in Bakersfield, California. Prior to that, he spent five years at Lightspeed Software as director of database marketing. From 1985–1990, he was associate editor of *Access to Wang* magazine, a vertical market computer publication covering Wang Labs. He currently lives in Bakersfield, California, with his wife, Elizabeth; their daughter, Michaela; and their dog, Polo.

Michael Willis is president and principal designer at Willis Design Studios. For the last 19 years, the focus of his studio has primarily been print design and advertising. In 1996, he landed a new client called Lightspeed Net, a local Internet provider. There he met a Webmaster by the name of Vincent Flanders. Vincent introduced Michael to HTML and Web design. Contrary to popular belief, he has never worked as a secret agent for the United States government. He lives in Bakersfield, California, with his wife, Nancy, and their two kids, Bentley and Sophia.

"I learned more from your site than *two* HTML books, *three* tutorials, and visits to hundreds of other sites. Once again, do not visit my site! Please—I don't want to be memorialized on WPTS."

"I've spent over 4 hours and a couple of six-packs (it's bloody hot down here in Australia) enjoying your efforts immensely. I've learned a lot, enjoyed a lot, woken up to some of my bad habits, but I've been kept glued to the monitor like no other site I have visited in the last couple of years. You deserve a bloody medal!"

"I am the Creative Director at a Michigan-based ISP with 15 years background in design and marketing. I discovered your site today and forwarded your URL to my entire sales staff and told them to 'read and learn.' Your site is a great resource. Keep up the good work."

"I stumbled across your site in the middle of making our personal home page, so there must be a God. We were in the middle of a royal battle about the coolness of black backgrounds. Anyhow your tutorial is not only educational but fun to read. Thank you!"

"I just wanted to compliment you on WebPagesThatSuck.com. I have to admit, when I first saw the URL, I thought it was probably just another obnoxious Web site written by yet another smart-ass teenager. I was very glad to see I was mistaken! You gave me a lot to think about in your lessons, and your use of frames was both elegant and logical."

"I am a fan/student of your 'tutorial.' In fact, I know many people here at Intel who subscribe to your site as the premiere teaching tool for intranet design."

Note: These really are verbatim quotes pulled from actual e-mail messages—trust us. We tossed the names to protect the innocent.

Flanders & Willis's Reality Check

If your site is for a business or nonprofit, you've got to make sure visitors have every opportunity to spend money at your site. This doesn't mean you have to be boring and conservative. It does mean you have to take extra care in designing your site so it looks professional, is easy to navigate, and gets marketed properly.

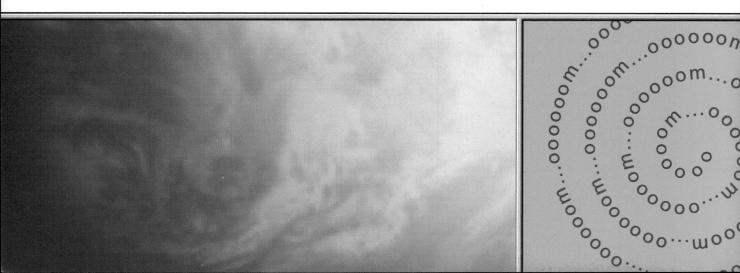

Ommmmmmm...   ...page

So, You Want to Create a Web Site

IN THIS CHAPTER

we're going to look at some of

the questions you need to answer

before creating your site and

we're going to provide you with

an outline of the issues you'll

face *when* creating your site.

In one of the old Mickey Rooney

and Judy Garland movies, there's

the famous line, "Hey kids, let's

put on a show!" Too many com-

panies utter the 90's version of

this line, "Hey kids, let's put

a Web site on the Internet!"

The company then hires someone

(or delegates the job to "the

person in Marketing who does

the brochures") to start coding their Web pages before they really think about why they're creating the site in the first place. They forget to ask themselves three very important questions: Why are we building a site? Who is our target audience? And what do they want from us? These—and other similar questions—should be answered before the first line of code is even written.

WHY ARE WE BUILDING THIS SITE?

Everyone who's contemplating putting a site on the Web needs to take the task of defining the reasons for their site's existence seriously. Quite often the reason is, "Because everyone else is on the Internet." Wrong answer. Yes, everybody should be on the Internet, but if that's the only reason you can come up with, then why don't you take the money you'll spend (in $1 bills) creating the site and throw it in into a crowd of people? At least you could get some amusement watching people fighting over your money—you sure as heck won't see people fighting to get into your Web site.

Sites Designed to Make Money

According to my own cumulative research, about 87 percent of the sites on the Web fall under this category, which includes corporations, small businesses, and many nonprofit organizations. Figure 1.1 shows a typical corporate site designed, ultimately, to sell goods.

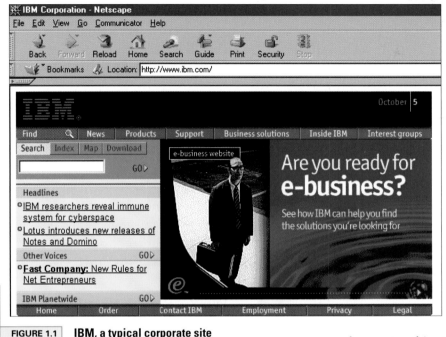

FIGURE 1.1   **IBM, a typical corporate site**
(`http://www.ibm.com/`)

We could give you some fancy reasons for creating a Web site, but there are only three simple reasons for creating a Web site:

1. To make money

2. To disseminate information or opinions

3. To stroke your little ego

It's important to know which of these three categories your site falls into so you can create an appropriate site. The last thing you need is an overly sophisticated 19th-generation Web site if you're trying to sell vitamins or if you're creating a site that lists everything you ever did up to age seven. Ask yourself what the purpose of your site is.

On the other end of the spectrum, Figure 1.2 shows a typical small business site. In fact, this site could be the archetype for sites that should be on the Internet. While the design leaves something to be desired, the Civil War Music Store serves a large vertical market where the customers are widely scattered throughout, not only the United States, but also the world. Vertical market sites are great because they understand the premise of selling on the Web—find a niche and market it to the world. The universe doesn't need another multilevel-marketing vitamin site.

Nonprofit organizations also want to make money from their sites. It's true they want to disseminate information, but they need money to survive and no self-respecting nonprofit organization turns down a contribution. (That's an over-generalization—there are some nonprofits that turn down contributions because they don't like the person or organization giving the money, but they're rare.) Figure 1.3 shows a typical nonprofit organization's site.

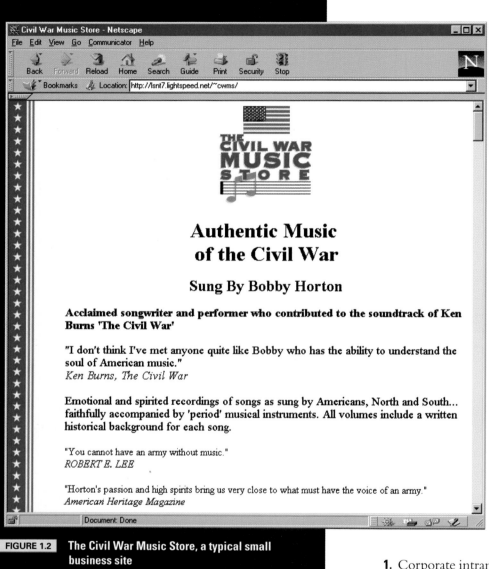

Authentic Music of the Civil War

Sung By Bobby Horton

Acclaimed songwriter and performer who contributed to the soundtrack of Ken Burns 'The Civil War'

"I don't think I've met anyone quite like Bobby who has the ability to understand the soul of American music."
Ken Burns, The Civil War

Emotional and spirited recordings of songs as sung by Americans, North and South... faithfully accompanied by 'period' musical instruments. All volumes include a written historical background for each song.

"You cannot have an army without music."
ROBERT E. LEE

"Horton's passion and high spirits bring us very close to what must have the voice of an army."
American Heritage Magazine

FIGURE 1.2 The Civil War Music Store, a typical small business site
(`http://Isnt7.lightspeed.net/~cwms/`)

Notice the first line of text at the bottom of the image. You'll see the word *Donations* to the right. Very nonpushy. While the site is more of an informational site, they also subtly remind their audience that they need money to operate.

Successful corporate, small business, and nonprofit sites share some common qualities:

> It's not about art.
> It's not about ego.
> It can and should be about information.
> It's mostly about money.

Sites Designed to Disseminate Information and/or Opinions

The three major types of sites that fall under this heading are:

1. Corporate intranets

2. Educational institutions

3. The hard-to-classify remainder—e-zines, some health sites, fan sites (could also come under ego-based sites), and the whole range of political/religious/social sites (any of these sites could also fall under the massage ego or make money categories).

Figure 1.4 shows an example of an informational site.

On the Web, it's often hard to differentiate among information, opinion, and outright lies. Don't fall for the line, "If it's on the Web, it must be true." To find out how gullible you are to Internet lies, take the online test offered by c | net at `http://www.cnet.com/Content/Features/Dlife/Truth/ss01.html`.

Sites created by fans of a rock band are often more interesting than the "official" sites. Fan sites are sincere and offer lots of information and links to other sites. The "official" sites generally offer the corporate viewpoint, but some offer extra features like unrecorded songs and the opportunity to win posters, tickets to concerts, and so on, which can't be offered by fan sites. On the flip side, official sites are almost always better designed. In fact, official band sites are often among the better designed sites on the Internet because a successful band can afford to hire the best talent.

Figure 1.5 shows the home page to a fan site devoted to the rock group Counting Crows, and Figure 1.6 shows the home page to the official Counting Crows Web site.

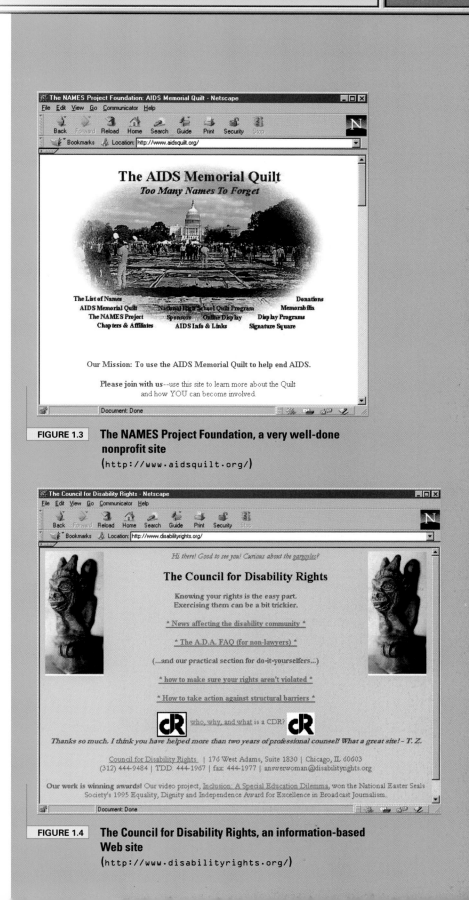

FIGURE 1.3 **The NAMES Project Foundation, a very well-done nonprofit site**
(`http://www.aidsquilt.org/`)

FIGURE 1.4 **The Council for Disability Rights, an information-based Web site**
(`http://www.disabilityrights.org/`)

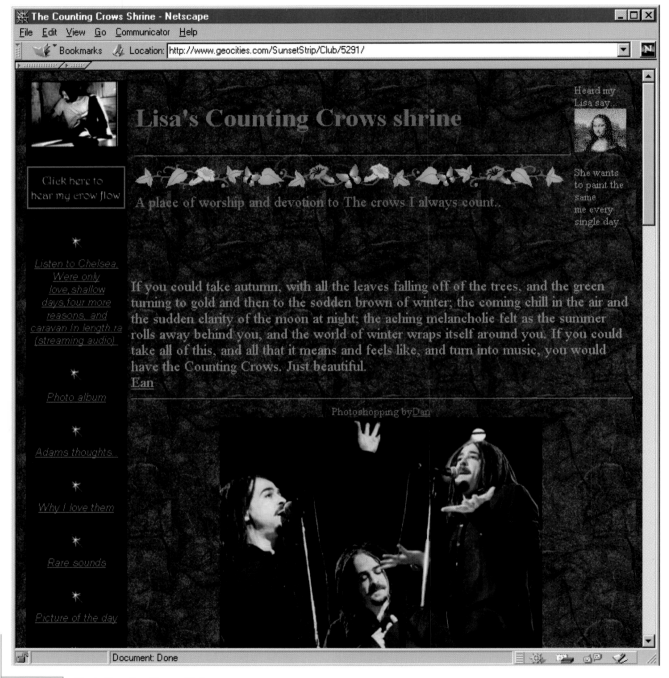

Lisa's Counting Crows Shrine
(http://www.geocities.com/SunsetStrip/Club/5291/)

Successful informational/opinion sites share certain qualities:

> It's not about art.
>
> It's not about ego
> (for informational sites).
>
> It's often about ego
> (for opinion sites).
>
> It's mostly about information.
>
> It's generally not about money.

Sites Designed to Stroke Your Little Ego

Well, it isn't too hard to figure out which types of sites qualify for this category—almost every personal page ever created and many opinion sites. Art, music, fan, and e-zine sites may fall under this category. Quite simply, if a site is not receiving advertising revenue or selling products, then there's a very good chance it's an ego site.

Figure 1.7 is an archetype ego site—a personal Web page.

Even sticking my own personal page in this book is just another stroke to my ego. Actually, the truth is I'm taking the easy way out. If there's one thing I've learned from WebPagesThatSuck.com, it's that people take their personal sites very, very seriously. You can tell someone their dog is ugly, their children are ugly—you can even tell them their spouse is ugly—but don't you dare tell them their personal Web page is ugly.

FIGURE 1.6   **The official Counting Crows Web site**
(`http://www.countingcrows.com/`)

Ego-based sites generally share these qualities:

> It can be about art.
>
> It can be about information.
>
> It's *always* about ego.
>
> It would like to be about money.

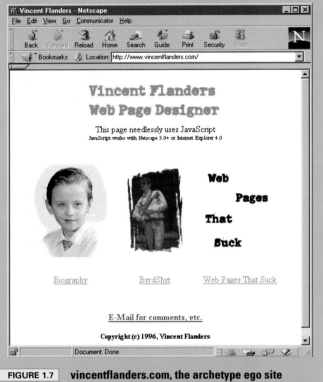

FIGURE 1.7   **vincentflanders.com, the archetype ego site**
(http://www.vincentflanders.com/)

How Does the Category Affect the Design?

If your site is a business or nonprofit site, you've got to make sure the visitor has every opportunity to spend money at your site. This doesn't mean you have to have a boring, conservative site. It does mean you have to take extra care in designing your site so it looks professional, is easy to navigate (we'll talk about navigation in Chapter 2), and marketed properly (we'll cover marketing in Chapters 9–11).

If your site is an informational or opinion site, you need to follow the graphics and text guidelines we'll cover in Chapters 4 and 5. An opinion site has more leeway because the expectation is that it won't follow "the rules" as closely as a business site. An informational site, however, has to focus on content delivery as much as possible. One of the most vexing problems facing an informational site is the glut of information already available—it's critical that these types of sites are organized so they are easy to navigate and aren't a mile long.

If your site is an ego site, then hey, you can use pretty much any design trick you want on your pages—streaming video, streaming sound, Java applets, huge graphics, and on and on. Of course, no one will visit your site because it will be ugly, take too long to load, and won't have any content. But other than that...

The key feature of any site should be restraint. Use just the necessary elements. Web design is a lot like the security industry; both of them rely only on what's "necessary." Rather than focusing on the technology (which is easier), the Web page designer has to focus on the target audience. The target audience should drive virtually every aspect of the site.

WHO IS OUR TARGET AUDIENCE?

Each of the three types of Web sites discussed in the first part of the chapter has more than one potential audience. For instance, a corporate site, such as the IBM site shown in Figure 1.1, might have current customers, investors, and recent college graduates looking for jobs visiting their site, while a non-profit organization, such as the Names Project Foundation site shown in Figure 1.3, might have potential donors, AIDs patients, and their families and friends visiting their site. You should know precisely who you are trying to lure to your site. And if you don't know who your audience is, neither will anybody else. Let's look at some of the potential audiences for business sites, nonprofit sites, informational sites, opinion sites, and ego sites.

Audiences for Business Sites

Some of the audiences for business sites include current customers, potential customers, investors, and the sales force, all of whom have different needs.

Current customers Provide any critical information about your product or service in a way that's easily accessible to your current clientele, who may be double-checking facts, verifying an order, or placing a new order.

Potential Customers Separate them into subgroups by level of interest or how they got to your site. Did they come from a banner ad on another site? Did they arrive from a search engine? Did they read a written brochure? You could have separate entrance pages for each of these arrival methods. For example, a potential customer who has read a brochure and accessed your site might go to a page detailing the product described in the brochure.

You want to convince these people to buy your product or service, so you can't afford to overload them with information. Every element of your site's design should tell your customer why they should buy your product. You need clear, functional navigational tools to make ordering as easy as possible. Including a search facility in your site is an excellent idea—everyone on the Web can attest to how frustrating it is to go to a site and *not* be able to find what you are looking for. Figure 1.8 shows you the Ziff-Davis site; the search engine button is toward the top of the of the page.

Web Page Design Is Like the Security Industry

In the security industry, the operative phrase is "Need to Know." Does Mr. X need to know that we're transporting $10,000 in cash to our branch office every day? If he doesn't, then he doesn't find out. It should be the same way with Web design; except the phrase should be altered slightly to "Need to Have." Does your page need this animated GIF? Does it need streaming video? If it does—because it will generate more income or some other tangible benefit—then it's your moral obligation to include it on the page.

It's easy to get sucked up into the Web design frenzy. Magazines talk about the latest technologies as if they were the second coming of Jesus. Well, they're not. A well-respected designer sent me the following e-mail about the design frenzy:

"I was recently at a trendy Web design party and someone came running up to me and said, 'Did you hear? They came out with streaming Shockwave and nobody knows it! Better learn it before everyone else does!' The latest technology has become a commodity in this town. People never ask if they should use it; they just do. They follow the trend, blindfolded, to the cutting edge.

Designers are not willing to embrace the Web as a design challenge; they have been fighting the basic tech-nology from the beginning, trying to make it like all desktop-publishing programs rolled up into one. Very few sites I've seen have bothered to get truly into content design or focus on what can been done with basic HTML. We are used to Photoshop and Quark, and we went to art school, not Stanford, so creating pretentious sites is in our blood."

FIGURE 1.8 The Ziff-Davis Find It search button is easy to find.

Figure 1.10 shows a much-improved Herbal.com page where you can now *order* the herbal products the site is pushing.

Investors If you're a public company, you're going to need to provide financial information to your stock-holders, potential stock-holders, and government regulatory bodies. (If my memory serves me correctly, there was at least one stock that was temporarily prevented from trading because a government agency didn't like some of the material that appeared on the company's Web site.) Every element of your design needs to convince people that you're the company in which they want to invest. However, you also have to keep within your government's regulatory guidelines. The guidelines may vary by country, but it's probably safe to say that you can't make promises you can't keep.

Herbal.com, a site I created awhile back, violates this principle—how stupid can I get? As Figure 1.9 demonstrates, here's a nice looking site that seems to have information to offer and products to sell; however, the designer and owner (in this case, me) forgot to put in a link so people can order products!

Nothing sucks more on a business site than forgetting to provide a way for customers to order products.

Your Sales Force These folks, which include distributors and agents as well, are a very important target market. However, you may want to put sales information on an intranet or a secure server. The information contained on your site should keep your sales force, dealers, and agents up to date with the latest price changes, policy changes, sales incentives, and so on. Look at every element of your design and ask if it will help them sell the product.

Audiences for Nonprofit Sites

Audiences for nonprofit sites include activists, information-seekers, and donors. People who visit a nonprofit's site are presumably interested in the organization's cause. As mentioned earlier, these organizations still need money to exist, even though they are nonprofits. The audience wants to learn how the nonprofit organization operates, who it serves, what it has accomplished, and what it believes in. The site's agenda needs to include disseminating this type of information *and* gathering funds. When talking to visitors at a nonprofit site, you want to gather them into your fold and encourage them to open their pocketbooks. Be sure every element of your site's design educates visitors about what you're trying to do and makes it easy for them to support you financially.

Audiences for Informational Sites

Audiences for informational sites generally fall into two categories: internal (those working on an intranet) and external (those accessing a public Web site).

For Intranets Employees and other people with access need to have available to them large quantities of information that's only available internally. These sites are very complicated and have needs, such as security, that we can't cover in this book, but are

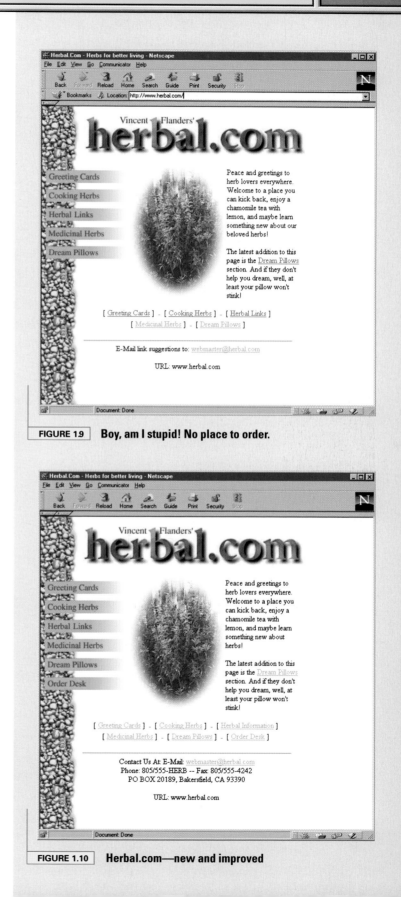

FIGURE 1.9   **Boy, am I stupid! No place to order.**

FIGURE 1.10   **Herbal.com—new and improved**

well-worth understanding before you begin your intranet. Additionally, corporate intranets have access to higher bandwidth than the average Internet user is accustomed to, which brings up issues like audio, video, VRML (Virtual Reality Markup Language), and database access. While that's far beyond the scope of this book, the main point still remains—design your intranet to meet the needs of your audience. If VRML and Shockwave help drive important issues home for your audience, by all means use them. Otherwise, practice restraint—even with this increased bandwidth. (If you want to learn more about setting up an intranet, see *Mastering Intranets: The Windows 95/NT Edition* by Pat Coleman and Peter Dyson.)

Students, Information Seekers, and the Curious

This crowd wants information. Because you have so much information to share and there are so many other sites vying for this group's attention, the most important thing for you to concentrate on is organizing your information in the best possible way.

It really sucks when sites with great information are set up so poorly that nobody wants to bother trying to navigate them.

Audiences for Opinion Sites

The audience for opinion sites is, quite simply, anyone who holds an opinion for or against a person or issue. Here in the United States, we have a radio personality named Rush Limbaugh, who is extremely popular with that segment of our population who espouses conservative politics. As you would imagine, there are several sites devoted to Mr. Limbaugh.

Ironically, he doesn't seem to have his own official Web site (as of the date this book is being written). Figure 1.11 shows a site set up in his honor.

Of course, what makes the Web so great is that for every action there's a reaction. A number of sites don't think highly of Mr. Limbaugh's viewpoints. Figure 1.12 shows one of these sites.

Audiences for Ego Sites

The audience for personal pages is basically only one person—the creator of the site (and possibly their family and more tolerant friends), so there are no real restrictions on presentation or content. Although "anything goes" on personal pages, you have to remember that a Web page is the first impression you're giving the world about yourself. If you've got a badly designed personal page, people are going to have a bad impression of you and that's something most people don't want.

To my knowledge, I only critique one personal page in the whole book (in Chapter 7, "The Bleeding Edge"), and I only use that page because it belongs to one of the world's richest men. Even if he got depressed because I didn't like his page (like he cares), he could just get in a plane and fly to Tahiti to work out his angst. In fact, he could probably *buy* Tahiti.

Okay, you've figured out why you're creating a site and who your target audience is. Let's move on to the next pressing question.

WHAT IS OUR AUDIENCE LOOKING FOR IN US?

I'm always amazed that so many businesses spend a great deal of time and money trying to figure out who the target audience is but ignore the obvious question: What is our target audience looking for in us? The answer is simple.

People want to do business with people they believe to be professional.

Many companies and organizations put mission statements on their sites to try to promote the fact that they're professional. After all, big corporations like Johnson & Johnson have mission statements (J&J has a credo that has almost attained legendary status). They want their visitors to feel they're doing business with good people—not a bunch of Internet hoodlums, so they create what Michael and I call a "sincere site." The problem is it's dangerously easy to go overboard on the sincerity and end up creating the opposite effect—a site that seems insincere. For our feelings about mission statements and their purpose, see the sidebar "Mission Statements" at the end of this chapter.

If we buy the premise that our target audience wants to deal with professionals, how do we go about creating such a site? Well, that's what the rest of the book is about. We'll start off by talking about site design and navigation. After all, if visitors can't easily navigate around your site, they probably won't have any difficulty finding the Back button.

TOO COOL

A GOOD MISSION STATEMENT

One of the visitors to WebPages ThatSuck.com sent Vincent a great story about mission statements. Here's what he said:

"When I lived in Japan for a year I visited the Suzuki factory to buy my motorbike. They had an enormous banner with Japanese symbols draped over the end of the shop floor. I asked the salesman what it meant. With a chuckle he told me, 'Smash Yamaha.' Now that's a mission statement."

We agree. You can stick that kind of mission statement on your home page—unless it would bring up anti-trust considerations.

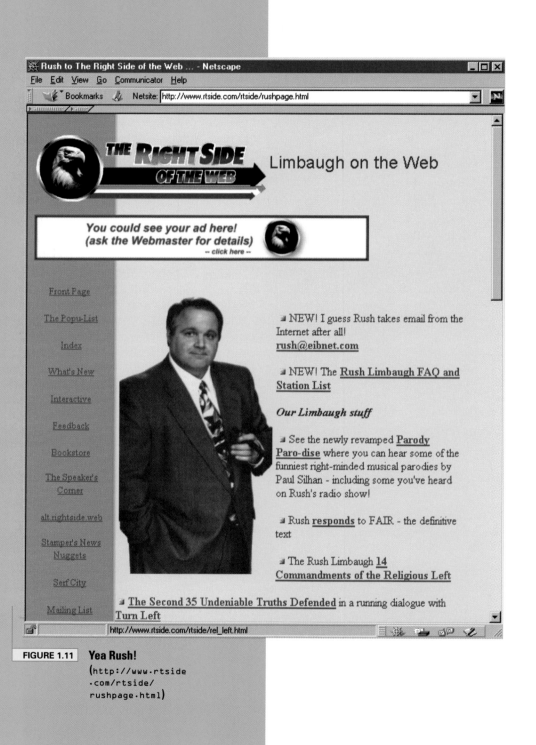

FIGURE 1.11 **Yea Rush!**
(http://www.rtside
.com/rtside/
rushpage.html)

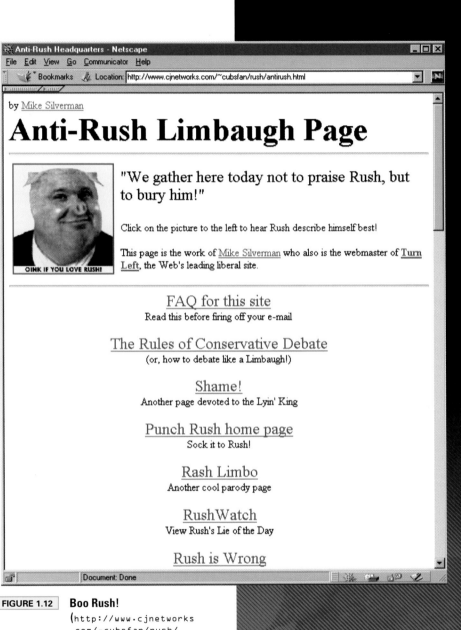

FIGURE 1.12   **Boo Rush!**
(http://www.cjnetworks
.com/~cubsfan/rush/
antirush.html)

OH NO

MISSION STATEMENTS

For the record, Michael and I hate mission statements with a passion—particularly when they show up on the home page of the site as in the example shown here.

Mission statements should be abolished or hidden away in some dark corner of your Web site. Every mission statement ever written can be summarized in the four words uttered by the great American philosopher, Chris Rock: "All babies must eat." Well, of course, they've got to eat—isn't that obvious? It's the same situation in the American Academy of gymnastics' mission statement—they're stating the obvious: "[We] seek to establish the highest-quality gymnastics program possible..." Of course they want the highest-quality gymnastics program possible. Stating the obvious is one of the major problems with mission statements.

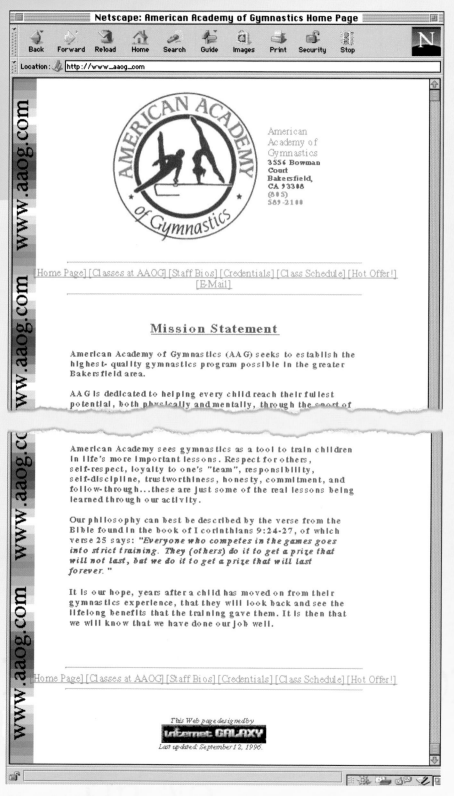

A long-winded mission statement

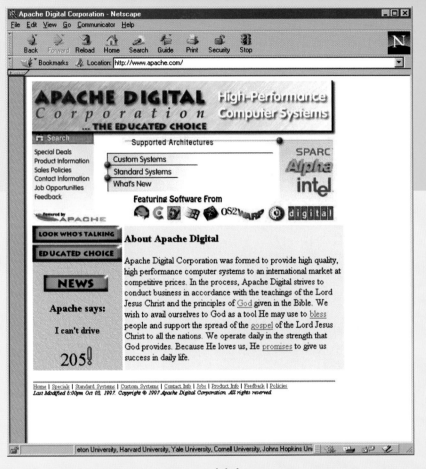

Religious mission statement on a commercial site

If you must have a mission statement (your boss insists), make it a link from your home page so visitors can decide whether or not they want to read it. It's the late 90s. People are cynical. Don't put your mission statement on your home page.

An even more objectionable type of mission statement appears on Apache Digital's site.

Normally, we wouldn't discuss this site with a 10-foot microphone. Religion is a touchy subject under the best of circumstances because it is a personal issue. I'm in an even more precarious situation given my personal history with religious authority http://www .vincentflanders.com/suspend.htm, which you might have stumbled across if you've visited WebPagesThatSuck.com. If it weren't for the fact that several people have e-mailed me about this site and for the fact that there are some serious design problems, I would have let this site go gently into that good night.

The problem with this type of mission statement is simple—there's going to be a group, a rather large group of people, who are turned off by this profession of faith. I just saw a story about Lou Gerstner, the head of IBM, that mentioned he went to Catholic mass every week. He downplayed the whole issue by saying it was personal. Now that's the way to

handle the topic. I think the public would be turned off and might take their business elsewhere if Mr. Gerstner started issuing public manifestos about religion.

As if the religious connotations aren't bad enough, this site will offend anyone who isn't a Christian (I think). If you click the God link, you'll get their definition of God (the fact that they even have such a definition is mind-boggling):

"GOD: Elohim, plural of Eloah, Deity; God, the Divine One. The Supreme God; the Creator, Elohim indicates the relation of God to man as Creator, and is in contrast with Jehovah which indicates Him in covenant relationship with creation."

I'm not a theologian, but I think it's fair to assume that this could piss off Jewish, Muslim, Buddhist, Hindu, Sikh, and so on, populations here in the United States, and I'm sure international visitors would be equally offended.

But, once again, it's a personal issue, and if these folks understand they might be turning off customers—or if a public profession of faith is more important than money—fine. But I feel they've taken a bad concept and made it worse: "All babies must eat and go to heaven."

Flanders & Willis's Reality Check

If your home page fails to entice because the images are too large, you're using sound files for no reason, the page takes forever to download, there's offensive material, the text isn't readable, and so on—then your visitors will hit the Back button faster than a politician changes position on the issues.

CHAPTER 2

Site Design and Navigation

IN THIS CHAPTER

you'll build upon some of the

"big picture" issues covered in

the last chapter. Here, you'll look

at two of the nitty-gritty issues

facing a designer when creating

an overall design for a Web site:

■ Designing a home page that

acts as an effective site guide

■ Designing a site that's easy

to navigate

To learn about these design issues, you'll hear about some navigational tools; then you'll look at some sites that suck and some that don't. From there, we'll move on to organizing your own site by creating storyboards. By the time you're through, you'll be able to tell a poorly designed site from an exceptionally well-designed one.

Okay, now that you know where I'm going in this chapter (a principal of good design), let's start navigating our way through this chapter by taking a look at the home page for Cigar Aficionado Magazine, shown in Figure 2.1.

To really understand what's good about this page and why it's an effective site design, I need to first talk about the concept of the home, main topic, and subsidiary pages, and the importance of making your site easy to navigate. Figure 2.2 shows how the pages on a Web site should be organized. The organization is quite simply a hierarchy with the most important page (the home page) on top and subsidiary pages below.

Why Does This Page Suck?

It doesn't! The bad boys of Web design just threw you a curve ball.

FIGURE 2.1 **Cigar Aficionado magazine**
(http://www.cigaraficionado.com/)

You can learn a lot about site design by looking at Cigar Aficionado's site, which you'll do later in the chapter. To start off though, here are some of the tips you can pick up from this site:

1. The designer did not sit down and start coding first thing. The designer sat down and figured out what important elements should go on the home page; then they figured out what went on the main topic pages and each subsidiary page. In other words, they scoped out the "big picture."

2. The designer put the most important elements on the first screen of the home page and the other main subsidiary pages.

3. The designer created significant content—a topic covered in Chapter 3.

4. The designer has a sense of aesthetics—the graphics and layout are first rate. No cheap clip art was used, and the *single*—repeat *single*—animated GIF (the animated cigar) is very high quality.

5. Most important, the designer created a home page that presents a professional image to the world. As soon as you go to the page, you know exactly what to expect and you know how to find the information you want.

THE HOME PAGE AS A SITE GUIDE

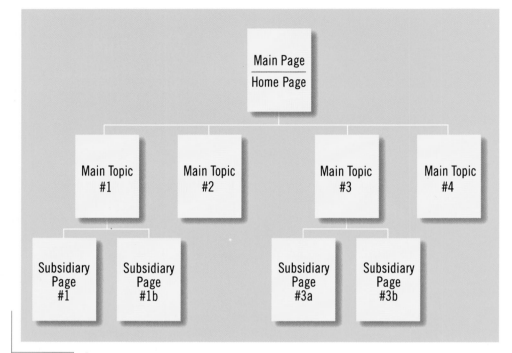

FIGURE 2.2 **Organization of a Web site**

Quite simply, the home page (or, as it's also referred to, the *front page*) is the gateway to your site. It's the road map, the index, the table of contents that tells visitors where to find the important information they need to make their stay at your site enjoyable and profitable.

A good analogy is that the home page of a Web site is similar to the cover of a newsstand magazine. You may not be aware of this fact, but the return rates to the magazine publisher for newsstand magazines are quite high. Unlike a magazine subscription, which is purchased long in advance, a newsstand magazine has a limited period of time to entice the general public to buy it off the rack. The most important factors that influence sales are the cover and the subject matter. The same is true for your Web site.

The home page is the most important page on your site because it's generally a visitor's first impression of your company or organization. If your home page looks professional, ethical, artistic, appears to have interesting content, and doesn't have any elements that would chase a customer away, then there's a good chance your visitors will stay. Hopefully, they'll purchase something from you. If your home page fails to entice because the images are too large, you're using sound files for no reason, the page takes forever to

The Web pages on a site are broken down into three main groupings:

1. Home page

2. Main topic pages

3. Subsidiary pages

This organizational structure, which is simplified to its lowest elements, forms the foundation of a Web site. However, the most important navigational tool in the developer's arsenal is the home page because it is, generally, the first page seen by your visitors.

download, there's offensive material, the text can't be read, and so on, and so on—then your visitors will hit the Back button faster than a politician changes position on the issues.

There are three things a home page should convey to the visitor:

1. The site's purpose—the who, what, when, where, and why

2. What kind of content is contained in the site

3. How to find that content

The Main Topic Page

This is a page that the home page links to. For example, Figure 2.3 shows the home page for Lotus Development Corporation (`http://www.lotus.com/`). From this home page, you can link to the following main topic pages:

Downloads	Purchasing	Services
Support	Developers	Corporate
Events	Discussions	Solutions
Products	Partners	Media Catalog

This is a good home page because it is clear where to go from here.

The Subsidiary Page

Any page other than a home or main topic page is a subsidiary page. Generally, these pages are subsets of a main topic page. For example, a page on the Lotusphere 98 trade show (see Figure 2.4) is a subsidiary page to the Partners main topic page.

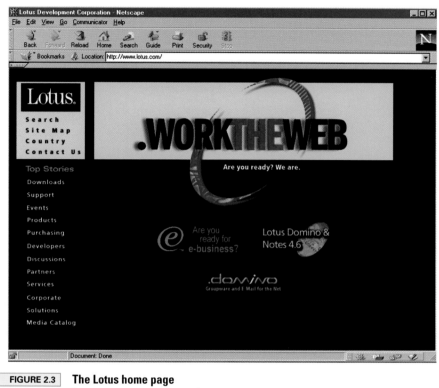

FIGURE 2.3 **The Lotus home page**
(`http://www.lotus.com/`)

From any subsidiary page, you want your visitors to be able to go to the home page so they can find out about your company and its products. You also want them to be able to go to any of the other main topic pages—especially a page where they can buy your products. Remember, you *always* need to make it easy for them to order.

For that reason, all your pages—home, main topic, and subsidiary pages—need to have links to the main topic pages on your site. In addition, you must include a link to the home page on all your main topic and subsidiary pages. Why?

Because you never know how a visitor arrives at your site.

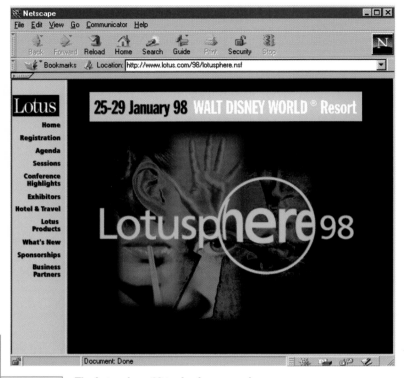

FIGURE 2.4 **The Lotusphere 98 trade show page is a subsidiary page.**

NAVIGATING THROUGH YOUR SITE

In navigating a Web site, you need to consider several factors:

> The first screen
>
> Navigational tools—graphics, text, frames
>
> Consistency

The First Screen—The Top's Gotta Pop or They're Not Gonna Stop

Don't let the cuteness of this little refrain sidetrack you from its important message. The first screen your visitor sees is the first impression they will have of your site. And keep in mind the first screen they see might *not* be the first screen of your home page. If your first screen sucks, they won't stop, and if they don't stop, they're not going to shop. Congratulations. You've spent a lot of money on a Web site where very few people get past the first page.

As I said in Chapter 1, you've got to put your most important informational elements in the first screen because some visitors have no more than four inches of screen real estate. Also, limit your home page to no more than two or three screens worth of material because people don't like to scroll forever and ever. Remember this phrase; make it your mantra:

Display important information prominently.

If it isn't important, then it shouldn't be on the home page. It probably shouldn't be on *any* page, but you have a little more leeway with subsidiary pages because you've got a little more space to maneuver.

Why is the first screen people see at a Web site sometimes a page other than the home page? Simple. Links on other pages, articles in magazines, a friend's suggestion or, most commonly, search engines. For example, a visitor might have conducted a search for the phrase **"Lotus Partners"** and ended up at http://www.lotus.com/partners.nsf, where they clicked the link and went to the page shown in Figure 2.4. Unless there's enough information on the Lotusphere 98 page, this visitor has no knowledge that the home page, shown in Figure 2.3, even exists or that Lotus has information on Lotus Products on another page. That information comes in the form of navigational links—graphic-, text-, or frame-based.

Navigational Tools—Graphics, Text, Frames

There are three main navigational tools, which you can use singly or in combination:

- Navigational Graphics
- Text
- Frames

Navigational Graphics There are two categories of navigational graphics:

- Buttons
- Imagemaps

A button is any graphic that's a link. Any time someone clicks a button, they should be taken to another page. Buttons make powerful navigational tools. Use them carefully. When you're using graphics, for example, make sure people don't confuse them with links. Figure 2.5 shows an image that looks like it should be a button, but it isn't.

An imagemap is an image that is treated by the browser as a navigational tool. When visitors click the imagemap, they are taken to a new page. Make sure it's clear to your visitors where they are going when they click on on a particular location on an imagemap.

It's the reverse of a magic trick. In a magic trick, you show the audience your right hand and perform the trick with your left. In Web design, you tell them where you're going first—and then go there.

Text Text links make excellent navigational tools, although you can go a little overboard, as Figure 2.6 indicates. Even though the folks here are a little link happy, you've got to love them for creating a page that totals only 15.8K in size. You won't have to wait days for this page to load.

Text links are very, very important; they are even more important on pages that use graphics and imagemaps as links.

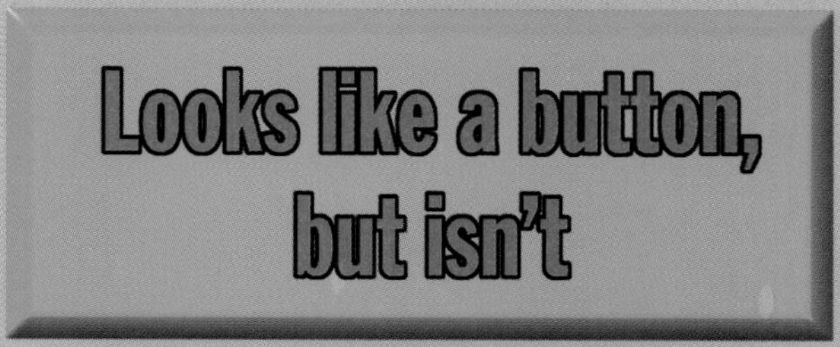

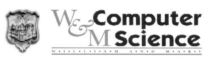

FIGURE 2.5 Confusing button

W&M Computer Science
WILLIAM AND MARY

Department Overview
Where we are located, our administration, the College we are part of, the Library, and our local community.

Programs
We offer B.A. and B.S. degrees in computer science as well as two graduate degrees: the M.S. and the Ph.D. Our graduate students can also pursue an M.S. with a specialization in Computational Operations Research or a M.S. or Ph.D. with a specialization in Computational Science.

People
We have 15 faculty members, 3 staff, many graduate students and undergraduate concentrators. We are always happy to hear from our former students.

Reaching us
Where to send E-mail or regular mail, call us, or fax us. How to navigate to Williamsburg or through the campus.

What's going on
Upcoming events. We have speakers, student presentations, a prospective BitSwap newsletter, and the puzzler. Get the latest on ACM local chapter and graduate student CSGSA events. Read selected newsgroups. Learn about undergraduate research opportunities.

Teaching
We teach these undergraduate and graduate courses, based on this long-range schedule. Online material is available for selected courses.

Computing Facilities
Check out our system info and UNIX Lab Manual. We have seven labs in McGlothlin-Street Hall. The entire College is networked and maintains computers labs. We expect users to follow these sensible rules.

Table of contents

External web sites of interest

Last updated: September 1, 1997. Report suggestions and problems to: webmaster@cs.wm.edu

Home | Department | Programs | People | Reaching us | What's going on | Teaching | Facilities | Navigating

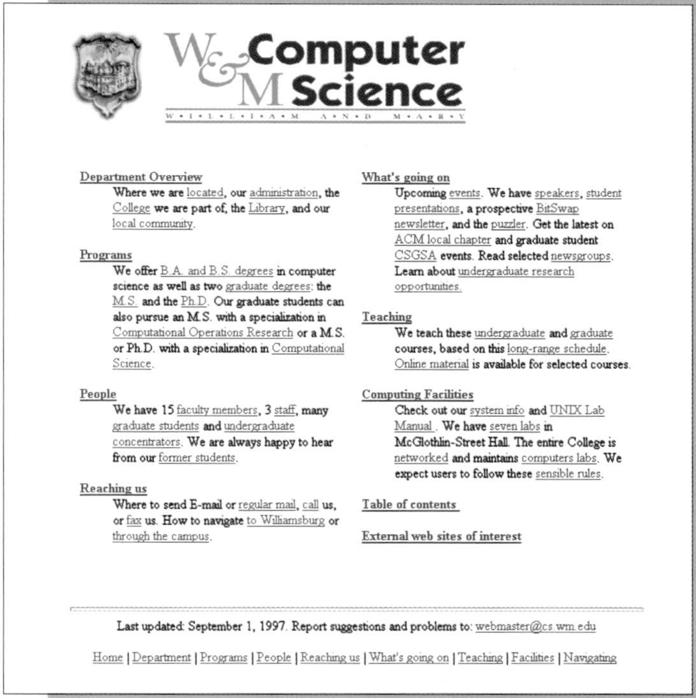

FIGURE 2.6 William and Mary Computer Science (http://cs.wm.edu/)

FIGURE 2.7   **Southwest Airlines**
(`http://www.iflyswa.com/`)

If you're using graphics or imagemaps as links, you must also have corresponding text links.

There are two reasons for this statement. The first is if you're being a bad girl or boy and the graphics on your page total more than 35K, the text will show up before the images and your visitors can happily click a text link and be on their merry way before the image

loads. The second reason is if your page has an imagemap and your visitor hits the Stop button before the imagemap loads, they won't know where they're going when they click. If there are no text links on the page, then they'll have to either reload the page or click and hope.

The big graphic in Figure 2.7 is a perfect example of a site that has an imagemap, but no text links. This is bad Web design. I'll talk more about this site later in the chapter.

Frames Frames were created by Netscape to answer the perplexing question, "How can I make my page easy to navigate?" Like so many other great ideas, this one also got perverted by the design community. When used properly, however, frames solve the dilemma of keeping the text links static so you don't have to constantly reload them. Figure 2.8 shows you how WebPagesThatSuck.com uses frames.

FIGURE 2.8   **Frames at WebPagesThatSuck.com**
(`http://www.webpagesthatsuck.com/begin.htm`)

The frame on the left is the navigational tool. When you click a link in the left-hand frame, the site in question pops up in the top right-hand frame while the witty, yet insightful commentary appears in the bottom right-hand frame. The navigational frame never changes.

Frames are controversial. Not so much because they are bad in and of themselves, but because people use them poorly. We'll examine frames in Chapter 6, "Frames and Links."

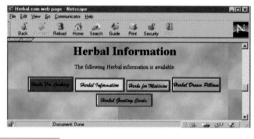

FIGURE 2.9   **The wrong way to do buttons**

Consistency

You need to be consistent in the design of your navigational tools. For example, the size and color of your buttons should be consistent. Figure 2.9 shows you the wrong way to use buttons. As you can see, using buttons with different colors and sizes looks unprofessional.

Figures 2.10 and 2.11 show two great examples of consistent navigational tools. The first page, shown in Figure 2.10, is a home page for a software product that converts word-processing documents into HTML. Notice the navigational bar on the left-hand side of the page; the depressed Home page button signifies which page you're visiting. Figure 2.11 shows the page for the Wang document conversion; as on the previous page, the Wang button is depressed to indicate you're on the Wang page. Total consistency.

Location When you place your navigational buttons on the page, make sure that if you place them at the

FIGURE 2.10   **The navigational button bar at the WebConvert home page**
(http://www.webconvert.com/)

FIGURE 2.11   **The navigational button bar at the WebConvert Wang Version page**
(http://www.webconvert.com/html/wang.htm)

top of your home page, they're on the top of every other page in your site. If you place them on the left-hand side of the home page, then they should be on the left-hand side of every other page. The WebConvert navigational tools, shown in Figures 2.10 and 2.11, follow this guideline. All of them are located on the left-hand side of the page.

It's a very simple concept— every navigational tool has to have a consistent look and location. Navigation should always be predictable. You want to create navigational tools that...

Are in the same spot on every page.

Have the same look. You don't want to use round buttons on the home page and square buttons on main topic pages and octagonal buttons on subsidiary pages.

Will get the visitor to the information in as few clicks as possible. I'm sure someone has researched the "Click Annoyance Factor"—the maximum number of clicks the average person is willing to perform to get to the information—but I haven't found this information on the Net. Personally, if I can't get to the information in three clicks and the site doesn't have a search engine, I'm ready to go somewhere else.

THE TOUR

Now that you understand how a site should be designed and how important it is to offer navigational tools, let's take a tour of some sites on the Internet and see how they measure up. We'll examine the first site thoroughly to make sure you understand the concepts of site design and navigation and then quickly run through some sucky and unsucky sites.

For each site, we'll check its

> Design
>
> Navigation
>
> Pluses
>
> Problems

Light Me Up! Cigar Aficionado Magazine

At the beginning of this chapter, we talked about how the first page of a site is like the cover of a magazine, so it's appropriate that the first site we discuss is actually a newsstand magazine.

The mystique of Cigar Aficionado magazine is sort of lost on Michael and me because, believe it or not, neither of us smoke cigars. (I tried to smoke Tiparillo's the end of my freshman year in college—but it *was* my freshman year.)

The most we can figure out, based on the Web site, is it appeals to those people who feel the "Good Life" consists of Art (their idea of art in the issue we looked at was Vargas, LeRoy Neiman, Frank Stella), Sports (golf, deep-sea sportfishing, tennis, boxing, bullfighting, hawking, polo), Music (samba), Fashion, Gambling (poker, hustling golf), Jewelry and Collectibles, and Leisure (expensive cars, model railroads, chess, dream boats, high-speed power boats, treasure hunting in the sea, high-end stereo equipment). On this list, I'm 0 for 7; Mike is 2 out of 7. Nevertheless, you don't have to understand the cigar lifestyle to understand the design.

Site Design at Cigar Aficionado   Michael and I both think the site design is superb.

Figure 2.12 shows the Cigar Aficionado magazine as it would appear on a 13–15-inch monitor. Let's examine how its design succeeds and, more importantly, how you can use the same principles to make your site a success.

The most important design element on this page is something you can't see.

The designer sat down and organized the site before they started writing the HTML and creating the graphics. If designers do their job properly, you won't even notice how successful they were. In this case, the designer broke down the elements of the magazine into different pieces and chose what was important.

Navigation at Cigar Aficionado In Figure 2.13, I've labeled the page so you can see the navigational structure of the home page.

The section marked "A" shows how the designer cleverly worked the most important topics into the top of the page. I stressed this concept back in Chapter 1 and again at the beginning of this chapter. These are the important topics I'm talking about here:

1. **Contact Us.** Make sure there's a way for visitors to contact you.

2. **Subscribe.** It's a magazine. They want you to subscribe. That's how they get money. Money is good. The fact that they don't offer subscriptions using a secure server is a potential security problem and would probably scare most people from ordering using their credit card. It would be interesting to know how many subscribers they've actually received from the Internet.

3. **Site Index.** If your site is divided up into many different areas, you'll want to include a site index (also called a *site map* or *site guide*). Your site index should be text based. Don't use graphics; they take too long to load.

The section marked "B" shows you a portion of a navigational bar where it looks like they've listed most of the important topics near the top. Interestingly, the Gift Shop is at the bottom, but that's probably okay because maybe they're trying not to look too pushy. Personally, Michael and I would have moved it closer to the top.

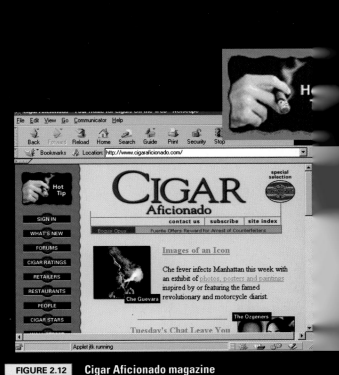

FIGURE 2.12 **Cigar Aficionado magazine**
(http://www.cigaraficionado.com/)

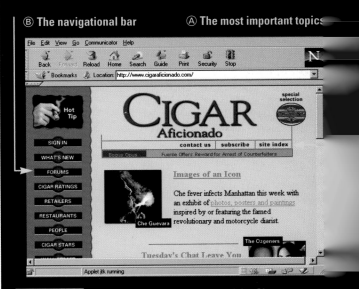

FIGURE 2.13 **The navigational structure of the Cigar Aficionado magazine site**

While a visitor must scroll down to see all the topics, there's enough information at the top of the page for them to get a good start on touring the important sections of the site.

Figure 2.14 shows the navigational structure of Cigar Ratings—one of the main topic pages. Notice that the round part of the label on the Cigar Ratings button has turned red. Obviously, you can look at the top of the page and see its title, but this touch is a nice one to add to the button. When you want to go to another topic, you won't click the Cigar Ratings button because it's turned red, which, as we all know, should make you want to stop. It's worth noting, however, that if you went to the Retailers page, there's no special marking to indicate you've been to the Cigar Ratings page. That's the province of text links. Nevertheless, the navigational information on this main topic page and on its subsidiary pages is excellent.

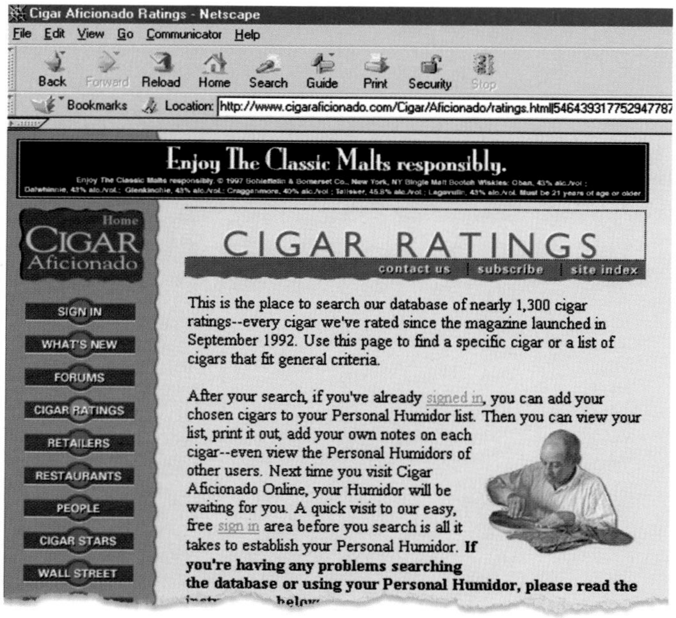

FIGURE 2.14   **Cigar Ratings page**
(`http://www.cigaraficionado.com/Cigar/`
`Aficionado/ratings.html`)

Pluses in the Cigar Aficionado Site First of all, the designer chose wonderful colors for the site based on the brown color of cigars. Most important, these colors are used in a consistent fashion throughout the site.

The link graphics are also wonderful—little cigar wrappers—and so very, very clever. The home page is uncluttered, and the other graphics add to the flavor (pardon the pun) of the page. There's one animated GIF image (the Hot Tip at the top of the left-hand navigation bar), but it's excellent (see Figure 2.12). While the graphic titled "Vote" is probably clip art, it's professional clip art (see Figure 2.1).

The site reeks (again, pardon the pun) of sophistication and elegance.

Problems in the Cigar Aficionado Site Even though we both like the page, there are six potential problems:

1. The HEIGHT and WIDTH parameters are not set for the images. As you will learn in Chapter 4, setting these parameters would cause the text to appear before the images on the page and give the viewer the opportunity to click a text link rather than wait for all the images to load.

2. Speaking of text links, *there are no text links on the front page*. Ooops. That's a design no-no. Michael and I suggest they put text links at the bottom of the page.

3. Dr. HTML (see the sidebar "Dr. HTML") reported that the page contained 84.8K worth of graphics and images on the day we visited. This means it would take between 24.1 seconds (on a 28.8Kbps modem) and 48.3 seconds (on a 14.4Kbps modem) to load the page (and probably longer because of the Java on the

page, but Dr. HTML doesn't measure Java applets). The people visiting this site probably don't care how long it takes for the page to load because of the content. (We could make a snide statement that the people who visit this site are all probably wealthy Republicans with ISDN connections, but we won't.) The cigar industry is a wonderful vertical niche market, and people who visit niche sites really don't care too much about download time.

4. It would be nice if there were a search engine facility on the front page. They have a link to their search engine tucked away at the bottom of the Site Index page, but they should really have one on the front page.

5. The site uses Java, and using it doesn't seem to enhance the site.

6. The site uses *Cookies.* These pesky little tracking devices basically track your movements on this site. I'm not sure why they need them, but using Cookies could turn off some visitors.

All six of these elements are flaws in the site's design, but numbers 1 and 2 are certainly the worst ones.

Let's stroll around and examine a few more sites to see if we can figure out what the designer was thinking when they designed the site.

TOO COOL

Dr. HTML

Dr.HTML *is one of the Most Important Sites on the Internet.*

The good doctor analyzes pages that physically reside on the Internet (have a URL) for errors and loading time. One of the many errors it looks for are missing HEIGHT and WIDTH parameters in images. In some of the examples used in this chapter, (Cigar Aficionado, United Airlines, and Lotus) these parameters were missing.

There are lots of HTML validation services on the Web—including those that don't charge fees. As always, check out Yahoo's page on the topic at `http://www.yahoo.com/Computers_and_Internet/ Information_and_Documentation/Data_Formats/ HTML/Validation_and_Checkers/`.

Dr. HTML
(`http://drhtml.imagiware.com/`)

FIGURE 2.15 **The Pepsi site**
(http://www.pepsi.com/)

You're Not Cool Enough. Go Away!

Figure 2.15 shows us Pepsi's home page.

This home page is stunning. Not stunning as in "stunningly beautiful," but stunning as in "I've just been poked by a stun gun, and I'm in a lot of freaking pain." As a Web designer, the last thing you want to do is keep people away from your site, but that seems to be the concept here. What this page is saying is, "If you don't have these plug-ins, then go away because we don't want you." Normally, I don't have a problem with plug-ins except that I often have to reinstall all of them every time a new release of my browser is issued—as one of the paragraphs of text on the Pepsi home page relates.

When I looked at this site, my first reaction was "The heck with this, I'm going elsewhere." But I decided to go to the next page and after fumbling around, trying to figure out where to click to get to the next page (the Pepsi World logo was the magic spot), I got the scare of my life. You have only to look at Figure 2.16 to understand.

After recovering from the shock, I tried to figure out where I was supposed to click to get to the next page. Basically, I had to move my cursor over the whole screen while looking at the status bar to figure it out. The four "magic spots" are those white circular scribblings. Bad, bad design.

As with so many other things in life, Michael, my partner in crime, initially held a contrary viewpoint about the Pepsi site. "I will admit at first glance I liked the layout. I wasn't bothered by all the plug-in requirements because I have them all—I like plug-ins! I'm a plug-in maniac! So I decided to peruse the site. Unfortunately it's a graphic behemoth! It looks like Photoshop puked here. If I had a day to spend (which I don't), I couldn't visit all the pages on this site, not because there are so many, but because it takes forever for the graphics to load. I had to take a Dramamine after viewing all their gut-wrenching animations! It's a good thing I didn't want to know anything about Pepsi, because, as far as I could tell, there's nothing here specifically dealing with Pepsi."

Site Design at Pepsi Don't use any of the techniques you see here. If there's a worthwhile site design technique used here, neither Michael nor I can find it.

Navigation at Pepsi This is an oxymoron like "fresh frozen." This site fails Navigation 101.

Pluses at Pepsi None.

Problems at Pepsi The whole site.

Eight Miles High: United Airlines

Figure 2.17 shows you the United Airlines home page, another excellently designed site.

Site Design at United Interestingly, this is one the few sites that has the right to use the clichéd outer-space background and animated spinning-globe GIF and can make it work. More amazingly, their use of a globe actually makes complete sense. You can't tell,

FIGURE 2.16 **Holy moly, I've drunk too much Pepsi.**
(`http://www.pepsi.com/main/nav/home_main1.html`)

but the globe is animated, and it is actually one of the coolest animated GIF images Michael and I have seen (the word *Index* is stationary). Why can they get away with using these clichés? They're an airline. Airlines fly in the sky. United flies around the world. They can use these images. Joe's Air Conditioning can't.

FIGURE 2.17	**United Airlines**

(`http://www.ual.com/`)

Navigation at United Instead of using a list of links in the usual boring manner (on the left side), they came up with a clever and artistic way to present them— you click the planet and you go to the page. For example, clicking the pilot takes you to the Flight Info/Reservations page. It's easy to navigate to the main topic pages and subsidiary pages and back.

Pluses at United Nothing out of the ordinary. It's just a well–thought out site. It's very easy to navigate the site because the navigation tools are consistently placed and cover the main topics a traveler needs to use.

Problems at United While the animated spinning globe is really cool, what is seriously *uncool* about the image is its 130K size (the whole page is 176.8K). Way,

way, too big. After all, this is a site where you want people to make airline reservations on your carrier—right? Why make it difficult for them by making them wait? Michael and I know this animated image is very cool, but you can't fall in love with your own design. It's possible people won't wait long enough to book a reservation. Hmm. That defeats the purpose of the site.

Another minus is none of the images on the home page have the HEIGHT and WIDTH parameters set. Finally, there are no text links. If the imagemap doesn't load, you really can't surf.

Another Airline: Southwest Airlines

I'm sure that Southwest Airlines doesn't like being referred to as "another airline," but it's the second one we're looking at, so it's another airline. Figure 2.18 shows you their home page.

This site is where Michael and I pull our Siskel & Ebert routine (international readers, see the sidebar "Siskel & Ebert" for an explanation). I (Ebert) think the home page is okay, while Michael (Siskel) thinks it sucks like a bilge pump. If this were a TV show it would go like this:

> **Michael:** I'm sure someone put time into creating their ugly 46K "takes-forever-to-load"

navigational imagemap. By the way, if you hit the Stop button before it loads, you won't be able to go to the *bleep* (pejorative term deleted) president's message page—which is too bad because he's manually indicating the number of people that have ever visited his page.

Vincent: Yeah, no text links certainly sucks, but I don't mind the motif of the ticket counter. Besides this home page loads faster than United Airlines. And I think having the president's face there is a nice touch.

Michael: You find him attractive?

I then rush over and start beating on Michael's head with a copy of *Creating Killer Web Sites,* which Michael usually has hidden in a drawer. Pandemonium results, and the whole scene ends up being shown on CNN.

Site Design at Southwest Artistically, it's not as pleasing as the United Airlines site, but, then again, it's 49K in size versus United's 176K size. Hmm. Also remember that Southwest prides itself on being an inexpensive carrier, and the minimalist design here works just fine. The pages load quickly.

A case *can* be made that the site looks as if it was made on the cheap. Since Southwest prides itself on being a low-cost carrier, that's consistent with their corporate philosophy of providing value.

Navigation at Southwest Once again, they've taken the minimalist approach, and it seems to work. They don't have buttons for all their topics, just the ones that count (translation: the ones that will bring in money)—Reservations, Flight Schedule, Frequent Flyer Program, and so on. Very nice.

Pluses at Southwest The main pluses about the site are the fast loading times and easy navigation. Look, it ain't pretty folks, but it's functional. There's something to be said for functional. Yes, it could be prettier and still load fast, but I don't think anyone but Michael is going to gag at the look of this site.

Minuses at Southwest Michael thinks it looks cheesy, and a case can be made for that viewpoint. One reason it's cheesy is the tacky blue border around the picture; they should have turned the border off around the picture. While the desk is nicely rendered (it has dimension to it), every other piece of art is flat and one-dimensional. Southwest is trying to have a realistic look, but then they add the flat art work and it causes dissonance—or as Michael phrased it: "That's an awfully big word to use for *dorky.*"

While the concept of a virtual ticket counter is excellent, the execution is poor.

Siskel and Ebert

Later in the book, you'll hear about avoiding jargon in your Web site. If you need proof that it's a good idea to keep jargon and nation-specific information out of your Web site, this Siskel & Ebert reference is a perfect example.

While many Americans will catch the reference, most, if not all, international visitors will be left out in the dark. So, for those nice international readers, here's a short explanation.

In the United States, Gene Siskel and Roger Ebert are two movie reviewers who work for different newspapers in Chicago, Illinois—hence, they are competitors. One of them won the Pulitzer Prize (a big deal in America) and periodically reminds the other he never won one. Siskel is the tall, balding guy, and Ebert is the short, stocky man with lots of hair. Sort of a Mutt and Jeff combination—oops, another reference even many Americans won't catch. Forget the Mutt and Jeff reference.

Siskel and Ebert have a TV show where they sit in a faux movie theater balcony and rate the movies coming out during the week. The premise is they don't really like each other, and sometimes they argue in a reasonably civilized manner about why the other one wouldn't know a good movie if it came up and bit him on the ass. Everyone who watches the show does so partly because they hope that one day, one of the two will snap and start choking the other one. Like ancient Roman emperors, they give a thumbs-up or thumbs-down sign to the movies they like or dislike respectively.

As I said, jargon and nation-specific references make for a bad Web page.

Siskel and Ebert's Web site is at `http://siskel-ebert.com`.

FIGURE 2.18   **Southwest Airlines**
(http://www.iflyswa.com/)

Out-of-Place Graphics: Kenwood Home and Car Audio

Figure 2.19 is the home page for Kenwood Home and Car Audio. Michael and I actually agree about the design.

Site Design at Kenwood The page uses graphics in a consistent manner, and the designer certainly thought about the organization of the site. But, as Michael so aptly put it, "I think marble backgrounds went out of style in the 70s or were they ever in? And what's up with the homeless looking guy in the picture? And what does that picture say about audio systems? I'm stumped." I wasn't thrilled with the concept either. Why are they using a hotel as the motif? If you go to the Kenwood Gear page, the motif is a laundry room—yes, Kenwood t-shirts need to be laundered, but the concept of a hotel is a stretch and poorly thought out.

Navigation at Kenwood The navigational tools used are well done, and the site is easy to navigate. Notice how the designer put the most important pages at the top of the directory—Catalog, Build a Home System, Build a Car System, Contests, and Product Help Center.

But there's one flaw that just drives me crazy. On the directory, the very first link is the Lobby. You've got to have that on the other pages, but not on the home page—if you click the link, you just reload the page.

Pluses at Kenwood Nothing I haven't said before.

Problems at Kenwood The home page takes up a little over 63K in size—that's over even the Microsoft recommended amount. Also, the images don't have the HEIGHT and WIDTH parameters set.

Text Is Just All Right with Me: Red Hat Software

All of the previous sites have been graphics-based. Figure 2.20 shows that Red Hat Software can design a reasonably effective site using text-based navigational tools.

Site Design at Red Hat Software

As you can see, the folks at Red Hat have taken a text-based approach to their site. The links on the left seem to be in logical order and also seem to cover the major topics:

> Secure Server (how they get paid)
> FTP Server
> Products
> Support
> Company Info
> Linux Info

The nicest part about their text-based approach is the page is only 22K in size and loads quickly.

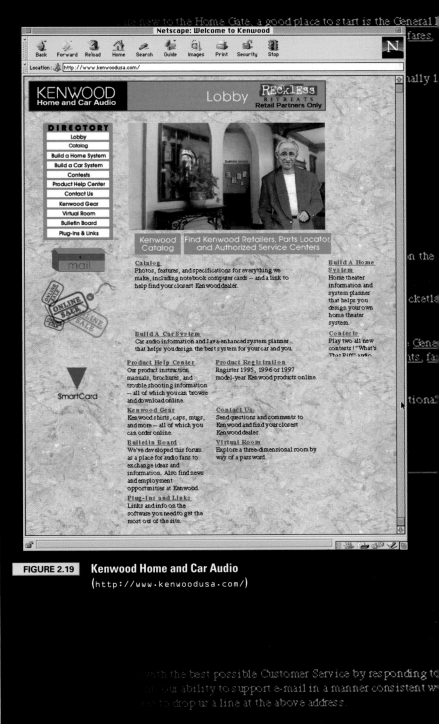

FIGURE 2.19 **Kenwood Home and Car Audio**
(http://www.kenwoodusa.com/)

Even though the site takes the minimalist approach to the use of graphics, it is, nonetheless, fairly effective. Yes, it's plain and not very exciting, but that's okay. This approach would not work with Cigar Aficionado, but for a software site it's fine. Later, in Chapter 4, you'll read about another software company who went way overboard and has a site that can't hold a candle to Red Hat.

Navigation at Red Hat Software The navigational aspects of Red Hat Software could be a lot better, as Figure 2.21 demonstrates. This figure is a little deceiving. There are image links to Support, Linux Info, and Company Info. However, you always need to have a link to the money page—the page where a visitor can order your products. It's also a good idea to have a contact link on each page so your visitors can contact you. Red Hat has such a link, but it's at the bottom of the page, and the links at the bottom should really be at the top of the page. If you're going to have your graphic links at the top of the page, then the links at the bottom of the page should be textual duplicates of the links at the top.

Pluses at Red Hat Software Nothing out of the ordinary. The pages load quickly, and you can find your way around the site without *too* much trouble. It's a very Spartan site, but being Spartan isn't bad.

Problems at Red Hat Software The designer at Red Hat may have taken the concept of text just a little too far. I realize that UNIX is a "text-based system" and UNIX wonks like nothing more than to read those technical UNIX books—you know, the ones with the animals on the cover. However,

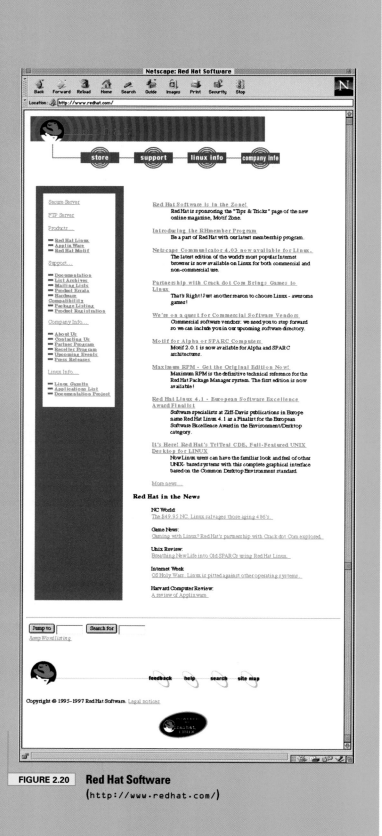

FIGURE 2.20   Red Hat Software
(http://www.redhat.com/)

there's just a little too much text on the pages to make me feel comfortable. Figure 2.22 shows a typical page on the site.

Well, that should cover it for the general tour. Next, we're going to look at some bad home-page design techniques.

Bad Home-Page Design Techniques

No, you're not going to see a whole slew of badly designed home pages. You're just going to look at some techniques that impede the visitor from visiting your site.

Forcible Entry: Herbal.com

Figure 2.23 shows you a technique Michael and I don't see much anymore on commercial or educational pages (thank goodness). But just because we haven't seen it in awhile doesn't mean it doesn't exist or won't make a comeback. It most frequently shows up on personal pages (why it's even used there is beyond us), but there's no valid reason why it's necessary under any circumstance.

What's evil about this page is the JavaScript on the Herbal.com site that requests a name be entered before the visitor proceeds. On a commercial or informational site, you don't want to do anything that impedes your visitor's progress into your site. You don't want to chase them away.

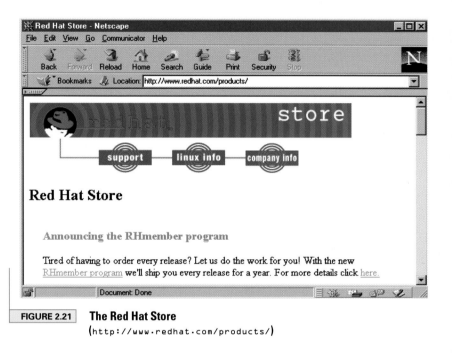

FIGURE 2.21   **The Red Hat Store**
(http://www.redhat.com/products/)

FIGURE 2.22   **Too much text at the Red Hat Store**
(http://www.redhat.com/products/)

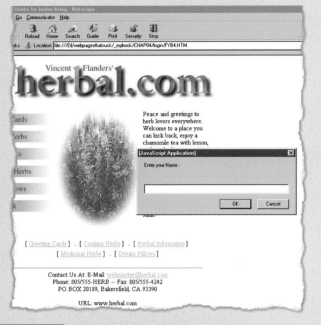

FIGURE 2.23   **Why oh why? Herbal.com goes weird.**

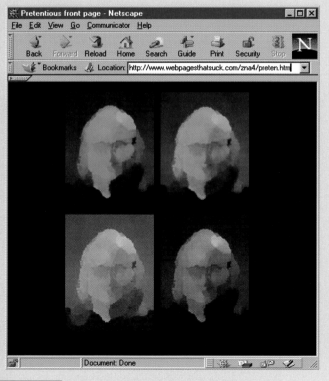

FIGURE 2.24   **The old splash page for vincentflanders.com**
`(http://www.vincentflanders.com/old)`

While Michael and I realize that there are very few absolutes in Web page design, this technique is an absolutely bad one to use. For that reason, we're going to:

NUKE IT!

What Do I Do Now? vincentflanders.com

Figure 2.24 shows the former *splash page* at my personal Web site. A splash page is different from a home page. A splash page is traditionally used for a first "splash" of art, which then transports you automatically to the "real" home page. In some instances, the user has to click to gain access to the home page. Splash pages can be confusing to visitors unless there are specific instructions on what they should do to gain entry to the home page.

This page is a parody of a famous Web designer's splash page. I parodied this look on his page because...that's the kind of guy I am.

There are, however, a few problems with this type of splash page:

1. The visitor is never sure when the page has stopped loading, and that's frustrating.

2. Because there are no text links to click, the visitor has to wait until they see the Document Done message in the status bar before proceeding.

3. The visitor doesn't have any idea where they're going when they click a picture. This adds nothing to the design of the site.

You don't ever want to confuse people when they go to your site. They need to know where they are and what they should do.

Exceptions As always, there is an exception, and this one actually makes sense, as illustrated in Figure 2.25.

The one exception to the rule is the type of site that has both an artistic sense and also downloads quickly. The Surface Type home page is about 12K in size—small enough to load quickly—and the designers have a great artistic sense, which they better have if they're going to design typefaces.

While it's artistic and doesn't annoy us because it loads quickly, imagine how you'd feel if you had to wait for 60K worth of images to load?

Now that you've seen several different aspects of design, I bet you want the answer to the question: "How do I design a site?" The answer: "Storyboards."

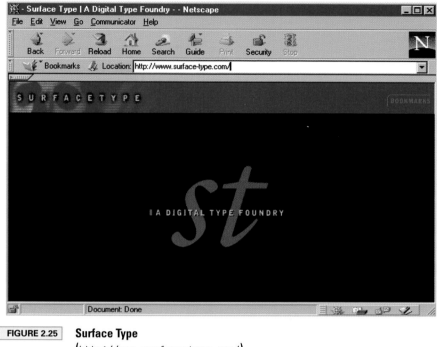

| FIGURE 2.25 | **Surface Type**
(`http://www.surface-type.com/`)

DESIGNING YOUR SITE USING STORYBOARDS

It's easy to look at the sites in this chapter and say, "Yes, that one is good" and "Yes, that one is bad." What's difficult is putting what you've seen about good design and navigation into practice on your sites.

Because you can easily get instantaneous feedback by writing HTML, there's a tendency to fall into the trap of "code before you think." Your problem is you need to create a home page. Your solution is to start writing HTML as fast as your stubby little fingers can type. This approach is the "There's never time to do it right, but there's always time to do it over—and

over and over again" approach to Web design. You waste both time and energy. (Of course, if you're billing by the hour and your client is dumb and rich...)

If you just sat down and planned your site, however, you wouldn't end up with a dozen iterations and wasted hours—but this takes organization, a quality some of us lack.

To show you how the storyboard approach works, Michael and I will use Michael's WillieBoy.com site as an example. Michael bought the domain name willieboy.com for his line of surf wear. Next, he decided to throw together a placeholder page in case somebody accidentally wandered into his site. Figure 2.26 is what Michael ended up putting on his placeholder page.

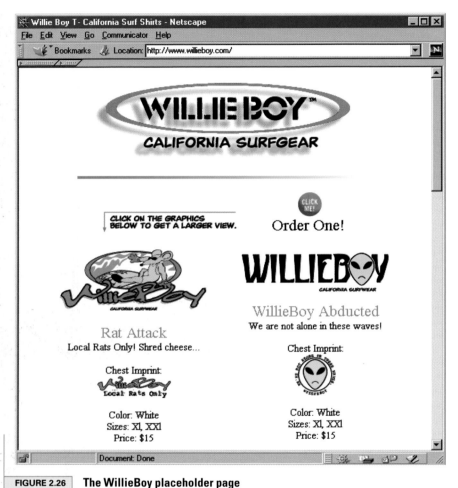

FIGURE 2.26   **The WillieBoy placeholder page**
(http://www.willieboy.com/)

puts it, "You can use any program that allows you to draw little boxes and put type in them. Of course, the old-fashioned 'pencil and paper' works fine, too." Because I use Windows NT, I use a copy of Visio 2 I purchased years and years ago to storyboard.

Storyboard—Step One

Michael's first step is to talk to me about the site. My background is in marketing, so I'm great at coming up with ideas for other people to implement <grin>. There didn't seem to be a lot of content to draw people in on Michael's placeholder page, so I told him that he'd better add something or he'd get a bunch of people who'd visit only once. The obvious starting point for content would be surf-related information, such as surfing condition reports, surf music lists, and so on. I also suggested adding a page showing different surfer tattoos, but Michael misunderstood; he thought I said he should create a line of "temporary tattoos with a surfing theme." I quickly confirmed that's what I actually said. Sometimes it pays to slur your ideas.

There's not much here. You can click the thumbnail images and see a bigger version of the image. The only link to another page is the Order One button, which takes you to a form that is *not* on a secure server.

This placeholder page is good enough until Michael decides to start marketing his clothing line on the Web. Now that Michael has decided to really create the site, he must go through the process of storyboarding. He takes an unusual approach by creating his storyboards in Illustrator or PageMaker. As he

Storyboard—Step Two

Next, Michael had to figure out what the main topic pages were going to be. Here's what he decided:

Garments

Order Form

WillieBoy's Favorite Surf Links

Tour of the Shirt Shop

Photo Contest

Photo Contest is actually a misnomer. It will really be a photo gallery where Michael will display photographs of people wearing WillieBoy t-shirts—a very clever marketing concept where visitors get their 15 minutes of fame on the Net.

If you're thinking of having a real contest on your site, you'll need to consult with a lawyer about the different legalities.

Storyboard—Step Three

With these ideas in hand, Michael starts the WillieBoy storyboard; the first version is shown in Figure 2.27, and the second version is shown in Figure 2.28.

Let's see what he was thinking when he created his first version. Michael drew the first box, which represents the home page. Then he drew the row of major topic pages with links to the subsidiary pages.

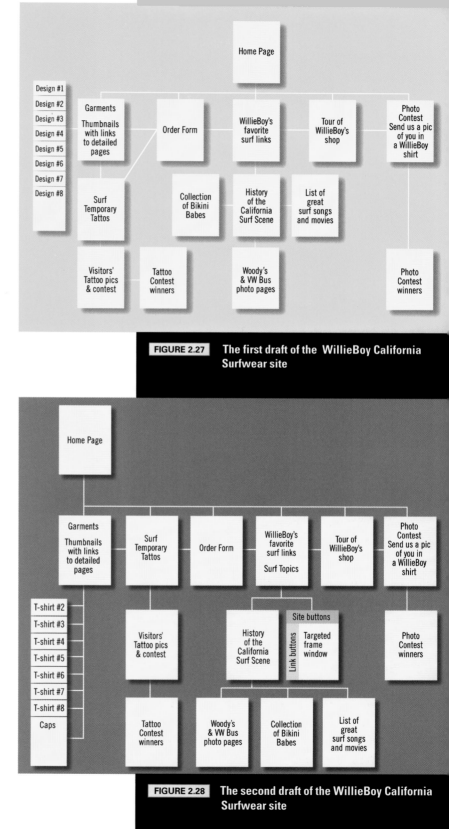

FIGURE 2.27 The first draft of the WillieBoy California Surfwear site

FIGURE 2.28 The second draft of the WillieBoy California Surfwear site

FIGURE 2.29   The final sketch for WillieBoy

Storyboard—Step Four

Michael then e-mailed me the TIF image file of the storyboard, and we discussed what changes should be made. I thought the temporary tattoos should be moved up from a subsidiary page and made a major topics page. Michael expressed concern about WillieBoy's Favorite Links page. He didn't like the fact that people could just click a link and leave his site—"Perhaps never to return again!"

How did Michael solve this problem? He explains: "Vincent came up with the layout for the links page. On this page, I wanted to feature daily surf reports, related articles, and so on, but I didn't want my visitors actually leaving. Vincent's solution was to use frames. In most cases I hate frames, but here it really made sense. When a visitor clicks a link, it will target my frame window, but my WillieBoy buttons/links will still be visible."

The revised storyboard is shown in Figure 2.28.

The total time spent creating the two storyboards, including consulting with me, was one and one-half hours.

Creating the Home Page

After creating the storyboard, Michael sits down in front of the TV and sketches the design for the home page on tissue paper while watching back-to-back episodes of *Seinfeld*. (Another strictly American reference. *Seinfeld* is best described as a very strange comedy only Americans would like.) While watching the show, he sketches three or four possible designs. If he gets a new idea, he slaps a new sheet of tissue paper on top of the old piece, traces the elements he wants to keep, and then adds the new elements.

During this process, Michael puts the different elements into a page grid because he knows that great Web sites are created using tables. After he makes the mock up, he'll put all the elements into a table so his grid design will translate to the screen. Figure 2.29 shows that the page is a simple table that consists of only one row and two columns.

This book assumes some basic knowledge of HTML, so if you need to learn how to make tables, an excellent online source is Table Tutor at http://junior.apk.net/jbarta/tutor/tables/index.html.

Time spent on the different versions of the home page was one hour; total time invested so far is two and one-half hours.

Besides watching two episodes of *Seinfeld* and sketching the layout of the home page, Michael decided on the following elements:

> **The color scheme** Michael wants to use bright "retro" colors for the links, the background, and the graphics, and he wants to use browser-safe colors. You'll learn about browser-safe colors in Chapter 4, but here's a quick explanation.

There are 216 "safe" colors a designer can use that will be seen by both Windows and Macintosh users without the image being messed up (the technical term for *messed up* is *dithered*). While 216 colors sounds like a lot, it isn't. You have to make a choice—"Do I design my pages for everyone or do I design them to please myself (or my client)?" Of course, if it's a client you have to please, let the client make the final decision.

> Michael is "stuck" with using the black and red colors of the WillieBoy logo because the logo was created long before the Web site was a gleam in his eye. If you're a Web page designer, you'll find out that preexisting logos will be the norm. While it can be hard to turn them into browser-safe colors, I'll discuss a way around the problem in Chapter 4. Michael chose a browser-safe autumn gold color for the navigation bar. Because he's using different gradations of teal in the image at the top-left of the page, he won't be able to use browser-safe colors on the image at the top left (this will be a surfer image).

> **The fonts** Michael is stuck with using the default fonts for the text, but he decides to use the same font used in the WillieBoy logo for the navigational text. He also decides to use a third font for headlines, the top headline being "We Found the Missing Links!"

> **The look of the images** Because this is, obviously, a surf-oriented site, the images need to have a surf flavor.

After making these decisions, Michael creates his home page in Photoshop. Yes, Photoshop. (Normally, a designer creates the graphics individually in

Use Your Images
More Than Once!

Michael will use the original navigational images throughout the site. Why?

Because the first time a page is loaded, the images will be stored in the visitor's cache. The next time the images are needed they won't have to be fetched from a faraway server, they'll be pulled from the cache and will therefore load more quickly than they loaded the first time. Repeating images throughout the site also adds the element of consistency to the design.

Photoshop and then aligns them in the HTML page by creating tables. Michael's approach is different because he creates the whole page as one large graphic.) Figure 2.30 shows the first rendition.

FIGURE 2.30   **The WillieBoy home page—created in Photoshop**

Obviously, Michael already had the logo, so he creates the navigational items and then the text. At the moment, he inserts nonsense text until he comes up with what he actually wants to use. This is, after all, a mock-up.

After he's happy with how the page looks, he'll cut up one large Photoshop image into separate graphic elements and insert them into an HTML document using tables to align them. Michael learned this slick technique from another designer. Because Michael is going to use the images on his site, he doesn't just spit them out; he spends about four hours on the page. The total time spent so far is six and one-half hours.

The reason I said the page is a first rendition is that Michael made one mistake and left one thing out. Looking back at the storyboard in Figure 2.28, you can see he left off WillieBoy's Favorite Surf Links/Surf Topics. I also think he needs a contact button after Photo Contest. You always want to give your visitors a way to contact you—even if it's just by phone.

Michael will repeat the navigation bar on the second page. Why? It makes the page load faster.

Creating the Rest of the Site

Michael will go through the same process for each of the main topic pages and subsidiary pages. His task is easier because the important design decisions have been made. The only major work that's left is adding the actual content and creating whatever new images are required.

The Value of Organizing via Storyboards

It should be obvious that organizing the design process by using storyboards can save a significant amount of time. There were only two iterations of the storyboard, and there were just two iterations for the home page. This sure beats the "code before you think" approach, which is similar to the joke about the airline pilot who gets on the speaker to inform the passengers, "Ladies and gentlemen, this is your captain. I've got good news and bad news. The good news is we're making record time. The bad news is we're lost."

Now just because your visitors won't get lost navigating your Web site, doesn't mean you can sit back and congratulate yourself. You've got to bring that plane in for a landing. Unless your site has content—the most important element in Web design—your visitors might leave in record time. In the next chapter, you'll learn why Content Is King.

TOO COOL

Tip Worth the Price of the Book

This tip is so simple, it's almost insulting to have me mention it— spend 99 cents to get yourself a notebook. Why? You need to keep track of everything that's specific to your site. Because two hours after you finish a project, you're going to forget every parameter you set.

What You Need to Keep Track of

Graphics.

Colors (both hexadecimal and RGB values).

Image sizes.

Fonts used for the text (if applicable) and the font size, leading, spacing, color, and style.

Filter settings—bevels and their parameters. Try to reproduce that bevel angle or that drop shadow two days from now. It's very, very important to write down your filter settings. You'll thank me.

Anything else you'd forget in a month—the login name and password for the FTP site, for example.

Flanders & Willis's Reality Check

Update your site as often as you can afford the time and/or money. Seriously, we can't stress this enough. Ask yourself this important question: Why would anybody in their right mind want to visit my site a second time?

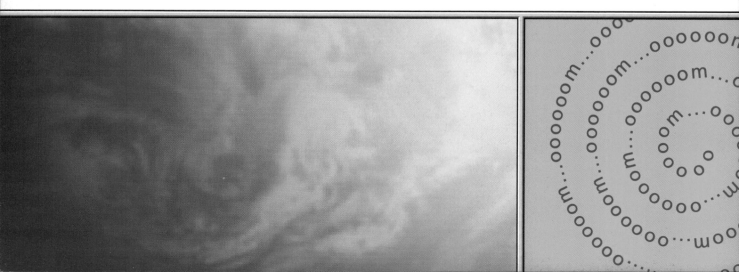

CHAPTER 3

Content Is King

IN THIS CHAPTER

we're going to talk about the most insidious mistake made in the field of Web design: thinking your site has content when all it has is a collection of words and images that, to quote Shakespeare, "are full of sound and fury signifying nothing." For some reason, even more so than you might find in other art forms, it's difficult for people involved in Web site design to take an objective look at their creation.

Designers and site owners can be infected with "Web Content Blindness"—they see their site as being the most content-driven site in the universe when it is, at best, just a poster or brochure.

As you're beginning to see, there are lots of ways you can screw up your site. In Chapter 2, you saw how a site can become almost impossible to navigate. In this chapter, we're going to examine sites with and without content and find ways to add content when it's needed. Let's start off by taking a look at the Slovinia perfume page (shown in Figure 3.1).

EVERYBODY THINKS THEIR SITE HAS CONTENT

To find out if your site really has content, ask yourself the *second* most important question you can ask about your Web site.

The Second Most Important Question You Can Ask about Your Web Site:

Why would anybody in their right mind visit my site a second time?

Seriously. Ask yourself this question and answer it honestly. Don't give me this: "My site shows people a great way

Why Does This Page Suck?

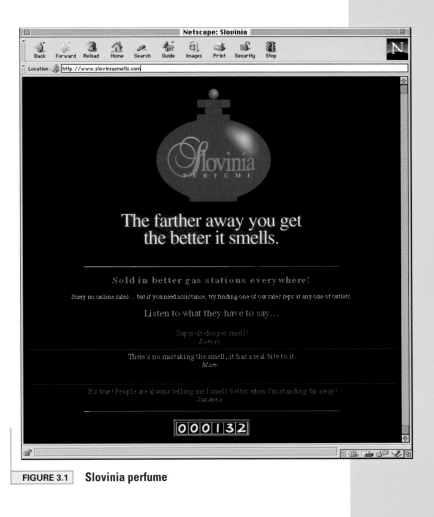

FIGURE 3.1   **Slovinia perfume**

At best (and I'm really stretching here when I use the word *best*), the Slovinia perfume page is a "brochure-ware" page — it was taken directly from a brochure or pamphlet used by the company and stuck up on the Web because, "They need to be on the Internet yesterday."

Obviously, there is no company called Slovinia Perfume (although there is a country called Slovenia). Michael created this sucky little masterpiece to bring home the most important message in this book:

Content is king. If your Web site doesn't have content, you don't really have a Web site.

I have to say he's done a great job creating a really bad page. The Slovinia site consists of one page that gives vague directions on how to purchase the product ("Sold in better gas stations everywhere!"). There's no real promotional material other than a few endorsements from people who are unimportant; no phone number, fax number, or e-mail links; and there's certainly no reason to stay at this site. It sucks. It sucks because there's no content. The counter at the bottom of the page is living proof the site sucks—132 visitors and most are probably from the designer checking to see how many people didn't visit the site.

However, it is a pretty funny idea, for what it's worth.

OH NO

PORNOGRAPHY: THE ULTIMATE WEB CONTENT?

I realize pornography is a touchy subject (pardon the pun) for many people, but we need to look at it in a cool, rational manner because, like it or not, pornography is the kind of content people will crawl through sewers and beg to buy. It certainly is the best-selling content on the Web. It's been estimated that between 80 and 90 percent of all commerce on the Internet involves porn—or "adult sites" as they're euphemistically known.

Right now, porn is where the money is on the Web, and there are people who are making $20,000 a month profit—not by selling pornography, but simply by selling banner ads on their sites to these pornography sites.

Like it or not, pornography is the ultimate easy sell because it's something people will pay to see. They might not pay to read Michael Kinsley's *Slate* magazine, but they might pay to see him naked. Well, maybe that's a bad example. You know what I mean.

to get involved in multilevel marketing so they can achieve independence and wealth." That's crap, not content.

Obviously, the "Second Most Important Question You Can Ask about Your Web Site" implies there is a *most* important question.

The Most Important Question You Can Ask about Your Web Site:

Why would anybody in their right mind visit my site a third, fourth, or fifth time?

Obviously, certain sites are one-trick ponies; however, repeat customers are the only way a company survives. There's an old marketing adage that it costs five times as much to sell to a new customer as it does to sell to a current customer. It's called relationship building. You need to build a relationship with your customer.

In Chapter 10, "Search Engines and Directories," you'll see how unscrupulous Internet scum can trick people into visiting their site. The problem with tricking people is simple: they'll visit—once—and never come back.

It's the same for a site without content. People might find your site listed in a search engine or directory, and they might be persuaded to visit—once. But the trick is getting them to come back a second, third, fourth, fifth time. What's so special about your site that's going to make people *want* to come back?

"Content is the ideal product...the ultimate merchandise. No sales talk necessary. The client will crawl through a sewer and beg to buy."

William Burroughs, as paraphrased by Vincent Flanders

Does your site have the kind of content that people are willing to crawl through sewers to get?

Let's take at look at some of the other types of sites that offer the kind of content people might want to return to.

A Newspaper Has Content

Figure 3.2 shows one of my favorite sites, The Onion.

I start with The Onion—which won the 1997 Cool Site of the Year award for writing—because I figured you were expecting a site like the ones displayed in Chapter 2—IBM, Lotus, United Airlines. The Onion is a hilarious satirical newspaper for those of us who are over the age of 18. It's one of the best humor sites on the Web. Yes, the site exists to sell subscriptions to the newspaper version of its magazine, but they're putting content on the site—it isn't a brochure-ware page that says, "Buy our cool newspaper" and consists of nothing more than the scanned-in front page of the newspaper.

Speaking of scanned-in sites, Figure 3.3 shows a great example of a scanned-in, brochure-ware site. Not only did they scan in a brochure, they accidentally (I hope) cropped off the right edge.

One thing The Onion has going for it is the fact that it's updated weekly. (It isn't weekly in the summer because the staff seems to take about a month off for vacation.) The Onion offers a reason to come back. It's a newspaper—it gets updated all the time. Almost every newspaper/magazine/newsletter on the Web has content because that's the business they're in—providing content. On the other end of the spectrum, the Sunset Hall Retirement Home doesn't seem to have much content.

Updating your content is insanely important. Update it constantly. That's an order. Assuming your site is worth visiting, it's the best way to get people to come back again and again.

FIGURE 3.2   The Onion: America's Finest News Source
(http://www.theonion.com/)

FIGURE 3.3   Sunset Hall retirement home
(http://www.free-thinkers.org/)

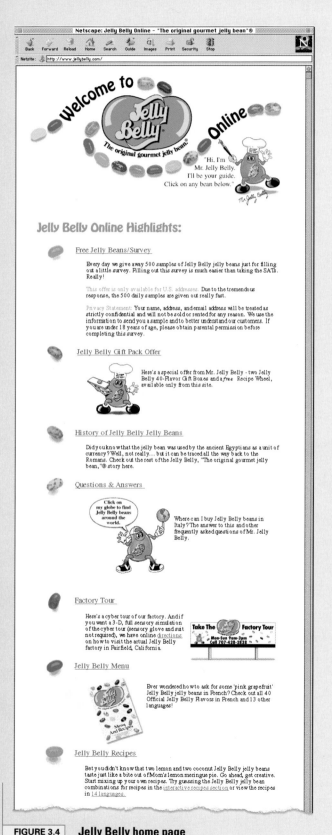

FIGURE 3.4   **Jelly Belly home page**
(http://www.jellybelly.com/)

Jelly Beans Have Content

Figure 3.4 shows us a business site that has content—the Jelly Belly home page. Jelly Belly jelly beans are gourmet jelly beans made popular by former President Ronald Reagan. A trip to their home page shows a site that's functional, yet fun.

While not the most colorful design in the world, it certainly serves its purpose—to make us feel good about jelly beans, which are really nothing more than flavored sugar that's going to screw with our metabolism, make our teeth rot, and make us gain weight. When we go to their site, we forget this—that's good design.

The designer could very easily have made this site look like the Slovinia perfume site—one page saying "Buy our candy at finer stores everywhere!"—except I'm sure their designer wouldn't have used a yucky black background and tacky rainbow bar dividers like the ones that appeared at the perfume site.

If you think about it, the Jelly Belly company is a perfect candidate for a one-page site. After all, they're only selling jelly beans and that's not really the type of product that does well on the Web, right? Wrong. By putting content on their page, they've made it a site worth visiting and revisiting again and again.

The site is divided into the following sections:

Free Jelly Beans/Survey (this is how they get you to come back)

Jelly Belly Gift Pack Offer (this is how they make sales)

History of Jelly Belly Jelly Beans (content)

Questions & Answers (content)

Factory Tour (content)

Jelly Belly Menu (content)

Jelly Belly Recipes (content)

Jelly Belly Art Gallery (content)

I'd like to point out my two favorite content sections—the Factory Tour and the Free Jelly Beans/Survey. When you take the factory tour, you learn how jelly beans are made. Demonstrations are a great way to add content to your site. Lots of people like to know background information about how a product is made or how a process is performed. Like everything else, there are exceptions: one that immediately comes to mind is a meat-packing plant. I don't want a tour. I don't want to know what goes on. Please, don't tell me what you do to old Bessie.

The Free Jelly Beans/Survey page is a contest where the company gives out 500 samples a day of their product. You have to fill out a survey to receive the prize, but they don't make you fill it out unless you're a winner—that's really brilliant. Imagine filling out a survey and then losing and then coming back and filling it out again. Well, you wouldn't come back. I don't know how many times I've tried to win, but I finally won, as Figure 3.5 demonstrates:

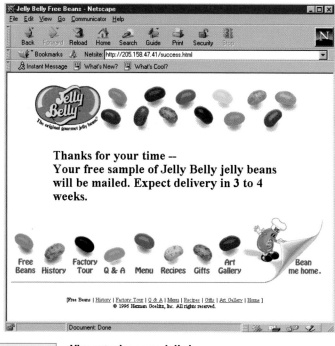

When I received my prize—a packet of free jelly beans, the Herman Goelitz company also included a color brochure with the official flavors and an invitation to join the Jelly Belly Taste Bud Club where for $4.95 I get various goodies, and for $10.95 I get various goodies, plus a T-shirt. Great marketing!

As a final note about content on this site, their Art Gallery is hysterical—all these works of art made out of jelly beans. Very clever.

The only complaint I have about the site is they don't seem to update their content often. Because you're only allowed to win once, there doesn't seem to be a reason to come back. I'm not sure what the solution is to this problem, but they should consider adding some new material.

A List Management Company Has Content

Figure 3.6 shows the home page for Edith Roman Associates, a well-known and well-respected list brokerage and list management firm. I know this because my background is in direct mail and if you're in the direct mail business, you know Edith Roman Associates.

Edith Roman provides some very compelling content. Notice the section Free Offers. *Free*—the word that makes Internet folk salivate. The first free offer is the List Catalog. Now, to get the free catalog or use their search facility you have to register because Edith wants your name—after all, she *is* in the list business.

If you've got content people want, you can get by with this tactic. If you don't, try the second tactic used in the Literature Downloads sections—give them content free of charge. There's one brochure, called "Stalking the Perfect High-Tech Sales Brochure," that gives you hints about how to put

FIGURE 3.5 **Vincent wins some jelly beans.**

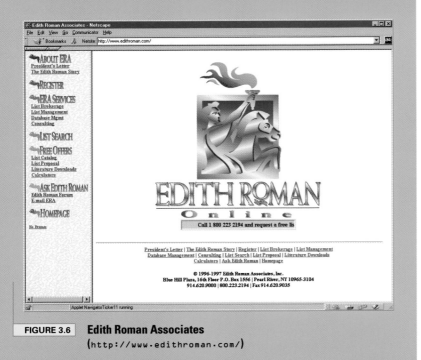

FIGURE 3.6   **Edith Roman Associates**
(`http://www.edithroman.com/`)

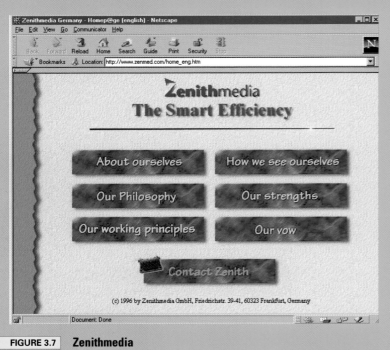

FIGURE 3.7   **Zenithmedia**
(`http://www.zenmed.com/home_eng.htm`)

together a successful high-tech sales brochure. All of these brochures can be helpful in your marketing efforts, and they make you feel kindly toward Edith Roman. And when you feel kindly toward her, you might just order one of her lists.

Her best feature, however, is her Calculators section, where she offers visitors free calculators. Everybody in the direct mail industry has these calculators in spreadsheet format. I suspect most people on the Web aren't in the direct mail industry and so these calculators will be new to the majority of visitors—that makes them a valuable marketing tool for Edith Roman. The "Return on Investment" calculator is an especially nice feature. As the page states, "This easy to use calculator will determine the cost and projected profit of your next direct mail campaign." Of course, you have to know certain figures, such as the amount of bad debt you allocate per unit sold, but you have these figures at your fingertips anyway, right?

After using the calculators and reading the literature, you decide that your visit to Edith Roman's site has been very positive. You feel good about it, and while you didn't initially want to register, you now feel that registering is a good idea because Edith Roman has been very helpful and you'd like a catalog. Ta-ching! It worked! Compelling content.

Let's compare this to a firm whose site content seems to be nothing more than a tooting of its own horn. Figure 3.7 shows the English version of Zenithmedia's home page.

The problem with this type of site is it's strictly self-congratulatory. Visitors don't care how great *you* are. What they want to know is what you are going to do for *them*. If this were a personal page, then it's okay to devote your site to your ego, but it's not okay for a business site to do this.

Other Types of Content

Whenever I get depressed and start feeling that the Internet has become one vast cyber–strip mall, I open the latest issue of *Yahoo! Internet Life* magazine or *The Web* magazine or any of the other news-stand magazines dealing with the Internet. Right there in front of me are hundreds of sites with content because these magazines can't afford to list sites without content. Even the weird sites they list, such as the Interactive Ego Booster, shown in Figure 3.8 (`http://web.syr.edu/~ablampac/ego/index.html`), and Ugly Earrings, shown in Figure 3.9 (`http://www.wco.com/~nelsnfam/uglyearing.html`), have more content than half of the business sites on the Net.

While a lot of this content has little applicability to your business, there are at least two ways you might be able to incorporate the concept into your site—putting valuable links to sites or paying to incorporate material into your site—which we'll discuss later in the chapter.

Obviously, if your site doesn't have content, you're going to have to spend some time, energy, and money rectifying the situation. Let's look at how you can add content to your site.

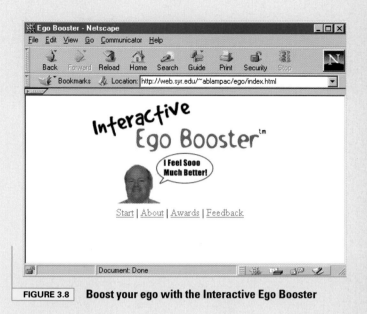

FIGURE 3.8   Boost your ego with the Interactive Ego Booster

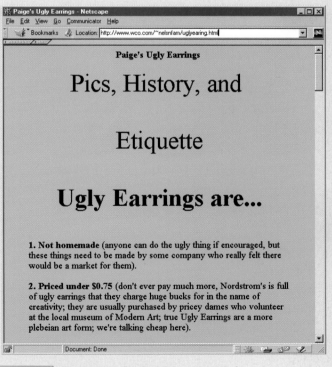

FIGURE 3.9   The beauty of ugly earrings revealed

ADDING CONTENT TO YOUR SITE

There are no shortcuts when it comes to adding content to your site. The word *adding* implies that you've got to exert some effort. Basically, there are two types of content you can add to your site:

1. Content you or your company creates

2. Content you buy or license

Adding Content You or Your Company Creates

The Jelly Belly site, shown earlier in Figure 3.4, is a perfect example of a site where the content was developed internally. They offer a virtual tour of the jelly bean creation process, a history of the jelly bean (notice it wasn't a boring history about the company and how cool great-grandfather was to come up with the concept), and a contest to win jelly beans.

But what can you do to add content to your site when you feel there really isn't any content? I can't restrain myself from asking the obvious question, "If there is no content, why are you even building a site?"

Let's take my stereotypical favorite type of site—a company selling vitamins. What kind of content could anyone possibly come up with that will make a vitamin site interesting to the public?

Look back at the sites discussed earlier in the chapter that I felt had content. What did they offer? Frequently updated information, contests and sweepstakes, tours, demonstrations, recipes, art made from the product being sold, questions and answers, history, free offers, and unique information.

And there are a few items that didn't appear in those sites that are also great ways to add content:

Links

Coupons

Tie-ins

Frequently Updated Information *Update* your site as often as you can afford the time and/or money. Seriously, I can't stress this enough. I feel somewhat guilty because I'm not spending pages and pages explaining this topic, but it's really a simple concept—update your content. Please remember one small detail. New crap is still crap. Add content.

And don't stick *placeholder* pages up and just leave them there. (A placeholder page is a page that says "Coming Soon" or "This Site Is Under Construction" and none of the links go anywhere.) A prime example of a placeholder page is the Web site for the Mayor of Portland, Oregon. I don't know how long the page shown in Figure 3.10 has been like this, but it's been this way for almost all of 1997.

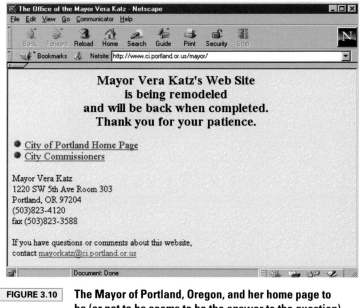

FIGURE 3.10   **The Mayor of Portland, Oregon, and her home page to be (or not to be seems to be the answer to the question)** (http://www.ci.portland.or.us/mayor/)

Contests and Sweepstakes Contests are a great way to generate interest in your site—for at least as long as you're having the contest. How the Jelly Belly folks set up their contest is very clever—they're giving away their product. The theory is the winners will like the jelly beans and then go out and buy only Jelly Belly jelly beans.

Michael and I wanted to have a contest promoting this book. We came up with the two perfect prizes:

> **First prize:** One week in Bakersfield, California (or $1,000)
>
> **Second prize:** Two weeks in Bakersfield, California (or $500)

We chose Bakersfield because that's where we both live and the town has been the butt of so many jokes about hicks. In fact, that was the rationale for the prizes: Bakersfield is such a hell-hole that the second place winner would have to spend more time here because he or she didn't win the first place prize. We thought it was a very funny way to promote the book.

It seems like such an easy concept: have a contest to give away money, vitamins, or whatever. The problem with contests and sweepstakes is they involve serious legal issues; they are a lot more complicated to conduct than you might think. The Arent Fox Web site (`http://www.arentfox.com/features/sweepstakes/faq/faq.html`) discusses some of the issues you have to consider before holding a contest or sweepstakes; for instance, can you limit participation, can the prize be a charitable donation, do you need to post a bond and register?

If you're considering having a contest or sweepstakes on your site, this site should be one of your first stops.

Everything is complicated, isn't it?

Tours I'm not sure a site *selling* vitamins is a candidate for a tour ("Hey, wanna see my studio apartment?"), but if you're manufacturing vitamins, you could certainly provide a tour of the plant on your Web site. My father worked for a television station. Because I got to go to the station a lot, it wasn't a big deal to me, but to my friends, a TV studio was an exciting place. They wanted to know what each piece of equipment was for, how the sets were built, how the shows were filmed, and so on. To some people, even a vitamin factory can be interesting. Let those desk-bound white-collar workers see how the rest of the world makes a living.

Demonstrations If you sold vitamins, you might want to show how they're made. If you have an herb shop, then your demonstration might take on a different form, such as showing your visitors how to make an herbal wreath or how to use the branches from the herb rosemary to make a great chicken kabob.

A demonstration should provide the visitor with information they wouldn't find anywhere else.

Recipes A recipe is, in a certain sense, a demonstration. Obviously, a computer store doesn't need to provide recipes, but recipes can add spice to sites you might not think of: a bridal shop (newlywed cooking on both sides often leaves something to be desired), a fireplace shop (food to eat while you're sitting by the fire), or a garden center (this is a little more obvious because they sell vegetables and herbs).

Speaking of garden centers, one of the best known herb growers, Richters Herbs, would be a logical candidate for a recipe page. As Figure 3.11 demonstrates, they don't have any links on the topic (they

FIGURE 3.11   **Richters Herb Specialists**
(http://www.richters.com/)

FIGURE 3.12   *American Gothic* made from
Jelly Belly jelly beans

do have links concerning other uses of herbs). Herb lovers will definitely find the site worth visiting.

Art Made from the Product Jelly Belly may be one of the few sites on the Web that can use this technique (see Figure 3.12 for a Jelly Belly version of *American Gothic*). However, there are some fun things you can do that are sort of related to your business. My ex-boss owned a software company, and he had a bunch of old Wang minicomputer terminals lying around the basement. Several of the employees tossed around the idea of filming a programmer riddling the terminals with bullets and then putting the video up on the Web. Sort of a Terminator motif. Okay, it was a slow day, and we were bored. There may be some amusing things you can add to your site that would make people visit. Even the antigun lobby might enjoy seeing a computer shot up, but try to keep the art tied to the company and make an effort not to alienate people.

Questions and Answers A FAQ (Frequently Asked Questions) page is always a good idea. Any time you sell a product on the Web people are going to have questions they want answered. Using the vitamin site as an example, obvious questions would concern dosage, usage—things like that. Be careful of what you say, however, because you're dealing with health issues and you're probably not an M.D.

History If done well, a history-of-the-company page can be enlightening. Of course, there's a much greater chance a history page will bore the living daylights out of the reader so you have to know what to use and what to lose. For God's sake, please don't include mission statements. I talked about this in Chapter 1. And whatever you do, don't let the president or a committee pass judgment on the history page. In fact, the fewer committees you have to deal with, the better your life as a designer will be.

Free Offers If there's one thing people who use the Internet love more than life itself, it's almost anything that's free. It's the old something for nothing concept that keeps people entering contests, filling out forms, heck, even buying lottery tickets. (In the United States, lotteries are used as a tax on the math-impaired portion of our population.) If you can come up with a free offer that's legal (and I stress the word *legal* here) like the Jelly Belly people did, then you'll be able to hook those suckers—I mean, attract visitors to your site.

Unique Information This is the name of the game, folks. What kind of unique information can you bring to your Web site to entice people to visit? Obviously, cigar sites can tell you how to light the darn things; record companies can let you listen to songs and tell you all about the artists (however, the sites I've seen are so sanitized they make the musicians look like Mother Theresa); cooking sites can post recipes; and auto sites can let you see images of the cars currently in stock.

While I like to banter on about content, the fact is there are some sites where it's pretty darn tough to come up with anything. If you've got to create a site for a company that furnishes car wash equipment—such as Dilling-Harris, Inc., the company shown in Figure 3.13—then creative ideas are hard to come by. They offer a typical car wash layout for prospective customers, but this isn't the place to put a link to recipes. A history of the car wash *might* entice readers—notice the emphasis on the word *might*. Visitors might also be interested in seeing the car wash equipment in action through a Quicktime movie or some other movie format. Although I'm usually against the practice of needlessly adding bandwidth-devouring applications, a video with the song "Carwash" playing in the background might make sense here—as long as you keep it short and sweet.

As far as adding content, Michael thinks a page outlining the money-making potential of the car wash business would be fascinating. Another concept would be a page outlining the advantages of automatic self-service car washes over tunnel car washes. A good title for the page might be "So, You Want to Get into the Car Wash Business."

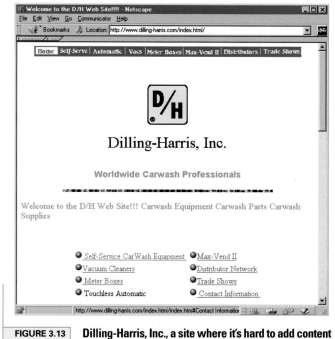

FIGURE 3.13 **Dilling-Harris, Inc., a site where it's hard to add content**
(`http://www.dilling-harris.com/index.html/`)

Links In the "old" days, it was a no-brainer to add links to your page—hey, it was the Internet; links were what it was all about. Then came the commercial success of the Internet, and everybody got so damn touchy, lawsuits erupted, and the concept of whether anyone has the right to link to an outside site without the permission of the outside site came into question. It has yet to be settled. If I remember correctly, Microsoft wanted to provide TicketMaster content within its Sidewalk sites. TicketMaster didn't

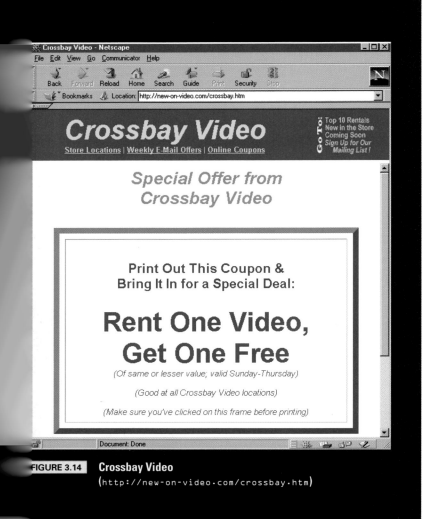

FIGURE 3.14 **Crossbay Video**
(`http://new-on-video.com/crossbay.htm`)

In fact, it doesn't take a whole lot of thought to come up with a list of links that might be valuable to add. Let's say you're a computer-training company; you might want to add links to the home pages of different hardware and software vendors (you might not depending on whether they actively promote *their* training services). An insurance company might want links to different weather-related or homeowner sites. A real estate site has an interesting set of problems creating links. Initially, you'd think it would make sense to link to the local newspaper and TV and radio stations. Wrong. These are the last places a real estate company wants to link to. These media generally only talk about the bad things that are happening in town— "Three dead in latest turf war. Sports scores on page 59." If, or when, the link issue gets resolved, links might be a good way to add content to your site. However, don't start adding links to other sites like they're salt on your popcorn. You need to assess the risk. The problem with outside links is that they invite people to leave your site and never return.

like the terms, and after much wrangling, the deal fell through. Microsoft linked to TicketMaster (using trademarked images) anyway, implying endorsement and direct cooperation through Microsoft. Not so— hence a legal battle.

Until a final decision is rendered—if it ever is—I really can't advise you on what to do. If the courts rule that it's okay to link, then you should definitely link to sites that might be useful to your business but aren't competitors. If they were competitors, they wouldn't really be useful, would they?

It's not a bad idea to send a quick message off to the Webmaster requesting to put a link to their site on yours. Maybe they'll even feel obligated to put a link back to yours!

Coupons Figure 3.14 shows a classic example of a coupon on a video-rental store's Web page. If your site has a local presence, coupons are a total no-brainer way of adding content to your site. There are lots of people who like to use coupons, and offering coupons on your site is also a good way to track how well your Web site is doing.

Keep in mind, however, that coupons work best if you have a local business, such as a tire store, restaurant—well, just about anything works.

Tie-ins A tie-in is similar to a link except that you, the site owner, get paid for putting in links to outside pages. Besides getting paid, you also make your site more valuable because you're adding content to your pages.

Figure 3.15 shows you the Bridal Timeline page for the French Shop, a bridal salon located here in Bakersfield, California. Logically, it isn't enough just to list the products available for sale. You need a way to entice visitors; for instance, the French Shop provides a list of "Things to Do" before the wedding.

While the list provided here is nice, the site owner could probably add a special page that would only be available for clients of the shop. This page would include links to local businesses that are bridal related—*and that have paid the owner to be listed.* Using our bridal example, possible links would include: beauty shops, caterers, decorations and accessories, florists, groom's wear, guest accommodations, invitations, jewelers, music, photographers, videographers, reception locations, transportation, travel agents, and wedding cakes.

The owner could charge more for a site placed at the top of the list or they could charge for including a link to a site, or—well, you get the point.

Take a look at your site and determine which of these techniques you can implement. Then implement them.

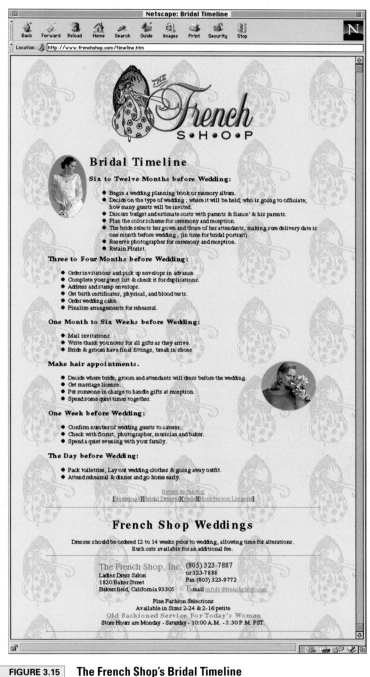

FIGURE 3.15 **The French Shop's Bridal Timeline**
(`http://www.frenchshop.com/timeline.htm`)

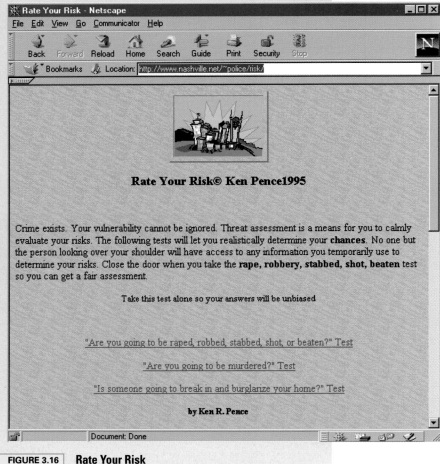

FIGURE 3.16 **Rate Your Risk**
(`http://www.nashville.net/~police/risk/`)

Adding Content That You Buy or License

Sometimes it's easier just to buy someone else's content or license its use on your Web site. Let's say you're an insurance company and you'd like to scare your customers into buying more life or home insurance. You could create a link to the site shown in Figure 3.16, or you could possibly arrange to license this material to include in your site; then you'll look like you were the genius who came up with the idea.

On the Rate Your Risk page, there are three tests you can take.

1. "Are you going to be raped, robbed, stabbed, shot, or beaten?"

2. "Are you going to be murdered?"

3. "Is someone going to break in and burglarize your home?"

Talk about scaring the living daylights out of someone—these titles are wonderful! Figure 3.17 shows the first part of the "Are you going to be murdered?" test.

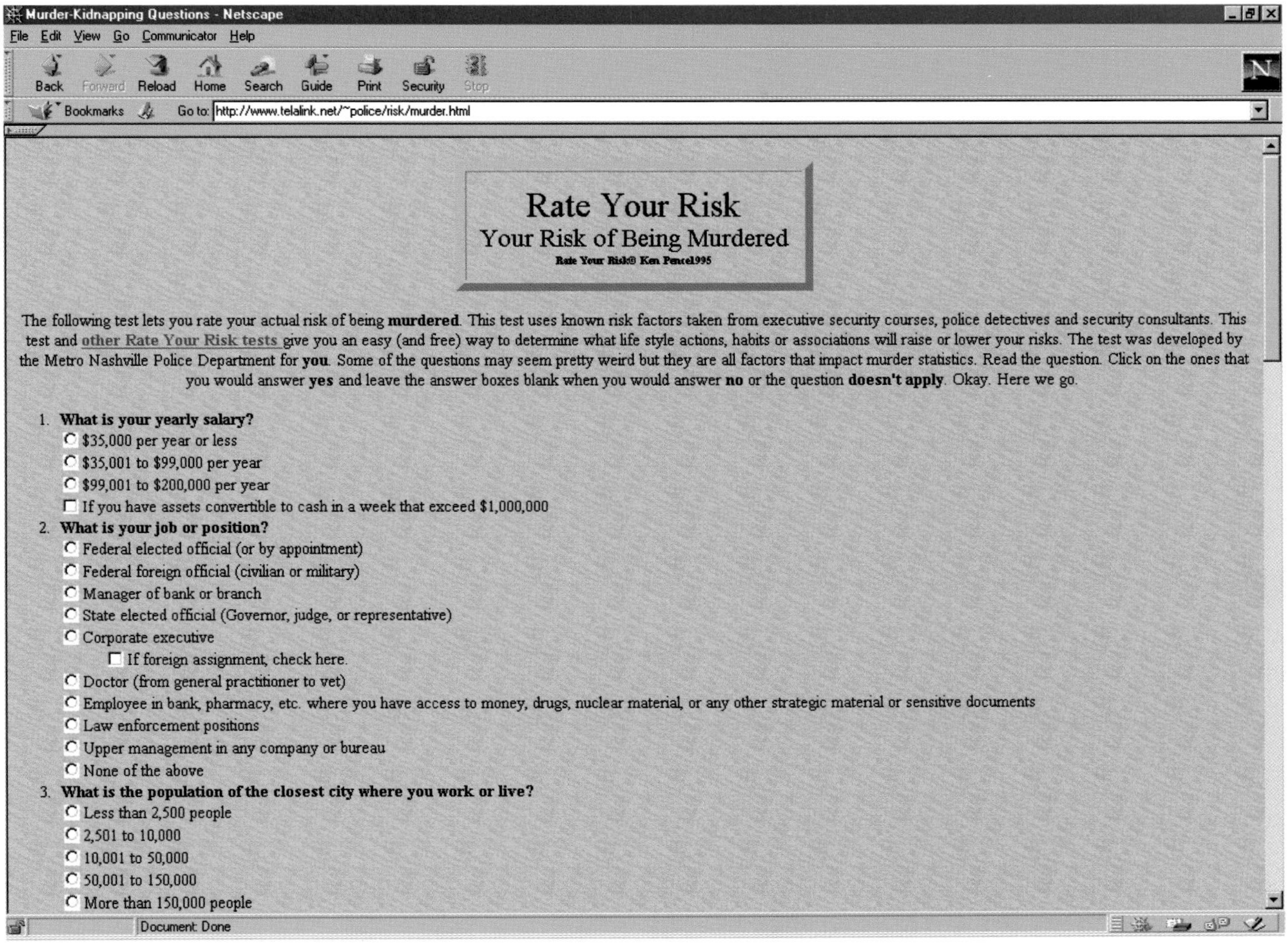

Rate Your Risk
Your Risk of Being Murdered
Rate Your Risk® Ken Pence1995

The following test lets you rate your actual risk of being **murdered**. This test uses known risk factors taken from executive security courses, police detectives and security consultants. This test and other Rate Your Risk tests give you an easy (and free) way to determine what life style actions, habits or associations will raise or lower your risks. The test was developed by the Metro Nashville Police Department for **you**. Some of the questions may seem pretty weird but they are all factors that impact murder statistics. Read the question. Click on the ones that you would answer **yes** and leave the answer boxes blank when you would answer **no** or the question **doesn't apply**. Okay. Here we go.

1. **What is your yearly salary?**
   - $35,000 per year or less
   - $35,001 to $99,000 per year
   - $99,001 to $200,000 per year
   - If you have assets convertible to cash in a week that exceed $1,000,000
2. **What is your job or position?**
   - Federal elected official (or by appointment)
   - Federal foreign official (civilian or military)
   - Manager of bank or branch
   - State elected official (Governor, judge, or representative)
   - Corporate executive
       - If foreign assignment, check here.
   - Doctor (from general practitioner to vet)
   - Employee in bank, pharmacy, etc. where you have access to money, drugs, nuclear material, or any other strategic material or sensitive documents
   - Law enforcement positions
   - Upper management in any company or bureau
   - None of the above
3. **What is the population of the closest city where you work or live?**
   - Less than 2,500 people
   - 2,501 to 10,000
   - 10,001 to 50,000
   - 50,001 to 150,000
   - More than 150,000 people

Document Done

FIGURE 3.17 **"Are you going to be murdered?" test**
(http://www.telalink.net/~police/risk/murder.html)

Isn't this great? This site is a perfect candidate for an insurance firm that wants to license some content.

Search the Internet to see if there are any interesting sites that would be willing to license their content to you. It could be a lot cheaper—and certainly a lot easier—than creating it yourself.

Hopefully, this chapter has inspired you to put (again and again) lots of content on your site. Next, we'll examine the area where Web designers make a lot of mistakes—graphics.

Flanders & Willis's Reality Check

We're not here to insult you, your dog, or your CEO, but we can't think of any image you could possibly put on your page that someone would wait minutes to see. Actually, we can think of a couple—for some reason people will wait forever to see pictures of naked or dead bodies. But if your site doesn't have one of these images, don't expect them to wait. Period.

CHAPTER 4

Bookmarks Netsite: http://www.pepsi.com/main/nav/home_main1.html

Fixing Your Graphic Problems

IN THIS CHAPTER

we're going to examine Herbal
.com, a site owned by me, co-
author Vincent Flanders. Both
Michael and I spent a lot of time
trying to create a Web page full
of graphics errors—errors that
are common to a lot of Web
pages on the Internet. We'll see
what's wrong with this page,
why it's wrong, and how to fix it
so it doesn't...well...so it doesn't
look so bad. Although it's a man-
ufactured page, we'll critique it
as we would any other page.

Toward the end of the chapter, we'll cover some other graphics mistakes, like *bevelmania* and *clichéd* images, which are not in the Herbal.com Web page but do tend to litter the Internet landscape.

HERBAL.COM

Herbal.com, shown in Figure 4.1, was created to sell holistic products via the Web. While the designer appears to have had some good intentions, the imple-mentation basically sucks. Before getting into the specifics, there are two Golden Rules all Web designers *must* keep in the forefront of their minds: First, faster is better, so don't make visitors wait too long for your graphics to download or they'll leave. Seriously. Second, once a page downloads, it better not be ugly. Herbal.com violates both of these rules—and then some.

FIGURE 4.1 The first design for Herbal.com

Why Does This Page Suck?

Herbal.com has the following design flaws:

1. The graphics are way too big.

2. A GIF image was used instead of a JPEG.

3. The HEIGHT and WIDTH parameters were changed, not the actual image size on the plant image.

4. The HEIGHT and WIDTH parameters weren't filled in on the button images.

5. The page is too long.

6. The background image sucks.

7. It doesn't use browser-safe colors.

8. The page also commits a not-so-obvious graphics mistake: The ALT parameter wasn't used (trust us, once you read the ALT parameter section, you'll see why this is important…).

9. It uses some bad graphics.

We'll spend the first half of the chapter looking at each of these issues in detail. Then we'll move on to other types of graphics problems and end it all with a makeover of the Herbal.com site.

1. THE GRAPHICS ARE WAY TOO BIG

The most significant improvement you can make to your site is to *limit* the physical dimensions and/or the physical size of your graphics files.

This is the *number one* design mistake on the Web. Repeat:

The number one design mistake made on the Web is using large graphics, and almost everybody is guilty of committing it.

A friend, who owns a company that puts out an esoteric product for the software industry, asked me to talk to his Web page designer as he planned their site. During my mini-design seminar, I stressed the importance of keeping the images small, which the designer seemed to agree with.

Three weeks later, I surfed to the new site and discovered that the home page had 135K of great looking graphics, which would take 35.9 seconds to download with a 28.8Kbps modem (kilobytes per second) and 71.8 seconds with a 14.4Kbps modem! Obviously, the designer just did not get it. Great looking graphics are fine, but nobody—and I mean *nobody*—is going to wait to see 135K worth of this-company-is-great pictures.

This rant brings me to the picture of the Lion's Tail plant (*Leonotis leonurus*) that is the centerpiece of the Herbal.com site in Figure 4.1. The image is 902×1072 pixels and takes up 356,338 bytes (356K). Bad.

So why are big images bad? In the September 1997 issue of *Windows Sources Magazine*, Paul Bonner said:

"Pages that take a minute or more to load just don't cut it with the average Web surfer whose attention span for new sites has been measured at only about 8 seconds."

UUNET, one of the largest providers of Internet bandwidth, ran an ad that sums it up: "Someone just clicked on your Web site. The next fifteen seconds will make you or break you." We should basically split the difference and say the average attention span is 10 seconds—tops <grin>.

The Average Joe on a Modem

So how long *will* it take the plant image (356K) to download? Using a 14.4Kbps connection, it will take approximately *four minutes* to download just the picture. With a 28.8Kbps connection, it will take roughly two minutes. I'm not here to insult you, your dog, or your CEO, but I can't think of any image you could possibly put on your page that someone would wait two minutes to see. (Actually, I can think of some. See "The Graphics That People Will Wait to See" sidebar.) If visitors can't load your pages quickly, they're going to leave. Period.

The typical designer's reply to this bit of information is often, "Hey, it loads quickly for me when I dial up the page on the Web, so what's the deal?" Well, if this page loads quickly for you, you've got a high-end connection to the Internet.

A high-end connection (128Kbps ISDN or greater) is the greatest curse bestowed upon any Web designer because they forget how the rest of the world lives. I had a LAN connection to a DS3 (45Mb/sec straight to the Internet); my 100K pages loaded just fine, thank you. But I soon heard from disgruntled customers that I wasn't surfing in the real world. So how does the real world surf? Well, according to a report by e-stats (`http://www.e-land.com/e-stat_pages/ net_usage_patterns_menu.html`), approximately 40 percent of Internet users surf at 28.8Kbps and, more importantly, *30 percent surf at 14.4Kbps.* That means 70 percent of Internet users are surfing at 28.8Kbps or slower.

If that doesn't convince you to use small images, consider this: the 6th WWW User Survey study, which is performed by the Graphics, Visualization, & Usability Center of the College of Computing at the Georgia Institute of Technology, found that 76.55 percent of Web users reported *speed* was the main problem with using the Web. Big pictures slow down the Internet. Big movie files slow down the Internet. Big sound files slow down the Internet. Is this getting through?

And don't think everybody's going to pay $40 a month to install a cable modem/ADSL/T1/___ (fill-in-the-blank) at their home so bandwidth won't be a problem. That'll be the day. Yes, cable modems exist for the lucky few, but as soon as bandwidth goes up, so will the amount of graphics on the average page, no doubt. Maybe Bill Gates's satellite system due in 2002 will solve our bandwidth problems. Maybe I'll get down to the weight I was in high school.

Is It Ever Okay to Use Large Images?

There are at least two situations where it's okay to use big images:

1. Certain types of pages—fan pages, e-zines, and special interest pages (art galleries, movie, music, scientific, photography, game sites, others of that ilk). People who go to these pages don't care how long it takes the page to load—they'll wait.

   My 13-year-old daughter is a perfect example. She'll wait forever to see pictures of this group called Hanson (see, it's a fan site). But the only reason she'll wait forever is because she's totally convinced—along with two million other girls—that she's going to marry Taylor Hanson.

   Remember: This type of site is the exception; if you're a business or a nonprofit organization, no one is going to wait for your images to load.

2. Your files are on an *intranet.* An intranet is an internal Internet where the speed of the connection is significantly faster. In that case, make 'em as big as your connection can handle; your users will tolerate it.

The Graphics That

People Will Wait to See

There are two more types of large images that many people will wait to see download and they both involve bodies—naked and dead.

People will wait forever to see pornographic images download because...well, never mind. Pictures of dead bodies also seem to fascinate people. If your site features naked or dead bodies, you don't need to worry about the size of the images—they'll wait.

Actually, there's also a third type of image people will wait to see: tasteless, sophomoric, and/or humorous images.

The image featuring the former American football star and current social pariah O.J. Simpson is just the kind of image some people will wait for.

O.J. with the bloody knife—a rather tasteless American piece of humor

How Much Is Too Much?

Keep the total size of your graphics below 35K *per page*. It takes approximately 31 seconds to download 35K worth of graphics using a 14.4Kbps modem or 15 seconds using a 28.8Kbps modem. While people will wait to see certain types of pictures download, keeping your images small will improve the quality of your pages more than just about anything else you can do. Well, besides adding content, as discussed back in Chapter 3.

If you've got content—*real* content, not some BS multilevel marketing story or other similar garbage—then you can put larger images on your page. If you don't, keep the size of the page small by keeping your images small.

Back on September 12, 1997, c|net reported that Microsoft was limiting the size of each of their pages to 60K and removing Java apps from the site. Obviously, their Java move could be interpreted as political, but not their decision to limit the physical size of their pages. Averaging 120 million hits per day, Microsoft realized it could save bandwidth by dealing with the size of the images on its 200,000 plus pages. Before you designers start whining, "Well, Microsoft thinks we can have at least 60K on a page," let me point out one fact: Microsoft has more content on their pages than 50 percent of the Web sites on the Internet. If you've got Microsoftian content—not some vitamin marketing site—then 60K is an acceptable limit.

Speed Doesn't Kill, Waiting Does

If you loaded Figure 4.1 from the CD into your browser, you would see a page that loads at a reasonable rate. If you were to copy it over to your hard disk and load the page, it would load very, very quickly.

Here's an important fact most beginners (and some old-timers) forget. Web pages load infinitely faster from your CD-ROM drive or hard disk than they load from the Internet!

Some of the better HTML editors (HotDog and HomeSite on the Wintel (PC) platform) have internal utilities that calculate the loading time for a document. For example, HomeSite says the Herbal.com page, shown in Figure 4.1, is 423.20K and will, under optimum conditions, take the following times to load:

Modem Speed	Time to Load (seconds)
14.4Kbps	264.5
28.8Kbps	132.3
57.6Kbps	66.1

To feel the full agony of loading this page, download it from the Internet (go to `http://www .webpages thatsuck.com/h0/bc1`). Compare the figures with your modem speed. Notice how agonizingly long it takes to load the page.

Optimizing the Size of Your Images

It's important to optimize the size of your images because the smaller the image, the faster it loads. Check out these sites for more information:

Bandwidth Conservation Society
(`http://www.infohiway.com/faster`)
This is one of the *most important* sites on the Internet. It is also one of the original sources on how to reduce the size of your graphics without reducing the quality of the images (or only minimally reducing the quality). Go here first.

Optimizing Web Graphics (http://www
.webreference.com/dev/graphics) The
folks at Webreference.com have an excellent
tutorial on all aspects of graphic optimization.

GIF Wizard (http://www.gifwizard.com)
Michael and I think this site is another one of
the *most important* sites on the Internet—even
though they charge for many of their services.
Businesses have to pay to use the service;
however, many functions are free for personal
pages. When I showed this site to Michael, he
said, "I love it so much, I'm willing to have
their baby." In light of this, let's take a closer
look at what GIF Wizard actually does.

So what does GIF Wizard actually do? Simple. You
give it the URL or the filename of a GIF, animated
GIF, or JPEG file, and it performs the calculations
and reduces the size of the image and shows you the
results online. You can then save the image to your
disk. The online display of the results is what sets this
site apart from the software that's available. You'll
achieve a 20–40 percent reduction with little, if any,
loss of quality.

Figure 4.2 shows an image whose file size is reduced
19 percent and 30 percent with little, if any, notice-
able loss of visual quality.

There are also several useful software programs; however, there's one caveat: All software is subject to
change and improvement—and no group of software
is more subject to change than Internet software. The
term *Internet time* signifies the shortened development
cycles on the Internet. In Internet time, there can be
as many as four major product revisions in the space
of a year; it's hard to keep up.

After trying just about every graphics-optimization
package out there on the Windows 95/NT platform
and finding most of them wanting in one area or

FIGURE 4.2 **GIF Wizard does its magic**

another, I sorta-kinda like these:

Ulead JPEG SmartSaver (`http://www.ulead.com`) It does a much better job than its counterpart Ulead GIF SmartSaver or its companion PhotoImpact GIF Optimizer.

DeBabelizer Pro (`http://www.equilibrium.com`) It's expensive: $595 list (approximately $390 Windows street price versus the $260 Mac price). It's a big, cumbersome, powerful program that is probably overkill for the average person.

HVS ColorGIF 2 (`http://www.digfrontiers.com`) This Photoshop plug-in is available for both Windows 95 and Macintosh; it has a really quick conversion to the Netscape 216 palette; and it costs $99. The major complaint is the preview window is too small, so you can't see enough of the image.

WebGraphics Optimizer (WGO) (`http://www.WebOpt.com`) This Windows 95–based shareware program can reduce the physical size of the file *and keep the quality.*

Finally, Michael thinks this graphics-optimization package is really cool:

PhotoGIF from BoxTop Software (`http://www.boxtopsoft.com`) They've got an excellent article about reducing GIF images at `http://www.boxtopsoft.com/Resources/tech101.html`. The Windows 95 version was available October 1, 1997. The Mac version costs $45.

If you don't want to buy a program like these, there's a real simple rule to follow: When you create an image, create it at the final size you need. This way, you're done and you don't have to worry about the problems inherent in reducing an image.

Cropping Your Images The best way to cut down the size of your image is to physically crop the image. Remember, all those extra pixels add up. See Figure 4.3 for an example of a graphic badly in need of cropping.

FIGURE 4.3 **This graphic needs to be cropped.**

Obviously, if you delete the extra white space in Figure 4.3, you'll cut down the size of the file, and cutting down the size of the file means your page will load faster. This is good. Really good.

2. A GIF IMAGE WAS USED INSTEAD OF JPEG

There's another problem with the picture of the Lion's Tail plant on Herbal.com (see Figure 4.1 at the beginning of the chapter) that isn't apparent unless you examine the source code—it's a GIF image, not a JPEG. There's a time and a place for using each file format.

GIF works best with images that use fewer, yet distinctive, colors, such as buttons, icons, and straight-edge images (cartoons and line-art), and textual images. It doesn't work well with images that have blurred edges. Photographs with degrees of shading are perfect examples of this. Table 4.1 gives you the lowdown on GIF images.

TOO COOL

 Select a larger picture of Sara Maria as she ponders her first snowman. Gu

Sara Marie's first snowman—and it's a dandy.

USING THUMBNAILS TO CUT DOWN THE SIZE OF YOUR GRAPHICS

A lot of designers reduce the HEIGHT and WIDTH parameters of the <IMG> tag to create thumbnail images. Don't do this!

The image file stays the same huge size. Take your image and either:

- Physically reduce the size of the whole image

    or

- Cut a portion out of the image

The absolute best use of thumbnail images on the Internet is located at `http://bizweb.lightspeed.net/~ham/sarade.htm`. Dave Waterman created a page about his visit to Germany to see his grand-daughter, Sara Maria. Ironically, the best thumbnail is on a personal page—not a business site.

Dave created a 2.9K (2,962-byte) JPEG image, shown above, as a link to a 26K image. (I'll talk more about JPEG versus GIF in the next section of the chapter.) Dave deserves an HTML pat-on-the-back

A little perspective makes all the difference.

for listing the size of the image in the descriptive text. You risk alienating your visitors if you don't tell them how big the image will be.

When you click the image, you'll see the best thumbnail on the Web.

Notice how the thumbnail made you think Sara's first snowman was a full-size snowman—not the cute little one you see above. Great editing.

Supports	Does Not Support
Only 256 colors	More than 256 colors
Transparent images	
Animation *(not necessarily good—I'll discuss this in detail later)*	
Comments *(these are hidden)*	
Interlacing *(a percentage of the picture is displayed at one time)*	
Lossless compression *(when the pixels are compressed and decompressed, no pixels are lost, so the image remains the same)*	Lossy compression *(when pixels are compressed certain pixels are removed)*
Royalty payments to UNISYS who holds the patents. *(this is somewhat misleading; end users or image creators don't owe royalty payments, licensing fees actually, to Unisys—only those who produce graphic-editing tools that can output GIFs)*	

TABLE 4.1   **The GIF File Format**

JPEG works best with color or with black and white photographs where there are a lot of smooth color changes. While black and white photographs work well with JPEG, straight black and white images don't unless there are at least 16 shades of gray. JPEG also doesn't work well with text. Table 4.2 gives you the skinny on the JPEG file format.

Supports	Does Not Support
16.7 million colors	Transparency
Interlacing	Animation
	Comments
	Lossless compression
	Royalty payments

TABLE 4.2   **The JPEG File Format**

Okay, what about the Herbal.com Web site? Well, as mentioned earlier, the plant picture was originally a GIF that took up 356K (365,338 bytes). I used Photoshop to change this image to the JPEG format, and the size of the plant picture is now "only" 120K (123,291 bytes)—a significant improvement, but still way too big. I haven't used any optimization techniques, however. You can see the "new and improved" image in Figure 4.4.

FIGURE 4.4   **The new and improved plant picture**

3. HEIGHT AND WIDTH PARAMETERS WERE CHANGED, NOT ACTUAL IMAGE SIZE

When my daughter was two years old, she tossed her blankie over her head and announced, "I'm invisible, you can't see me." To her young mind, if she couln't see us, then we couldn't see her. This sweet scene has its counterpart in the HTML world.

Web page designers somehow feel that if they reduce the HEIGHT and WIDTH parameters of the `<IMG>` tag (this tag is used to display an image on the screen), then the size of the file will automatically be reduced. It doesn't work that way. The plant image from Herbal.com is really 902 pixels wide—too wide for most screens—but changing the HEIGHT and WIDTH parameters of the `<IMG>` tag forced it to fit on the screen. Just because the parameter was changed so the image fits the screen doesn't mean the image is physically smaller— it's not; the file size is still 356K.

4. THE HEIGHT AND WIDTH PARAMETER WASN'T FILLED IN

For those of you unfamiliar with HTML, here's the HTML code for the picture of the plant:

```
<IMG SRC="plant1.gif" WIDTH=902 HEIGHT=1072>
```

Today, most HTML editors automatically calculate the HEIGHT and WIDTH parameters of the image for you. If you're creating your HTML files with an older editor or if you're a propeller head and use a text editor like Notepad, you'll have to figure out what the HEIGHT and WIDTH parameters are and fill them in yourselves. Windows users have the option of using a program such as HTML Power Tools' Image Tag Scanner, which will go through files and calculate the size of the images and insert this information inside the HTML documents. Go to `http://www.opposite.com/` to download Windows 3.*x* and Windows 95 versions.

Why are the HEIGHT and WIDTH parameters important? Because if they're set, the browser allocates space for the image, which it will fill in later, and then moves on to load the text. Assuming the parameters are set correctly, the text links will load before large *imagemap* graphics (an imagemap is an image that is treated by the browser as a navigational tool). The visitor can read the text links and click them before waiting to see the imagemap.

For your visitors' sakes, fill in the HEIGHT and WIDTH parameters so their browser will know what to do.

TOO COOL

HOW BIG *IS* THE WORKING AREA FOR A WEB PAGE?

The talented folks at Yale University have given this topic a great deal of thought (`http:// info.med.yale.edu/caim/ manual/pages/safe_area.html`) and have come up with some staggering conclusions.

Design pages for the lowest screen resolution possible: 640x480. Use safe areas. A safe area is the area where it's safe to design pages given either of the two following scenarios:

1. If you want the maximum screen area for graphics and are not concerned with people printing the pages, the dimensions are:

   Maximum width = 595 pixels
   Maximum height = 295 pixels

2. If you're designing your pages so they can be printed, the dimensions are:

   Maximum width = 535 pixels
   Maximum height = 295 pixels

Why so small when the screen size is 640x480? These figures take into account the amount of screen real estate a browser takes up.

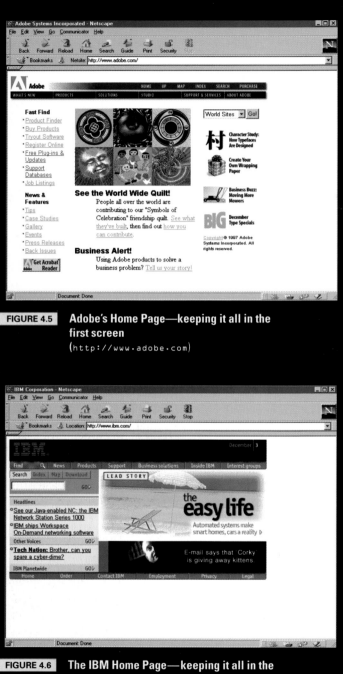

FIGURE 4.5 Adobe's Home Page—keeping it all in the first screen
(http://www.adobe.com)

FIGURE 4.6 The IBM Home Page—keeping it all in the first screen
(http://www.ibm.com)

5. THE PAGE IS TOO LONG

If you look back at Figure 4.1, you'll notice the page is really long and it features a common error: subjectivity. The designer fell in love with the graphics and wanted to showcase them more than the links to the rest of the site. (It's probably hard to believe the designer fell in love with these particular graphics, but most designers truly like the images they are using; they don't purposely pick sucky ones.)

As pointed out in "How Big *Is* the Working Area for a Web Page?" the length of the average monitor screen is roughly 295 pixels. At 1,836 pixels, this page is at least *six* screenloads long. Worse than the length is the fact that you have to scroll down *three* screenloads before you get to the links to the rest of the site. A lot of people don't want to scroll down more than two screenloads, so if you have a long page, you'll lose them.

Take a look at a couple of successful sites, such as the Adobe site shown in Figure 4.5 and the IBM site in Figure 4.6. The links are almost always in the first screen. If anyone bothered to wait to see the Herbal.com site load (remember, the page takes over four minutes to download), it's doubtful they'd want to wade through all the junk to get to the links. Don't fall so in love with your graphics that you make it difficult to find the links to the rest of your site.

THE IMPORTANCE OF TEXT LINKS

Along with graphic links, it's important to have text links on your site. This statement is even more important when you're using imagemaps. If the imagemap doesn't load or the server is acting up, clicking the image won't send the visitor to a new page. They'll be stuck—and most likely leave, never to return. Alas, you need a way to get your visitor to the rest of the site, and text links are the way.

6. THE BACKGROUND IMAGE SUCKS

One school of Web page design says you should never use background images. The rationale is that background images can make the text harder to read and can also make the Web page take longer to load. On the other hand, many people believe that background images can enhance a page. In the case of Herbal.com, visitors would have been better served if the designer had subscribed to the former philosophy—not only is the background image illegally large (31K), but it also doesn't tile correctly, so you see the seams. Figure 4.7 shows you the Herbal.com background and how the seams show in the background tile.

If you're going to use background images, you want them to look like one continuous image, rather than a bunch of squares. Speaking of bunches of squares, Figure 4.8 shows an example of a real site with a sucky background.

Remember, when you use a background like the one shown in Figure 4.1, you're telling the world "I'm an amateur," and nobody takes an amateur seriously.

There are any number of sites that discuss how to make seamless tiles. One site that gives a good explanation is `http://www.stink.com/web/webtile/`**. If that site isn't enough, go to the AltaVista search engine (`http://altavista.digital.com`) and search using the keywords** *"seamless tiles"* **(include the double quotes).**

Because sucky background images are so prevalent on the Web, let's spend some time talking about color and those little repeating striped backgrounds that make me want to pull what little hair I have out of my head!

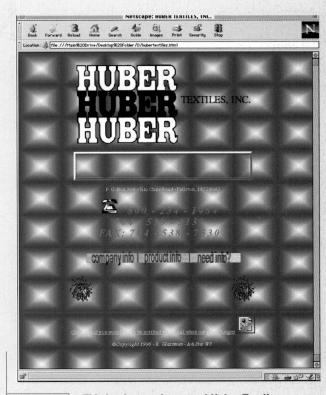

FIGURE 4.7   **Your seams are showing.**

FIGURE 4.8   **This background must go! Huber Textiles** (`http://www.arkstar.com/hubertextiles/`)

OH NO

AVOIDING SUCKY BACKGROUNDS

I'm not sure why, but a lot of sites (including business sites) use sucky backgrounds. Here are some examples of the types of sucky backgrounds you'll find on the Web.

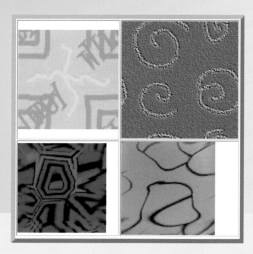

Some examples of sucky backgrounds you might find on the Web. Actually, these "bad" backgrounds Michael made are a lot nicer than the ones you'll normally see.

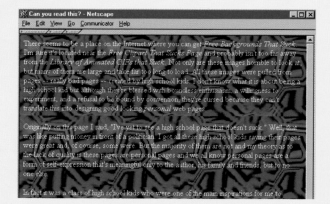

An example of hard-to-read text

Using the <H3> tag to make the text too big

While you'll find lots of sucky backgrounds on business pages, you'll most often find them on personal pages—especially the pages of high school kids. I don't know why teenagers like to use these backgrounds. Check out this next background; try to read the text on the page for more information about my experience with high school kids. The text was taken from the original WebPagesThatSuck. com site.

Because there's a fair amount of contrast between the background and the text, you can actually read the screen—but it's not easy. To try to make up for the background color, people either increase the <FONT> size or use <H3> tags on all the text to make the text larger, as shown in this example.

Don't be tempted to use this as a solution. If you can't read the text over the background image when the font is normal size, you need to fix the background—not increase the size of the font.

TOO COOL

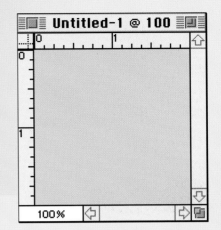

Step 2. The beginning image

MICHAEL'S QUICK AND DIRTY TIPS FOR MAKING A SEAMLESS TILE BACKGROUND

If you've used Photoshop, you probably know how to make a regular seamless-tile background. But, just in case you don't, here are my steps to success:

1. Create a new image at 96x96 pixels using 72 dpi.

2. Fill it in with a nice neutral color, such as the nice shade of brown used in the image shown at the top of the page.

3. Select the Noise (Filter > Noise > Add Noise) and add a value. I used 40 because it gives just enough graininess to the image. Check the monochrome box. Your image should now look like the second image, shown in the middle.

4. Apply the Blur filter (Filter > Blur > Blur). You can see the result in the bottom image.

5. For a less grainy image, press Ctrl+F twice (Ctrl+F, Ctrl+F) for Windows' systems or Command-F twice for Mac. This applies the Blur filter two more times and will give the image some contrast so the text is easier to read.

6. Convert the image to Index Colors (Image > Mode > Index Color). When converting, the settings should read:

Pallete	Adaptive
Color depth	5-bits/pixel
Colors	32
Dither	None

There you have it—a simple way to create compelling backgrounds without getting caught up in all of the needless bells and whistles.

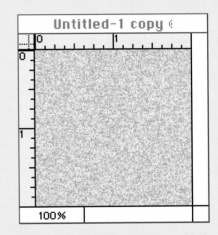

Step 3. The graininess has been added.

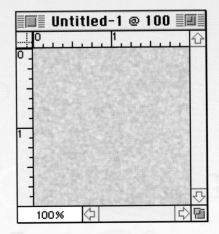

Step 4. The "edge" has been taken off the grain.

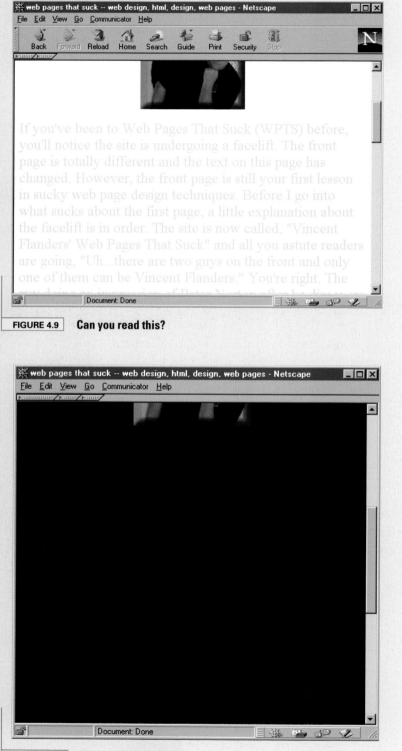

FIGURE 4.9 Can you read this?

FIGURE 4.10 Can you read this?

Background, Text, and Link Colors

Color is an important topic because so many people screw up and assign colors to their text and links that do not work with the background they've chosen. While there isn't space to discuss color theory, there are a number of sites that do a good job.

One of the best sites that discusses color theory is, logically enough, called "Color Theory" at `http://www.andrew.cmu.edu/user/dw4e/color/index.html`.

Of course, there's always Yahoo (`http://www.yahoo.com/Arts/Criticism_and_Theory/Color_Theory/`) if you want a list of current sites that discuss color theory.

Speaking of color and color choices, let's take a look at Figure 4.9. Can you read it? If you're a normal human being, you can't.

Lesson: Don't put light-colored text on a light background!

Now, you might think that nobody on the Internet would create a page like this, but you're wrong. There are many sites like this—but there are even more like the example shown in Figure 4.10.

Contrast The key word to remember when you're dealing with color is *contrast*. Don't use dark text colors on dark backgrounds. The text color must contrast with the background color or your visitors won't be able to read the text. This is why black backgrounds suck. Even if you make the text white, you still must fill in the other link parameters of the body tag with values that contrast to the background because the default values won't be seen by many browsers. The following are the default values for each link parameter in Netscape Communicator 4 (it may vary by browser):

LINK (unvisited link)	Dark blue
VLINK (visited link)	Purple
ALINK (active link)	Red

It's difficult to see the LINK and VLINK values, and it's important for your visitors to see these links so they know which links they've already visited and which ones they haven't been to.

When all else fails, you can't go wrong by putting black text on a white background (or a light ivory background). After all, that is what most magazines and newspapers use.

ColorCenter The site shown in Figure 4.11 is one of the more important sites on the Internet. Color-Center (`http://www.hidaho.com/colorcenter/`) lets you pick different background, link, and text colors, which you can then test on-screen. It also displays the `<BODY>` tag, so you can copy it and use it in your HTML documents. The only requirement for using the site is you have to have a browser that supports JavaScript. If you're not color-blind (amazingly, 10 percent of the male population is), you don't need to buy books about how to design using color; you can just go to this site.

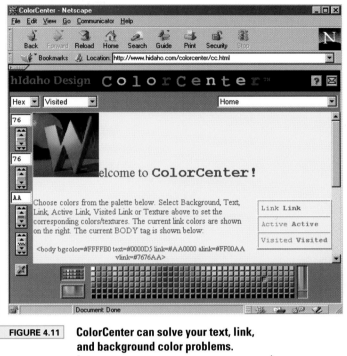

FIGURE 4.11 **ColorCenter can solve your text, link, and background color problems.**
(`http://www.hidaho.com/colorcenter`)

The Wrong Colors Can Get You Killed In California, the wrong color choice can get you killed. If you're in certain parts of certain cities and you're caught wearing the blue color of the Crips...well...you don't have to be a Stanford grad to figure out what's going to happen. The same holds true if you're caught wearing the red color of the Bloods in an area dominated by the Crips.

You're probably wondering what this has to do with the Stanford University home page shown in Figure 4.12? Well, as one irate alum wrote: "Stanford's colors are Cardinal (like 'Crimson' but with nicer weather) and White. Our arch-nemesis, Cal, uses Blue and Gold. What background color did the folks we paid (a large sum of money) decide to use for our site?" Gee. Looks like blue to me. Rat-a-tat-tat.

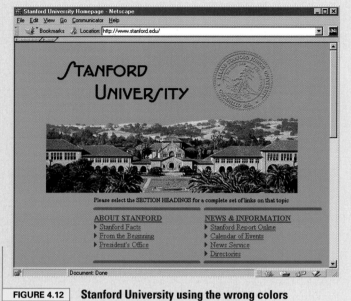

FIGURE 4.12 **Stanford University using the wrong colors**
(http://www.stanford.edu/)

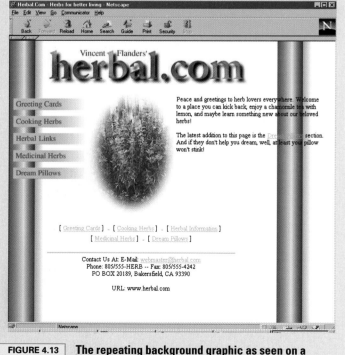

FIGURE 4.13 **The repeating background graphic as seen on a high resolution screen**

There are a couple of other problems that should be noted about this site. At 84K, it's a touch heavy on the graphics. The seal at the top of the page is also crooked—a fact you could verify by going to any of the other pages.

Angry alumni can be dangerous. The only hope for this Web page designer is the Artist Protection Program. I hope he or she makes it in time.

Avoid Using Short, Little, Repeating Striped Backgrounds

I realize Michael and I are going to sound like spoiled little rich boys, but there's nothing more annoying than seeing a striped background bar repeat itself on a 21-inch monitor with a high resolution graphics card. Yes, both Michael and I have large screen monitors and many designers make their background images 600-, 800-, even 1,024-pixels wide. One of the more frequent problems, however, is that designers forget there's an increasingly large segment of the population using high-resolution graphics cards. Look at Figure 4.13 to see what happens when a page with a 640-pixel-wide background is viewed on a high-resolution graphics card. The background pattern repeats itself, the text flows over the border, and well, it sucks.

This week you're probably safe making your background image 1,281 pixels wide (1,280 is the width of a high-resolution graphics card, so you add one pixel and it won't repeat). But because graphics cards are always changing, 1,600 pixel cards might be common two weeks from now, so you'll have to make your image 1,601 pixels wide. Ah, the ever-changing nature of the Web.

7. IT DOESN'T USE BROWSER-SAFE COLORS

One of my least favorite topics is browser-safe colors. Basically, the premise is simple: there are 216 "safe" colors a designer can use that will be seen by both Windows and Macintosh users without the image being messed up (the technical term for *messed up* is *dithered*). While 216 colors sounds like a lot, it isn't. You have to make a choice—do you design your pages for everyone or do you design them to please yourself (or your client)? In the case of pleasing the client, let the client make the final decision.

A whole book could be written about color, browser-safe colors, and the Web. Wait, it has. *Coloring Web Graphics* by Lynda Weinman and Bruce Heavin is a great resource. It goes into detail about every aspect of color and the Web, so if you're serious about Web graphics, this book is one you need.

There are also several Web sites that cover the topic of browser-safe colors:

The Browser Safe Color Palette (a great explanation of the whole issue is provided here) `http://www.lynda.com/hex.html`

The Discriminating Color Palette `http://www.adobe.com/newsfeatures/palette/main.html`

The 256, oops, 216 colors of Netscape `http://www.connect.hawaii.com/hc/webmasters/Netscape.colors.html`

The Safety Palette `http://www.microsoft.com/workshop/design/color/safety.asp`

Computer Graphic Techniques (an excellent and thorough site) `http://www.mvassist.pair.com/Graphics.html`

Web Engineer's Toolbox (provides a clickable 216-color palette) `http://lightsphere.com/colors/`

Dougie's Color Picker `http://www.phoenix.net/~jacobson/colorSel.html`

There's also a really great tool for both the Mac and Windows 95/NT that will help you finesse the browser-safe color problem. The utility is called ColorSafe (`http://www.boxtopsoft.com`). Very slick program. Michael turned me on to this one, and I've been grateful ever since.

What's the bottom line? Well, it's a good idea to use browser-safe colors when you're initially creating GIF images for your Web page (it isn't necessary to use them for JPEG). However, it's just not worth your time to sweat over every image just to get the colors right. It's more important to shrink the file size.

Because Herbal.com is a high-end site, targeted toward the Martha Stewart crowd with monitor cards that have 16.7 million colors, let's go on our merry way to the next graphics problem: no ALT parameters.

8. IT DOESN'T USE THE ALT PARAMETER

One of the frequent mistakes people make (and I make it all the time) is not putting in a description of the image in the ALT parameter of the `<IMG>` tag. The ALT parameter is the descriptive text that is displayed when an image is broken or when a visitor has set his or her browser so graphics are not displayed. On later versions of Netscape and Internet Explorer, the text used in the ALT parameter is displayed when the mouse passes over the image.

When people surf with the images turned off (these are impatient types who don't want to wait for images

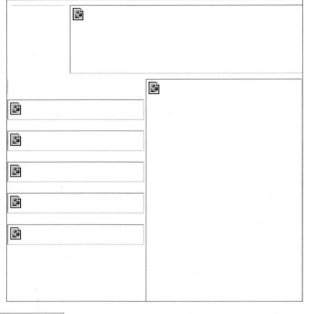

FIGURE 4.14   **What the screen looks like when you surf with the graphics turned off.**

9. IT USES SOME BAD GRAPHICS

After looking at all the various aspects of the background issue, we need to examine the other graphics used on the Herbal.com page. The word that comes to mind is *ugly* when I look at the images on this page. For example, the Vincent Flanders and Herbal.com images, shown in Figure 4.15 and in Figure 4.16, are horrific.

FIGURE 4.15   **The always classy Vincent Flanders**

FIGURE 4.16   **The sophistication of Herbal.com**

to load, but considering how long some pages take to load, they're smart), they won't see all your pretty pictures. Figure 4.14 shows what a page looks like when the images are turned off in the browser.

Without the ALT parameter, you can't tell where you should click and you have no idea how to navigate the site. People don't like to waste their time, and it's possible that when they click, they'll be taken to a place where they don't want to go.

Choose the text you use for the ALT parameter wisely. You might like to use text like "Subscribe to the Indianapolis Star/News by clicking here" or "Sports Page—Get the latest scores." Make sure you tell the person where they're going to end up if they click the graphic. There are other uses for the ALT parameter; in Chapter 10, you'll learn an important trick about what kind of text to use—it's not as obvious as you might think.

First, each one is using a different text font—remember we talked about the importance of consistency in Chapter 2—and second, each image is on a white background, which contrasts terribly with the blue background. When I surf, I'm always amazed at the lack of artistic talent out there. I'm no artist, but I know what sucks. A white square on top of a blue background is very tacky. At least make the image transparent so it will look like the one in Figure 4.17.

FIGURE 4.17   **The logo shown in Figure 4.15 is now transparent.**

Almost every graphics program has a transparency option. Find it. Use the Help files.

Too Many Animated GIFs

Not only is the Herbal.com image in a different font than the Vincent Flanders' image, it's an animated GIF—a horrible animated GIF—although you can't tell that from looking at the image shown in Figure 4.1. In addition, the two rainbow divider bars and the construction sign are animated GIFs.

If you look at most successful sites, they'll have animated GIF images (generally ads), but those animations are extremely well-crafted and they're not overpowering. However, there's something about personal pages that make people go out and steal other sites' animated GIFs and shove as many on a page as is humanly possible.

Of course, there are some business sites that cram their pages full of animated GIFs as well. You'll see one in a moment. Generally speaking, the more animated GIFs on a page, the suckier the page. Take a look at Figure 4.18 and bear in mind that all of the images are animated.

To adequately appreciate Figure 4.18, view it in your browser. As you can see, it sucks. It sucks bad.

Figure 4.18 is a made-up site; Figure 4.19 isn't. It shows a real site from a software company whose designer is desperately fond of animated GIFs.

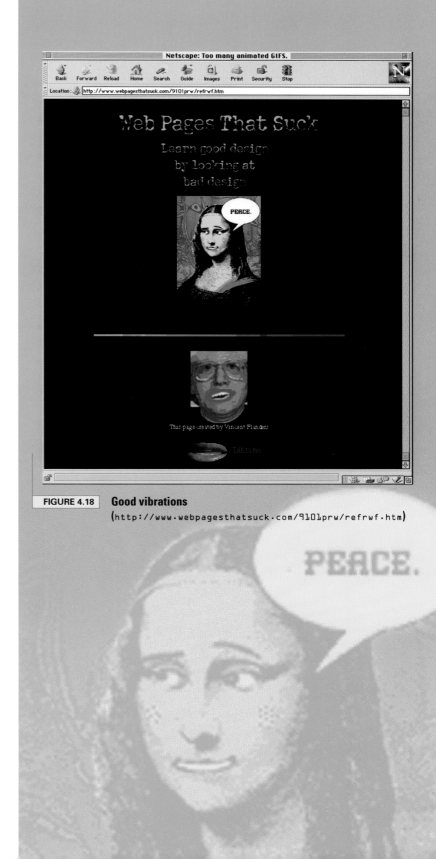

FIGURE 4.18   **Good vibrations**
(`http://www.webpagesthatsuck.com/9101prw/refrwf.htm`)

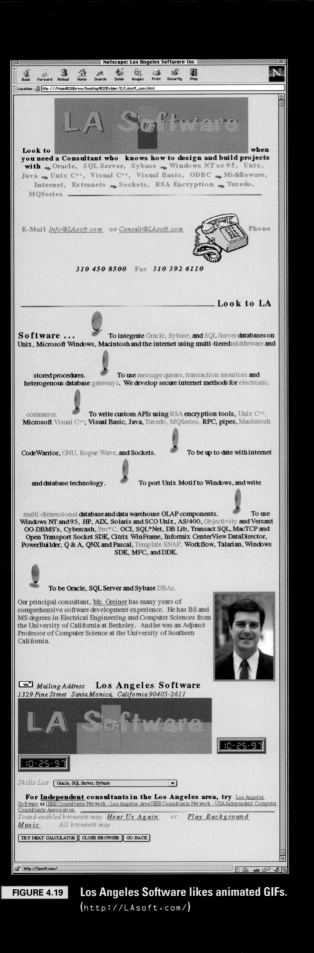

FIGURE 4.19 Los Angeles Software likes animated GIFs.
(`http://LAsoft.com/`)

Animated GIFs are like sweets. They're great in small quantities, but eat too many and you'll get sick.

Now don't get me wrong, animated GIFs can be *extremely* powerful tools in the right hands. The best Web designers from each coast met to design a Web site for the Washington, DC chapter of the Literacy Volunteers of America. The winning entry used a remarkable animated GIF on the home page. Figure 4.20 shows the different cells of the animation (it starts at the top and works its way down). Because you can't show an animation on a printed page, this is as good as I can do, but it doesn't compare to the real thing. You can see it at `http://www.fray.com/lva/`. It is so brilliant it will make you hate the sucky animated GIFs that permeate the Web even more than you already do. Thankfully, animated GIFs don't animate when you use them as background images. Thank your lucky stars for small favors.

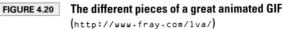

FIGURE 4.20 The different pieces of a great animated GIF
(`http://www.fray.com/lva/`)

THE BEST SOFTWARE FOR CREATING ANIMATED GIFS

There are tons of programs for creating animated GIFs, and depending on my mood and what needs to be done, I would choose one of the following:

GIF Construction Set

(http://www.mindworkshop.com/ alchemy/gifcon.html) The first program I ever used to create animated GIFs.

GIF Movie Gear

(http://www.gamani.com/) You saw it in action in Figure 4.20. I especially like the way it lays out the frames so you can see how the animation works.

Ulead's Animation SmartSaver

(http://www.ulead.com) It can optimize both animated and regular GIF images, but you can't preview the results on-screen.

Ulead's PhotoImpact GIF Animator

(http://www.ulead.com/ webutilities/ga/ga_main.htm) The latest version (2) offers some incredible transition effects.

For the Mac, Michael likes:

GifBuilder

(http://iawww.epfl.ch/Staff/Yves .Piguet/clip2gif-home/GifBuilder .html) This program is very popular among Mac aficionados. It takes individual Photoshop layers and turns them into individual animated frames —something that can't be done on the Windows NT platform. Very, very cool.

INFORMATION ABOUT ANIMATED GIFS

There's lots of information about animated GIFs for you to peruse as you surf the Web:

c|net's article on GIF Animation

(http://www.cnet.com/Content/ Features/Techno/Gif89/) c|net gives a very good introduction into the process of creating animations.

Eyeland's Cel by Cel

(http://www.eyeland.com/thestuff/ how/cel/cel.html) Here you'll find out about some advanced techniques for designing animated GIFs.

GIF Animation on the WWW

(http://member.aol.com/royalef/ gifanim.htm) If there was one person who was most responsible for popularizing animated GIFs and eliminating most Java animations in the process, it was Royal Frazier. By the way, his site violates the "The Page is Too Long" tennant. Just goes to show that when you've got content, you can break the rules.

Yahoo!

(http://www.yahoo.com/Arts/ Visual_Arts/Animation/Computer_ Animation/Animated_GIFs/) Of course.

ZD Whole Web Catalog

(http://www5.zdnet.com/zdwebcat/ content/garage/gif89a/animation .html) Good article on how to create animated images.

THE BEST SOFTWARE FOR OPTIMIZING ANIMATED GIFS

Because animated GIFs tend to be large (remember, you're combining multiple GIF images into one image), there's a fertile market for programs that will optimize these images.

Webreference magazine had a contest to see which program could best optimize animated GIFs. The article, "Optimizing Animated GIFs," is technical, comprehensive, and tells you more than you probably want to know about optimization. You can read the complete article at http://www.webreference.com/ dev/gifanim/summary.html. However, the two programs that performed the best optimization were:

ColorWorks:WEB 3 by SPG Inc.

(http://www.spg-net.com/) Unlike other programs, this full graphics suite is very powerful. I like this program a lot. In my personal comparison tests, it kicked everyone's rear. For Windows 95/NT.

GIFmation by BoxTop Software

(http://www.boxtopsoft.com/) This program is cool, and BoxTop Software has some great articles on optimization. For both Mac and Windows 95/NT.

TOO COOL

MICHAEL'S QUICK AND DIRTY TIPS FOR CREATING BUTTONS IN PHOTOSHOP

1. Open a new file (choose File > New from the menu bar). My buttons are going to be 2" x .4" or 300x60 pixels, so I'll enter 2 in the Width text box and .4 in the Height text box.

Step 1. Setting the parameters for the buttons

2. Set the resolution to 72 dpi. I used a higher resolution for the images (150 dpi) so they would show up better in the book.

3. Select a browser-safe color from the swatch menu and fill in the background.

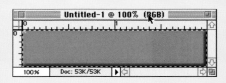

Step 4. The button with a browser-safe color and bevel

4. Use Alien Skin's bevel tool (http://www.alienskin.com) to create a perfect bevel in about five seconds, as shown above. Alien Skin's Eye Candy suite of Photoshop plug-ins is a "must-have" for serious Web button creators.

5. Use Photoshop's guide rules (new to version 4) to insert the type, as shown below.

Step 5. Putting on the type

6. Select the Type tool and click the center line. I chose a cool freeware font I found at http://charity .artificial.com/freefonts/ slumber.html and set it to 18 point and anti-aliased.

7. Now the cool stuff. Click the center line for the next button, and you'll notice Photoshop puts that type on a new layer. After you set the type, turn off Layer by clicking the eye icon. You'll see your new button clear as day, just like the one at the top of the next page. Repeat the typing process until you've created all your buttons. Now save your buttons as a native Photoshop file, so you can come back and add additional buttons later.

8. Next, duplicate the file for each layer (Image > Duplicate). In this case, I made five duplicates. Then I activated/deactivated the layers so each of the buttons were revealed, as shown in the second image on the next page.

9. Change from RGB to Index mode by selecting Image > Mode > Index. Photoshop will ask you if you want to flatten layers. Click Yes. Next the dialog box appears where you set the Palette choice (I chose Adaptive) and Color Depth (I felt it was safe to go with 5 bit or 32 colors, thereby giving me a small file but still allowing for some color depth).

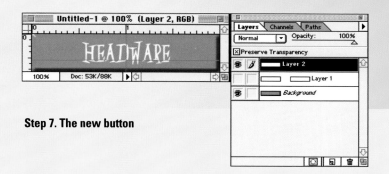

Step 7. The new button

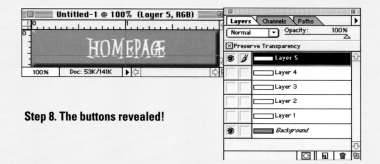

Step 8. The buttons revealed!

10. Save as a CompuServe GIF file. I like to name my buttons easy-to-remember names. I use the same first three letters, in this case *but,* so the buttons appear in my folder in alphabetical order.

buthome.gif

butothr.gif

butdecl.gif

buthead.gif

butshirt.gif

11. Optional, but very cool. Create a duplicate set of buttons to use as "selected" buttons. Just open up your original Buttons file. Select Background in the layers palette. Change your background color (in this case, I choose purple). Apply the bevel filter to it, and viola, you are ready to repeat steps 5 and 6 to create a second set of buttons. The complete set is shown in the image to the right. I add a number *1* to these names, so it will be easy for me when it comes time to do the HTML.

buthome1.gif

butothr1.gif

butdecl1.gif

buthead1.gif

butshirt1.gif

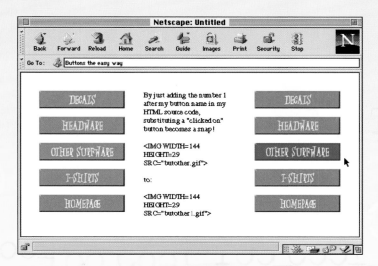

Step 11. The complete set of buttons

OTHER GRAPHICS PROBLEMS THAT, THANKFULLY, WEREN'T ON THIS PAGE

So far, this chapter has covered most of the serious graphic design flaws. If your page has any of the flaws already mentioned and you fix them, you're well on your way to creating a good-looking page. However, there are some other serious (and not-so-serious) mistakes that you should also be sure to avoid:

Globes and other clichéd images

Going overboard with effects and filters

Pretentiousness

Globes and Other Clichéd Images

Let's face it folks, if there's one image that's become a cliché, it's the globe symbolizing the *World* Wide Web. Michael and I—and almost every other designer—hate globes so much we decided not to even use one in this section of the book. If you want to make both of us scream, *make an animated globe.* It's the Web-graphics equivalent of fingernails on the chalkboard. Of course, if your site deals with flying or space—for example, the United Airlines page we saw back in Chapter 2—then it's okay to use a globe. Heck, NASA (National Aeronautics and Space Administration—home of the U.S. space program) only uses a little-bitty globe and it's their logo. If NASA feels they only need to use a little-bitty globe, you probably don't need to use it on your ice cream site. Some of the other clichéd images to avoid are spiders, webs, and folding envelopes for e-mail links.

Going Overboard

Okay, you've learned how to use your graphics program—or maybe you're already a professional graphics artist—and you're just starting to create Web pages. You've purchased some wonderful filters, such as Kai's Power Tools (KPT), Alien Skin's Eye Candy, and Auto F/X to help you create really cool graphics. But, you've forgotten the ommm page mantra, *and you're now a menace to Web society.* Take a look at Figure 4.21 to get a sense of how easy it is to go overboard with graphics tools.

This figure demonstrates the "High on Kai" syndrome, named after one of the best filter tools on the Internet. KPT's most amusing feature is called Page Curl. It's absolutely cool to use this feature once. I actually used Page Curl on a Web page (for a radio station), so I've reached my career limit and Page Curl is forever banned. The Page Curl in Figure 4.22 belongs to Michael. He's now done with curling. Kai's Power Tools Page is at `http://www.metatools.com/kpt/`.

When people first get KPT or any other graphics tool, there's a tendency to...ah...um... go overboard. It's called the "I've just learned how to (use KPT /make bevels /whatever) syndrome." We get a new toy, play with it, and then put the results on every image or on every page on our site.

In the world of graphic design, where 100Mb image files are not uncommon, Kai's Power Tools (KPT) from MetaTools has been a staple of great design for a long time. Because there's no limit to image size in the graphic arts world, you can easily create extraordinary effects; however, in the world of the Internet, you've got to be careful about the size of your images.

It takes a great designer with a good deal of self-control to use graphic tools and keep the images small. Then, of course, there's the whole concept of aesthetics. It's hard to fight the urge to make really complex images because, quite frankly, complex images look cool. Once again, it takes talent to make them fit in with the look of a Web page.

There are a few common special effects that can turn otherwise respectable humans into fanatics: bevels, shadows, and glowing text. If you remember only one thing from the next few pages let it be this: practice restraint.

Bevelmania Another set of filters that amateurs and a few professionals abuse is Eye Candy from Alien Skin software (`http://www.alienskin.com/`). Both Michael and I have been known to use Alien Skin's beveled-edge filters on occasion because neither one of us have found a program that creates better beveled edges. Like Kai's Photo Tools, these filters are abused because they're very, very good. At an approximate street price of $129, it might be a little expensive just to create bevels.

Whether it's appropriate to use beveled edges on Web pages is another controversial topic. Many designers avoid using them; others advocate infrequent use. Michael and I suggest that if you use them, use them only on buttons that serve as links to other pages. There's something about a beveled image that makes people believe it's a clickable image. *Please* don't bevel photos unless they're clickable.

This line from Michael's mouth puts the whole Web design issue into perspective. This next image is an art project. It's a labor of love and therefore fine for the artist to sweat over it for hours and hours.

The Juggler, by Michaela Marie Flanders, 1995

A Web page, with rare exceptions, is not an art project, so you don't need to spend hours optimizing images to squeeze the last pixel out of them or spend time creating animations. If you're spending hours tweaking, let go! Unless you've got a stupid client who loves to spend money, complete the page and get it out the door (or upload it onto the site, as the case may be).

We're not advocating a slam-bam attitude. Do a professional job, focusing on the important issues, and remember your client may end up hating what you've labored hours over.

Figure 4.22 shows what can happen when a designer gets carried away with a new toy.

Shadow Filters Another controversy exists about whether or not to put shadows on Web graphics. One design school feels it's passé. Another school makes the valid point that shadows make the image size larger, and these images can only be viewed correctly—without dithering—on monitors that support 24-bit color. A third school says, "Damn the torpedoes. Full shadow ahead!"

While Eye Candy makes great shadows, there are several filters that do a nice job with shadows, such as Extensis PhotoTools (`http://www.extensis.com`). But just because Eye Candy does a good job, hold off for a bit.

In addition to large image sizes and dithering, there is another problem with using shadow filters—an insidious problem that sometimes creeps into even the best Web sites: *shadows only come from one direction.*

Sounds obvious, doesn't it? But what happens is you'll create a new page and add a new image that has a shadow, and then you'll grab an older image and place it on the page without realizing the shadow goes a different direction! The Web page shown in Figure 4.23 demonstrates shadow overkill —if you consider shadows coming from four different directions overkill.

Even the big boys and girls can make this mistake. Figure 4.24 shows a real world example from Netscape.

Don't Use GLOWing Text Glowing text sucks for many reasons, but first and foremost, it sucks because it looks bad on all those low-resolution monitors found across the Internet. Believe it or not, 216 colors are just not enough to display the gradients used in

FIGURE 4.23 Red Dog to Sky Leader. We've got bad shadows at 11, 6, 9, and 1 o'clock.

these types of images without dithering badly. Figure 4.25 shows how good an image looks using a 24–bit graphics card, while Figure 4.26 shows how the same image looks using a 256–color graphics card.

FIGURE 4.25 We lie to the client.

FIGURE 4.26 The client lies to us.

FIGURE 4.24 Netscape's in the shade, too.

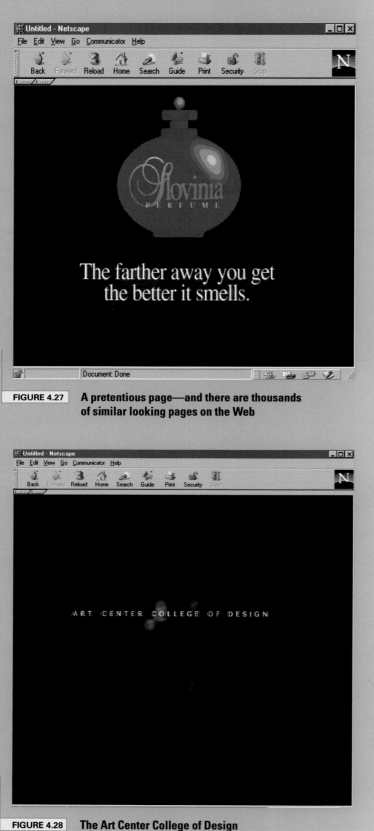

FIGURE 4.27   A pretentious page—and there are thousands of similar looking pages on the Web

FIGURE 4.28   The Art Center College of Design
(http://www.artcenter.edu/)

Pretentious Pages

Not only can you have a sucky Web page, you can create a pretentious page that just reeks, "I'm an Artistè." There's nothing wrong with artists. It's just that some of them have rather skewed world views. Because their only tool is a hammer, all problems become nails.

Figure 4.27 shows a home page Michael and I created for a "perfume." You can't really appreciate the absurdity of this page unless you view it from your browser. Both images are animated GIFs—as the text comes into focus, the perfume bottle "moves" farther away.

Unfortunately, many sites use this type of splash page. To get to the "real" home page, either you have to click the graphic or the browser will automatically take you to the next page using a variation of the META tag:

```
<head>
      <title>Web Pages That
Suck- Pretentious Front
Page</title>
          <meta http-
equiv="refresh" content="17;
url=home.html">
</head>
```

What the text in red signifies is that the browser will load a document called `home.html` after 17 seconds. Not all browsers support this feature, so you need to make sure you provide a text link for people to click. The site shown in Figure 4.27 did not. Bad, bad, bad.

One of the most perfectly pretentious sites on the Internet is shown in Figure 4.28. It's perfect because...well...it's an art school, and you'd think they'd know better than to design a site that looks like this. As one visitor to WebPagesThatSuck.com said, "It's a damn art school, it's supposed to look artsy-fartsy." The use of the "@" symbol to say "this is where it's @" is so precious.

All this talk about graphics makes Michael and me thirsty and brings us to a very important point, using graphics programs, which is our next topic.

USING A GRAPHICS PROGRAM

You wouldn't wire your house without some electrical experience (hopefully), so why would you create graphics for a Web page without learning how to use a graphics program? When it comes to graphics programs, Photoshop is the most recognized program and some say it's the most powerful. It's also probably one of the most expensive at $895 list and about $550 on the street. (An adequate version is often bundled with scanners, so check it out when you buy a new scanner. You can then upgrade to the full version for around $200.) Whatever you use, really learn to use it. Buy some books. There are only about five billion Photoshop books on the market.

You can download a demo version of Photoshop at `http://www.adobe.com/prodindex/photoshop/demoreg.html`.

Unfortunately, Mac users have fewer choices than Windows users, and they're more expensive. Michael, our Mac expert, also recommends Photoshop.

If you're running Windows and are on a limited budget, try Paint Shop Pro (`http://www.jasc.com/pspdl.html`). This program ($56 approximate street price) was the winner of the 1997 Ziff-Davis Shareware Awards "Program of the Year." Frankly, Michael and I started out with Photoshop, but we realize you may not have a lot of graphic experience. Because Paint Shop Pro only costs 10 percent of what Photoshop costs, we can hardly recommend the average person go out and spend $550 for Photoshop. Even if you throw in the cost of the two books written about Paint Shop Pro, you will have still spent significantly less than the cost of Photoshop.

Before you go out and buy a new program, you might want to try out some of the shareware and freeware that's available. Of course, if you're using FrontPage 98, then Microsoft Image Composer comes bundled with it and you already have a graphics editor.

TOO COOL

WHERE DO YOU FIND GRAPHICS SOFTWARE—ESPECIALLY SHAREWARE AND FREEWARE (AND DEMOWARE/ TRIALWARE)?

In the Windows/Windows95/ Windows NT, world I recommend:

Dave Central Software Archive
(`http://www.davecentral.com/`)

Tucows
(`http://www.tucows.com/`
for the nearest location)

Stroud's Consummate Winsock Applications
(`http://cws.internet.com/`)

ZDNet Software Library
(`http://www.hotfiles.com/`)

Shareware.com
(`http://www.shareware.com/`)

For the Mac, Michael, the guy who actually uses a Mac, recommends:

Download.com
(`http://www.download.com/`)

And Michael and I recommend these sites for all Internet-related software, not just graphics.

If you've never worked with graphics before and you're serious about creating quality artwork, I hate to be the one to break the news to you, but you're probably going to end up spending more money on graphics software and hardware than you spent on your PC. There are all these filters and plug-ins you'll find you *just have* to own. And when you buy these tools, you'll be tempted to use every one of them!

If you're a designer or you plan to have a site with lots of pages, you probably need to invest in graphics software. If you've got a one-shot site, such as a brochure-type site that probably won't change a lot, then it might be cheaper to hire a graphic artist to create your logo and buttons and other images.

GRAPHICS DON'TS

With respect to graphics, there are several things you don't want to do on your Web pages. Most of them should be pretty intuitive, but just in case, let's go over them quickly—it could save you a lot of needless embarrassment.

Don't Use Personal Pictures Unless You're a Model

Look at the picture of me in Figure 4.29. This picture was taken from the Herbal .com site. Need I say more?

FIGURE 4.29 **What happens to models after they discover carbohydrates.**

Don't Use Inappropriate or Offensive Images

Speaking of tasteless, sophomoric, and/or humorous images, the image ostensibly of O.J. Simpson holding the bloody knife that killed his wife and Ron Goldman, shown in Figure 4.30, might be considered inappropriate or offensive in certain contexts (the Los Angeles County District Attorney's office home page comes to mind), while it might be considered the height of humor on another site. The bottom line is: know your audience.

FIGURE 4.30 **I couldn't resist**

If your site caters to the international marketplace, it will be much harder to check your site for propriety, but it's something you'll have to take into consideration. For example, certain colors and numbers are offensive to different cultures. This isn't the place to go into how different cultures view these issues. If they're a concern, check it out.

Don't Use Cutesy Pictures

Figure 4.31 shows a picture of Michael Willis on the Herbal.com site. Michael Willis does not look like a happy face. I know; I've seen him. You've seen him in this book. Being cutesy is fine for personal pages, but not for professional pages. If you don't have a photo, skip the cutesy placeholder image.

FIGURE 4.31 **I am not Michael.**

We know some of you are thinking, "There's no way a site used that kind of picture." Wrong. This picture was based on a real, live, governmental agency Web page. Swear to God. The only difference was the person in the regular photo looked more...ah...bureaucratic. The original page doesn't exist any more, but it remains burned in our eyeballs.

Speaking of bad things on that governmental agency's site: They were the inspiration for the sound files we put on the Herbal.com site. Fortunately, it's gone—not the agency, but any trace of suckiness.

Don't Use Graphics as Dividers Unless They Look *Really* Good

Michael and I have mixed emotions about using graphics as dividers. There are cases where they look good, but more often than not, they don't. Plus, they're becoming less and less frequent on well-designed sites. Many sites are going to the IBM scheme where they have different colored sections that act as dividers—it's less obtrusive than divider bars. The red divider bar used in the Herbal.com site and shown in Figure 4.32 is a perfect example of a poorly made bar.

FIGURE 4.32   **A poorly done divider bar**

Check around. You'll find most well-designed sites don't use graphic divider bars.

Don't Use Free Clip Art That's on the Internet

There are two possible scenarios here. If you find clip art on the Internet that's any good, then everybody is using it and your site will look like everyone else's site. If the clip art is bad, you don't want to use it because you'll look stupid. Even though it's public domain, it might belong to someone else. Play it safe. Don't use clip art you find on the Internet.

Don't "Borrow" Images—or Anything Else

Although the images on Herbal.com are original, the truth is too many people go to someone's page and steal—I mean "borrow"—someone else's work (or someone else's stolen property). I was teaching Web design to this 14-year-old boy who gave a great explanation about why it's okay to steal images from other sites. Pointing to one of the huge images on his page (typical teenage page—black background, centered images, and light green text), he

TOO COOL

GOOD CLIP ART

Sounds like an oxymoron such as "freezer burn" or "clearly confused." There are lots of packages you can buy (Vincent and I have bought our share)—and not all of them are worth buying.

However, there are two catalogs you should start getting:

1. Image Club (800/661-9410 or `http://www.imageclub.com/`): Image Club is owned by Adobe so there's certainly an emphasis on type, which you won't find at the second catalog, Publisher's Toolbox. Image Club also offers monthly design tips. One month they offered a tip for designing seamless tiles. Image Club is my favorite place to find cool clip art.

2. Publisher's Toolbox (800/390-0461 or `http://www.pubtool.com/`): Publisher's Toolbox offers clip art and a whole lot more. Basically, if it's graphics related, they offer it.

3. I also like PhotoDisc (`http://www.photodisc.com/`): I don't use their products as much for Web pages as I do for regular commercial design, but that's only because I don't like to use photos unless they're really necessary to the content of the page. However, PhotoDisc has a huge selection of affordable photos.

FIGURE 4.33   The page tries to improve

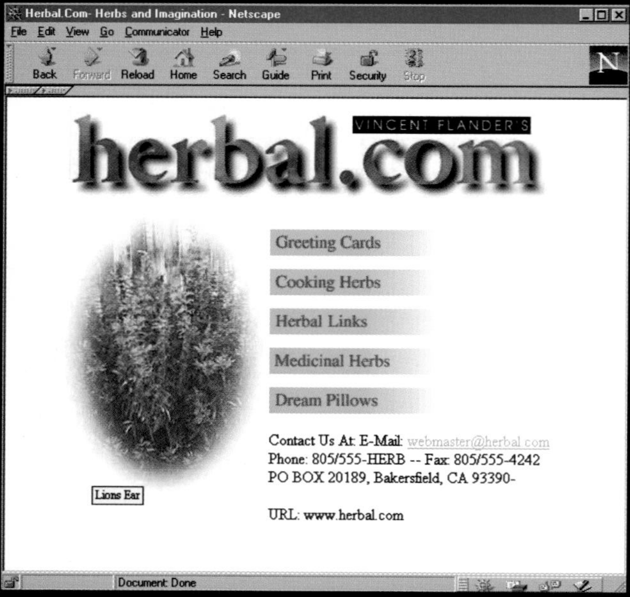

FIGURE 4.34   The second revision

said it was okay for him to use it because his friend, whose site he stole it from, had stolen it from someone else.

Ah, the logic of 14-year-old boys. Speaking of logic, I'll never forget the time I gave a talk to a group of teachers and educators about Web page aesthetics. When the speech was over, the first question asked was, in summary format, "How can I steal the images from another Web site?" And you wonder why your kids are turning out to be thugs. Don't steal another person's art. I know everybody thinks the Internet is free and therefore everything on it is free, but it isn't.

Seriously, you can get yourself in a whole lot of trouble by stealing images, sound files (even though it's you playing "Stairway to Heaven" on the kazoo, you've still have to pay to use the song), movie clips, and so on. One of the best discussions of this topic is by the law firm of McCutchen, Doyle, Brown & Enersen, LLP. Entitled "Unauthorized Content: Is It Worth The Risk?" the article can be found at `http://www.mccutchen.com/ip/unauth.htm`. The Internet is no longer merely the domain for weird nerds; it's a business platform, and as soon as money is involved, you know the lawyers will start showing up. Get used to it.

Forget that it's illegal to steal images and you could be sued. Almost everybody steals the same artwork—how many times have we seen the rotating, football-shaped "New" image? When you steal artwork, people are going to think, "How honest is a person who steals images?" People don't want to do business with people who steal.

Don't Use Under Construction Signs

Every site on the Internet should perpetually be under construction so you don't need to graphically represent this fact. Kill the signs—if they're animated, kill them quickly.

Now that we have some graphics knowledge under our belt, let's take a look at how the Herbal.com site evolved.

THE REVISIONS

Once a designer realizes that their page is atrocious, there's the tendency for him or her to have what is called the "minimalist reaction." They strip out everything from the page but the minimum elements necessary. There's nothing horribly wrong with the first revised version of Herbal.com, shown in Figure 4.33; it is certainly an improvement over the original design (back in Figure 4.1). This page actually looks better than many business pages out on the Web, but it's lacking that "professional look" and could stand some polishing.

How Does the Page Look Now?

Figure 4.34 shows the next revision of the site. It's a pretty major revision, so let's examine how the page was created.

While it's difficult to try to systematize the creative process involved in any grand work of art, here's the plan of attack that was used to create this page:

1. Begin with the logo.

2. Move on to the key image.

3. Move on to the buttons.

4. Finish up with the text.

Start at the Top with the Logo When a browser displays a Web page, it starts at the top left of the window and works its way down. When you revise your site, start at the top and work your way down.

Using the image of the Lion's Tail plant as a basis for the color on the page, Michael designed the logo. In choosing the colors, he decided not to use browser-safe colors because the audience for this market would be people who could afford high-end systems.

Notice how the previous page's two logos (Vincent Flanders' and Herbal.com—shown in Figure 4.33) were combined into one image. The obvious benefit is it cuts down on the length of the page.

The logo takes on an added importance because it is used to determine the width of the page. Everything after the logo goes into a table; therefore, the width of the table cells can't be wider than the logo.

Then Comes the Plant Image Next, Michael had to decide how to handle the plant image. First of all, he physically reduced the size of the file, and because it was a photograph, he put it into JPEG format.

Obviously, sticking with the block image of the plant isn't the most aesthetically pleasing way to go, so he decided to feather the image. Figure 4.35 and Figure 4.36 show us the two different approaches he took. To see how he created this image, see the "Feathering Techniques with Photoshop" sidebar.

After mulling it over, Michael settled on the vertical orientation.

FIGURE 4.35 **The plant with a horizontal orientation**

FIGURE 4.36 **The plant with a vertical orientation**

TOO COOL

MICHAEL'S QUICK AND DIRTY STEPS FOR FEATHERING WITH PHOTOSHOP

Most of you Photoshop folks probably know how to feather an image, but for those of you who don't, here are the steps:

1. Open the image in Photoshop.

2. Use any selection tool (Elliptical is used here) to select an area.

3. Choose Select > Feather under the main menu.

4. Enter the feather value. The higher the value, the softer the edge. I selected a value of 15, as shown in the image at the top of this page.

5. Click OK.

6. Choose Select > Inverse to choose the area that's not selected by the Elliptical tool.

7. Press the Delete key to delete the area around the selection. Now the image looks like this one.

8. Crop the image down using the Crop tool.

9. Use the Lasso tool to create organic forms. Some other variations are shown to the right of the feathered image.

Step 4. A feather value of 15

Step 7. Voilà—the feathered image

Step 9. An organically shaped image

Step 9. A star-shaped image

OH NO

OTHER TOOLS FOR PUTTING EDGES ON IMAGES

Look, square edges are...well...for squares. To give your images a professional look, put edges on them. There are two ways to put edges on your graphics: the Photoshop-do-it-by-hand approach just described or the way the pros do it but won't tell you because they want to keep it a design secret.

Michael used Photoshop to make the edge by hand, but he didn't have to do it that way. There's a great set of utilities out there to do most of the work for you.

Michael and many other artists are extremely fond of the three volumes of AUTO F/X PHOTO/GRAPHIC EDGES 3 filters from, logically enough, AUTO F/X (http://www.autofx.com/). These Windows 95/NT and Power Mac Photoshop plug-ins support Photoshop, Illustrator, Freehand, PageMaker, Fractal Design Painter, Corel Photopaint, PhotoDeluxe, Canvas 5, Paint Shop Pro, and other graphic design programs. Using these filters to give your pictures cool edges is a snap.

The good news about AUTO F/X filters is they work really well and they're incredibly simple to use. The bad news is each set costs $179 and there are three sets. Sometimes you can get all three for about $400—roughly a $140 savings.

Here are some examples of what you get from each set of filters. The top example shows you the original image before the filter was applied.

The next example shows the image after Filter AF232 from Volume 1—Traditional Edge Effects was used. (Because this particular filter is vertically oriented and the picture is horizontally oriented, the image was rotated 90 degrees so it would work with the filter.) Other than that, no tweaking was done.

This edge is the default. AUTO F/X has many parameters you can use to tweak the image, but as you can see, you can get interesting effects without using them.

It's important to note that many/most/all of the edge effects will not look very good on monitors whose graphics cards only have 256 colors. The gradations in color don't show up very well. Like everything in life, it's a trade-off. Great effects require great money.

Michael has already created some edges for you to use with Photoshop and other programs that have a Paste Into function. Michael's edges are not plug-ins, but use the same technique used in earlier versions of AUTO F/X. Detailed instructions on how to use these edges are included on the CD. The bottom example shows you our original picture with one of Michael's edges added.

The original image

Image after Filter AF232 from Volume 1 is applied

One of Michael's edges

FIGURE 4.37   **The original**

Then Come the Buttons Michael settled on the orange color of the plant's flowers for the background color of the buttons and on a shade of green for the color of the text. He could have reversed the colors, but chose not to. The truth is, it might have made the buttons more legible to have the text lighter than the button, but he felt the orange color added some warmth to the page. At this point, it's really a matter of taste.

Finally, the Text Michael had no text to work with, so he made space to include the important contact information. There's still some additional fine-tuning that could be done at this point, but we've made great progress on the graphics front.

Finished Product

Figure 4.37 shows the original version of Herbal.com, shown at the beginning of the chapter, and Figure 4.38 shows the finished product.

To recap, Michael made the following changes to the page:

1. Changed the logo. The name *Vincent Flanders'* used to be white text on a black background. He reduced it in size and made it blend in with the color scheme.

2. Created a rock border image on left side of screen. The rock border is a variation on a common theme you see on the Web—the color stripe going down the left side of the screen. This looks much better than that ubiquitous color stripe.

3. Moved the graphic links to the left side of the page and the plant image to the right side.

4. Inserted expository text. The page seemed a little bland so Michael came up with temporary filler text.

5. Added a color-coordinated divider bar.

6. Added the text links. Remember to use text links in addition to the graphics links. If you create your page correctly using the HEIGHT and WIDTH parameters, the text will load first and people can click the text links if they don't want to wait for the images to load.

While there are a host of other graphic quicksand pits you can fall into, the ones covered in this chapter are the most dangerous.

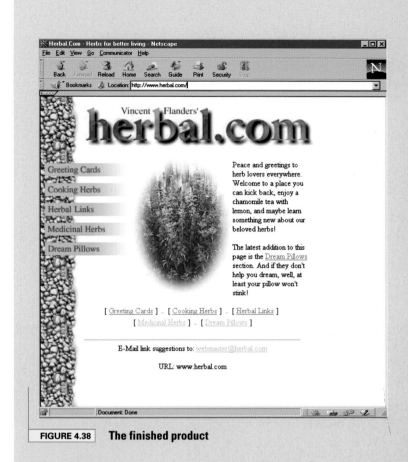

FIGURE 4.38 **The finished product**

INTERNATIONAL

HOW DO YOU SAY "SUCK" IN JAPAN?

The Internet is truly global and so are graphics no-nos. Before moving on, let's see how our neighbors across the Pacific are handling graphics on their Web sites. The following page is from an appliance company.

Rainbow dividers, an international no-no

Look—a globe. Bet you've never seen that before.

From which direction is the light coming— east or west?

With a sales income of approximately 320 billion yen, Best Denki's should cut loose of some of that yen and hire an artist to do the graphics.

NO LANGUAGE BARRIER HERE

Now, let's compare the Japanese site to another appliance company's site.

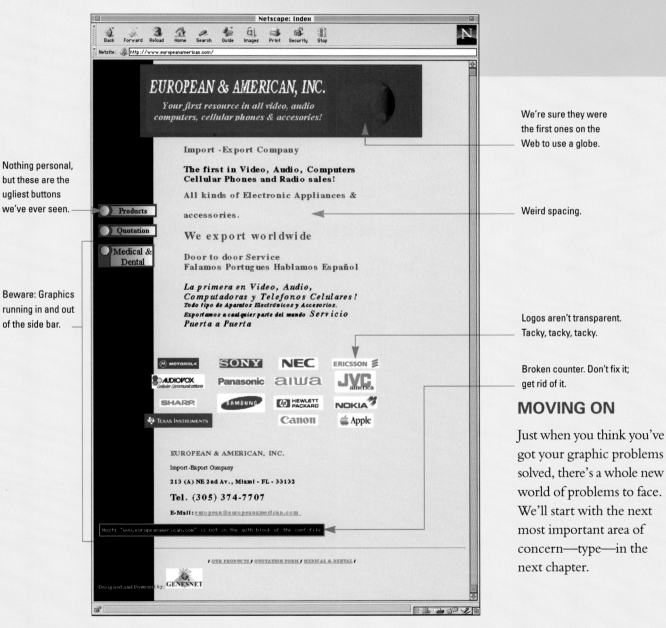

We're sure they were the first ones on the Web to use a globe.

Nothing personal, but these are the ugliest buttons we've ever seen.

Weird spacing.

Beware: Graphics running in and out of the side bar.

Logos aren't transparent. Tacky, tacky, tacky.

Broken counter. Don't fix it; get rid of it.

MOVING ON

Just when you think you've got your graphic problems solved, there's a whole new world of problems to face. We'll start with the next most important area of concern—type—in the next chapter.

This sucks—this sucks bad.

Flanders & Willis's Reality Check

The Byrds recorded a great song years ago called "Turn, Turn, Turn" where one of the lines is, "There is a season and a time for every purpose under heaven." It's the same for most of your text-based tags—**<B>**old, **<I>**talic, **<BIG>**, **<SMALL>**, **ALL CAPS**, and **<U>**nderline. There's a time and a season to use them—and NOT to use them—so choose wisely.

CHAPTER 5

Fixing Your Text Problems

IN THIS CHAPTER

we'll see how text mistakes can have a disastrous effect on the appearance of your Web site. Chapter 4 dealt with graphics problems—the Number One way a designer can mess up a Web page. Guess what the Number Two way is? That's right—text. As my dad always said, "It's not what you say, it's how you say it," and on Web pages, we generally say it with text.

Many Web page designers think graphics are the flash and sizzle of a Web page—the fun stuff—and too many of them feel text is "that boring stuff marketing gives us to stick on the page." This attitude can lead to sloppiness, and sloppiness can lead to design mistakes. However, with some careful editing, we'll help you shape up your site in no time at all.

THE ORIGINAL

The reason text exists is to communicate content. And we know that if we effectively communicate content, we'll get people to take an interest, and possibly buy, our product or service. To effectively communicate, your text must be simple, clear, and easy to read. For Figure 5.1, Michael took one of the original pages from WebPagesThatSuck.com and messed it up to show a whole series of text mistakes.

Visitors to the current WebPagesThatSuck.com site send e-mail asking if their page is okay. When I visit their sites, they often look astonishingly similar to Figure 5.1. While Michael may have created the "mother of all horrible text pages," don't be fooled into thinking that pages such as the one shown in Figure 5.1 don't really exist on the Internet—they do. There are dozens of similar pages scattered throughout the Net.

Why Does This Page Suck?

Web Pages That Suck - Netscape

File Edit View Go Communicator Help

Web Pages That Suck

LESSON 1

Well, you've just had your <u>first lesson in sucky web page design</u> techniques. The first thing that sucks on the front page is the JavaScript that makes the colors fade in and out. Earlier versions of Netscape allowed you to do the same thing with multiple <BODY> tags, but Netscape fixed that around release 2.0. *Now, some clever guy figured a way to get a JavaScript to recreate this very pretentious technique.*

LET ME RE-STATE THE LAST SENTENCE. IT'S GOING TO BE VERY PRETENTIOUS FOR ANYONE OTHER THAN THE ORIGINAL AUTHOR TO USE THIS JAVASCRIPT. THE ORIGINAL AUTHOR IS VERY TALENTED AND FOR HIM, IT'S OK TO USE THIS TECHNIQUE, BUT EVENTUALLY EVERYBODY IS GOING TO START USING IT AND THEN IT WILL BECOME PRETENTIOUS. WHEN I FIRST SAW THIS TECHNIQUE BACK IN THE SUMMER OF 1996 IT WAS REALLY COOL BUT IT QUICKLY BECAME OVERUSED SO LET'S STOP USING THIS TECHNIQUE.

THE FRONT PAGE FEATURES ANOTHER OVERUSED WEB DESIGN TECHNIQUE THAT COMES IN TWO VARIATIONS AND I USED VARIATION #1: When the animation stops, you can either click on the image (mine's a textual image -- it can be a graphical image) to go to the "real" home page or if you don't click, the <META> "refresh" command automatically takes the viewer to the next page. Variation #2 is the same, but it's just a regular image or imagemap, not an animated GIF

I'M NOT SURE WHO ORIGINALLY CREATED THIS TECHNIQUE. (PROBABLY WIRED MAGAZINE -- THEY'VE CREATED A LOT OF GREAT GRAPHIC TECHNIQUES) BUT, LIKE THE RAINBOW-COLORED DIVIDER, IT'S BECOME A CLICHE.

Speaking of cliches, pages with black backgrounds are a very, very popular cliche. Whenever I see a black background it's like the designer is lowering his voice and saying, *"This is a cool page. I'm pretty cool, too."* To be honest, I'd say maybe 5% of the sites with black backgrounds are actually cool and almost every one of those was designed by a *professional graphics artist*. If you're not a pro, black's not the way to go.

Document: Done

FIGURE 5.1 **It's all in how you say it.**

Once again, through a makeover of a sample page, we'll show you how to turn a problem page into a thing of functional beauty. We've also included other real pages from the Web, such as the one shown in Figure 5.2, to provide you with even more insight into how easily text can muck up a site. But first, let's delve a little more deeply into Vincent and Michael's Four Strong Suggestions for Successful Sites.

Looking at Figure 5.1, it's safe to assume that visitors to this site would not grasp its content because the text is impossible to read. Odds are, as soon as anyone views this page, they'll immediately hit the Back button. This page shouts "Amateur!"

You can learn a lot from this figure. Here are the Four *Strong Suggestions* for Successful Sites:

1. Avoid black backgrounds.

2. Don't mix text attributes.

3. Limit the number of text colors.

4. Resist the temptation to use blinking text.

The term *strong suggestion* is used courtesy of the IRS; they *strongly suggest* that you pay your federal income tax by April 15. Well, Michael and I *strongly suggest* that you implement these suggestions—right now!

FIGURE 5.2 **Color Me Silly. Tube World**
(`http://www.execpc.com/~tekman/parts.html`)

1. Avoid Black Backgrounds

In the previous chapter, you saw how a black background makes it challenging to read a page, even when white text is used. Figure 5.1 is in even worse shape. Not only is the background black, the text is multicolored—including dark blue—so it's incredibly difficult to read. Changing the background color to white is a small first step toward improving the page overall.

We should note that graphics professionals are able to use black backgrounds more successfully than the average Web page creator. Just like a chef could figure out how to take Twinkies™ and create a gourmet meal, a graphic professional can take what is normally a bad design technique and create a masterpiece. It helps when you have taste and talent. Those of us who aren't as proficient should be more hesitant to use black backgrounds. Remember this little rhyme: "If you're not a graphics pro, black's not the way to go."

2. Don't Mix Text Attributes

I'm not going to mince words here: Don't mix and match text elements. Mixing and matching fonts, font sizes, and text attributes (bold, underline, italic) is visually confusing. Generally speaking, you need to be conservative when using text elements. Keep it simple.

3. Limit the Number of Text Colors

Ditto.

Figure 5.3 demonstrates an interesting fact: a page appears differently on the Macintosh version of Netscape than it does on the Windows version of Netscape. Figure 5.3 shows the first copy Michael made of this page. Look for the text that's highlighted—that's the BLINKing text. That same text looks quite different when it's displayed on a Windows 95-based system, as shown in Figure 5.1.

Too many exclamation points (!) are the textual equivalent of `<BLINK>`. Don't use a bazillion exclamation points (!) on your pages. Thankfully, this is one of the few text mistakes not found on our example page.

FIGURE 5.3 Michael's first prototype as displayed on a Macintosh using Netscape 2

4. Resist the Temptation to Use Blinking Text

If my sources are telling the truth, Netscape originally created the `<BLINK>` tag as an inside joke. Unfortunately, it caught on with the HTML community. It's annoying beyond all belief, and, more importantly, I've never seen a place where it needed to be used. Don't use the `<BLINK>` tag. Generally, Michael and I try not to issue commands from atop Mount Internet, but the `<BLINK>` tag is an exception. Don't use it. Please.

Can It Be Saved?

Quite simply, Figure 5.1 is almost beyond fixing. When I first redesigned the page for this book, I removed *most* of the text tags (heavy emphasis on the word *most*) and came up with what you see in Figure 5.4.

The page still needs a lot of work. Much of the remainder of this chapter will show you what to do with a page like this. You can use these techniques to fix your site's textual look one step at a time and hopefully, avoid starting over from scratch.

Start your search at Yahoo.

If you don't know HTML, Yahoo!
has a list of beginner guides that
you can find at
`http://www.yahoo.com/`
`Computers_and_Internet/`
`Internet/World_Wide_Web/`
`Information_and_`
`Documentation/Beginner_s`
`_Guides/Beginner_s_HTML/`.

You'll find more intermediate-
and advanced-level guides at
`http://www.yahoo.com/`
`Computers_and_Internet/`
`Information_and_`
`Documentation/Data_`
`Formats/HTML/Guides_`
`and_Tutorials/`.

Some of the sites listed that
you should definitely check
out include:

**The Bare Bones Guide to
HTML**
`http://werbach.com/`
`barebones/`

A Beginner's Guide to HTML
`http://www.ncsa.uiuc`
`.edu/General/Internet/WWW`
`/HTMLPrimer.html`

HTML Reference Library
(this is a free Windows 95 Help
file) `http://www6.zdnet`
`.com/cgibin/texis/swlib/`
`hotfiles/info.html?fcode`
`=0008W1`

FIGURE 5.4 The text tags have been removed.

This book assumes the reader has *some* elementary knowledge of
HTML. If you need a tune up, see the sidebar "HTML Guides and
Tutorials" for some resources on learning how to code.

WHAT GOES INTO MAKING A BETTER PAGE?

Many/most/some books on Web page design operate on the following principle: "I'm going to show the little people how to make a cool page—I'll
even give them the code and show them my magic Photoshop tricks, but
they'll never be able to make a page that looks as good as mine." (Insane
laughter of the designer/author fades.) What these designers neglect to
mention is they often spend hours tweaking the pages, going through revision
after revision. What you see is the final version.

That's not how Michael and I operate. The best way to learn is to show
different iterations of the same theme—warts and all. Granted, this isn't
the Art God approach, but it's a much more effective teaching tool.

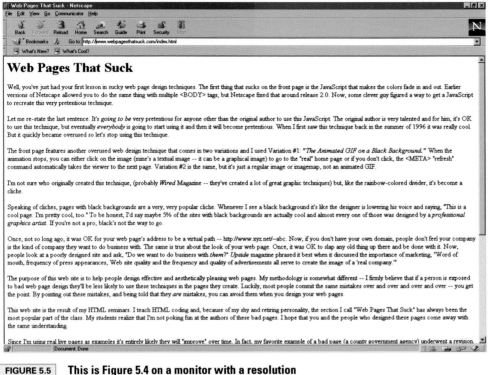

will arm you with some important information as you begin working on the text portion of your site.

FIGURE 5.5 This is Figure 5.4 on a monitor with a resolution of 1152 x 840 pixels.

Text Is the Basis of All Internet Life

Originally, the Web was a text-only medium, and there are plenty of people who would argue that it should have stayed that way. In fact, a lot of folks turn the images off before they surf. I suggest you try this some time because it significantly speeds up your Internet travels. The methodology varies by browser—it even varies between releases of the same browser. For Netscape Communicator, select Edit > Preferences > Advanced and then uncheck Automatically Load Images and click the OK button.

When the Mosaic browser was new, people crammed everything they could onto a Web page, making pages unbearably long. I'm guilty of this myself. See the sidebar "My Pathetic First Page."

The page shown in Figure 5.4 contains way too much text. Figure 5.5 demonstrates that even if you're blessed with a high-resolution graphics card, there's still too much text on the page.

As we know, the average Internet surfer doesn't have this kind of resolution. We need to break up the page into discrete units and make it less boring. The first step is to add some graphics.

As you can see in Figure 5.1, there are many ways to screw up the text on a Web page. But that's easy to fix—just remove the background color and most/all of the text attribute tags, as I did in Figure 5.4, and you're there, right?

Well, not exactly. See, if removing the extraneous tags would get you a great looking page, this book would have been written on the back of a matchbook cover: "Remove all extraneous tags. Thank you." Unfortunately, the page would still be pretty boring.

What else matters when you're working with text? Mostly, it's how you arrange the text on the page and what attributes you use, which is not as simple to do correctly as it might seem. The following sections

OH NO

MY PATHETIC FIRST PAGE

The very first page I ever created (and I got paid for this page) would probably qualify as the archetype page for illustrating the use of "Too Much Text." Here is this work of art.

Look, it was early 1995—three years ago—and based on Internet time, that's the equivalent of at least 12 regular years.

Remember what you learned in Chapter 2—most people don't like to scroll down more than two or three screens to see what's on a page.

100 INCHES LONG

**Vincent Flanders'
first Web page**

The Lightspeed Net Home Page is sponsored this week by:

American Communications Network

American Communications Network Inc.
Your Local Choice for Long Distance

Providing the best long distance service *and* Internet services to business.

Get There Fast!

If you don't have a full page monitor and don't want to scroll down the home page, click on one of the follow topic items and *Get There Fast*:

Autos - Aviation - What's Going on in Bakersfield - News, Weather, Sports - Business Topics - Cooking - Cool Stuff - Computers - Dancing - Education (HomeWork Research) - Entertainment - Fishing - Games - Gardening - Health and Medicine - Hobbies - HomeWork Research (Education) - Humor - Internet Resource - Internet Software - Jobs and Careers - Legal - Lightspeed Software - Maps - Martial Arts - Medicine and Health - Miscellaneous - Movies - Music and Musicians - Mother of All Lists - What's New - News of the Weird - Pets - Philosophy - Plants - Politics and Government - Real Estate - Religion - Restaurants - Rookie Corner - Searching the Internet - Shopping - Sports - Star Trek - Television - Tourist Info - Travel - Virtual Travel - World - We Know How to Make Clickable Images and Cool Guy Graphics Too - About this Web Page

Send questions or comments to:
WebMaster@lightspeed.net

- ## The Mother of All Lists

  If you only went to *one* page, this is the page. If you just picked the three check-marked items, you co get to almost anywhere on the Internet. If you want to free-form surf, go here.

  [back to the top]

- ## The Rookie Corner

  Just what it says. Learn about the Internet.

  [back to the top]

- ## HomeWork Research (Education)

  This includes sections for K-8 grades, High School Students, and College Students.

  The Other Education section also contains a wide variety of information and covers the following topic

  Agriculture
  Anthropology
  Archaeology
  Arts and Humanities
  Art Galleries
  Astronomy
  Atmospheric Sciences
  Biology
  Botany
  Chemistry
  Environmental Issues
  Geography
  Geology
  Herbs
  History
  Language and Linguistics
  Libraries and Reference
  Literature and Poetry
  Magazines
  Math
  Museums
  Native American Studies
  News and Newspapers
  Oceanography

Library is another great spot to start your research efforts..

[back to the top]

- ## Cool Stuff

  Cool is a matter of taste, but since Lightspeed Technologies is the coolest place in the world to work, are well qualified to present a small sampling of the cool stuff to be found on the Internet.

  [back to the top]

- ## Lightspeed Software

  The following information is available: Marketing info - Tech Support department - info about the cool software company in America - and the latest issue of the Lightspeed Link Newsletter.

  [back to the top]

- ## What's Going on in Bakersfield -- News, Weather and Sport

  If you woke up in Bakersfield and wanted to know what was going on here and the world, well you'd here.

  [back to the top]

- ## What's New

  What's new on the Internet and on this server.

  [back to the top]

- ## Business

  The following topics are presented: Corporations, General Business, Jobs and Careers, Legal and Rea Estate.

  [back to the top]

- ## Games

  [back to the top]

- ## Entertainment

  Contains the following topics:
  Drama & Theatre
  Hobbies (Autos, Aviation, Cooking, Dancing, Fishing, Gambling, Gardening, Martial Arts, Pets, Plants and Misc.)
  Humor
  Miscellaneous
  Movies
  Music & Musicians
  Star Trek
  Television

  [back to the top]

- ## Sports

  [back to the top]

- ## Politics and Government

- ## Politics and Government

  Includes: Government, Military, Politics, and California Government.

  [back to the top]

- ## Computers

  Information on Computer Companies, Computer Graphics, Programming Languages, Multimedia, Software and User Groups.

  [back to the top]

- ## Internet Resources

  Includes Internet Search Engines.

  [back to the top]

- ## Miscellaneous

  Includes: Maps, Medicine, Non-Profit Organizations, Philosophy, Religion, Shopping & Restaurants, Travel, Tourist Information, Virtual Tourism, and The World.

  [back to the top]

- ## News

  [back to the top]

- ## News of the Weird

  This is what everybody at Lightspeed Software Lives For! *News of the Weird* is a weekly syndicated column by Chuck Shepherd containing synopses of bizarre news stories reported in various sources a is carried in over 200 newspapers. There is also an "electronic edition" both in the form of a weekly electronic mailing list and an archive accessible via the WWW and ftp. Read this week's column to get idea of what it is all about. (Note that the online edition is delayed by 2 weeks to give papers a chance publish it first.)

  [back to the top]

- ## Software to Access the Internet

  Yes, we realize that if you're already here you don't need this software, but this site has Windows and Macintosh software for surfing the net. Give it a look.

  A third party site that has especially good access to software.

  Internet Software for the Macintosh
  Internet Software for Windows

  [back to the top]

About this web page

The guilty parties unmasked -- sort of.

[back to the top]

We Know How to Make Clickable Images and Cool Guy Graphi Too

OH NO

DO AS I SAY, NOT AS I DO

One of the problems with Web design books is that the authors always come across as Art Gods. Part of the reason is editorial. The book publisher wants the author to come across as "the expert"—the all-seeing, all-knowing person who never makes a mistake. This is what the public wants when they buy a book, right? Well, that's not how it works in the real world. Mistakes are made and because one of the premises of this book is to "learn good design by looking at bad design," I want to continually stress bad design techniques—even if it makes Michael and I look like less than Art Gods. Enough of the rant.

Anyway, I'm always asked what font is used for the WebPagesThatSuck .com logo. Well, I can tell you it's Schmutz Corroded, which I purchased from Image Club (see Chapter 4 for address).

All I can tell you about the logo are its physical dimensions. As I mentioned back in Chapter 2, keep track of the details of the graphics you create. For example, I should have written down the following details about the logo:

Point size

Shadow details (I used the Eye Candy filters, but I didn't write down any of the settings used)

Learn from my mistakes.

FIGURE 5.6 The logo for WebPagesThatSuck.com

There's Too Much Text! Add Graphics!

That's right! There's too much text in Figures 5.4 and 5.5. Figure 5.6 shows the graphics logo created for the top of the page. In addition to the logo for the title of the site, I added a subhead for some visual appeal and to give visitors more insight into what the site is all about.

Break the Text Up into Multiple Pages

While the graphic logo helps, there's still too much text. If you look at the actual document shown in Figure 5.5, you'll see the text goes on and on. Let's break the page up into smaller units (actually three pages). Figure 5.7 shows you the first of the three pages.

Horizontal and Vertical Text Figure 5.7 shows how the page looks on a 1152x840 pixel monitor. The first page looks better than the original. I solved the problem of too much vertical text, but I still have too much horizontal text.

Unless instructed otherwise by HTML formatting tags, the Web browser automatically fills the page with text and images starting at the top left of the screen and working its way across and then down to the bottom right. Text completely fills the width of the browser window.

If you were to check, however, you'd discover that a line of text in most books is about four inches wide and contains between 9 and 15 words per line. There are 35 words on the first line of the page shown in Figure 5.7. I don't know about you, but unless a Web page can tell me how to turn lead

FIGURE 5.7   I broke the original page into three pages; here's the first page.

into gold or has a magic formula that will make me 50 pounds lighter, I wouldn't try to read this page. It's just too difficult to keep your place.

Tables

Tables are how all the great Web sites are created. Why? Because they are the best way to limit the width of a Web page. They are the only way you can place elements in a grid-like pattern. (Technically, that's not true because Cascading Style Sheets (CSS) have similar capabilities. The implementation of CSS by Netscape and Microsoft is, as of now, not particularly stable. While it is the future of Web design, tables are the present.)

In the old days, HTML editors were pretty worthless because you had to basically code tables by hand. With the advent of WYSIWYG editors (What You See Is What You Get), you can easily create table-based pages. Even the non-WYSIWYG editors include special programs to create tables.

To illustrate the use of tables, I'm going to show you how the final version of one page from WebPagesThatSuck.com site was designed.

TOO COOL

TEXT TIPS

Remember the following text tips:

People don't really like to scan long sections of the screen to find information.

Break text into small, yet palatable morsels.

Keep your text to between 9 and 15 words per line.

Insert Table button

New Table Properties

Number of rows: 2   Number of columns: 2

Attributes

Border line width: 1   pixels

Cell spacing: 14   pixels between cells

Cell padding: 4   pixel space within cells

☑ Table width: 550   Pixels

☐ Table min. height: 100   % of window

☐ Table color: Choose Color

☐ Include caption: ○ above   ○ below table

Table alignment
○ Left   ⦿ Center   ○ Right

OK   Cancel   Apply   Help

Making Tables Using Netscape Navigator Gold

There are lots of programs you can use to create tables, but I chose Netscape Navigator Gold because it's readily available; however, the principles shown here are the same for many programs.

When creating tables, it's *extremely* important to lay out the design before you start. In Chapter 2, I mentioned the importance of planning your page, but it's even *more* important to lay out your tables before you create them. Why? Because tables are created one cell at a time starting from the top left and working across and then down the page. Because of the grid arrangement, it's difficult to modify tables. You have to insert a row or column, and then span the rows or columns and fill in the text. (If you don't understand or are uncomfortable with these terms, that should be proof tables aren't something to take lightly.)

If you need more information on how to create HTML tables, there's a great tutorial on tables. You can find Table Tutor at http://junior .apk.net/~jbarta/tutor/tables/index.html.

Assume the Position   Figure 5.8 shows the top of the main screen of Netscape Navigator Gold. Note the cursor is ready to click the Insert Table button.

After you click the Insert Table button, the New Table Properties dialog box is displayed. You need to fill in some parameters. Normally, it's a case of trial and error, but to keep this part of the chapter down to its right size, I'm going to play Art God and give you the "correct" numbers. They are shown in Figure 5.9. Set the Border Line Width to **1** so you can see how the elements in the table are placed. After the table is done, set the Border Line Width to **0** because you don't want the border to show; in most cases, having your border show looks tacky—very, very tacky.

Click the OK button to accept the parameters. Your screen should resemble the one shown Figure 5.10.

Fill 'Er Up Now all you have to do is fill up the table with your text and images. Personally, I always like to start with the text. I copy the text I'm going to use, put my cursor in the top-right cell, and then paste the text into the cell. The result is shown in Figure 5.11.

Picture This Next, add the pictures. First, position the cursor in the top-left cell, and then select the Insert Image button, as shown in Figure 5.11.

Because you haven't saved the document, selecting the Insert Image button brings up a message box that tells you to save the document in order to proceed.

After saving the document, you can insert an image. Figure 5.12 shows the Properties dialog box that appears after you have saved the document. In the example shown here, the only parameter added was the alternative text. Under Alternative Representations, I entered **A picture of Vincent Flanders all tied up**. As mentioned in Chapter 4, the ALT parameter is the descriptive text that is displayed when an image is broken or when a visitor has set his or her browser so graphics are not displayed. On later versions of Netscape and Internet Explorer, the text used in the ALT parameter is displayed when the mouse passes over the image. It's very important to fill in the ALT parameter.

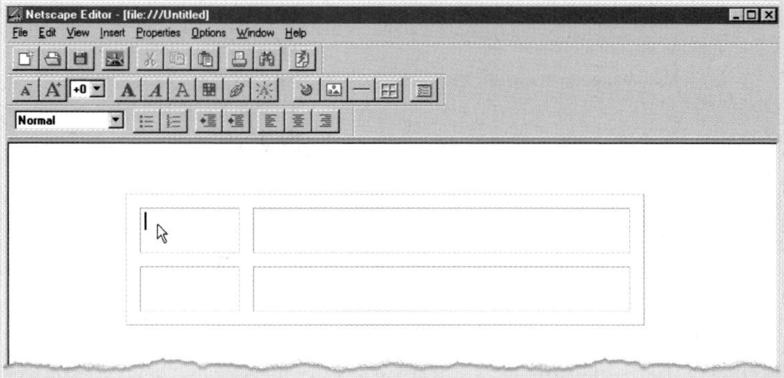

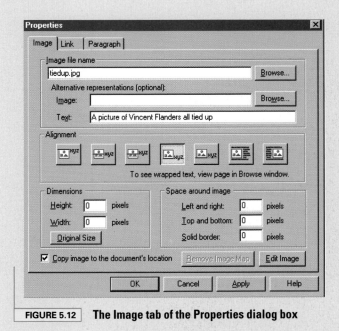

FIGURE 5.10 **Our basic table**

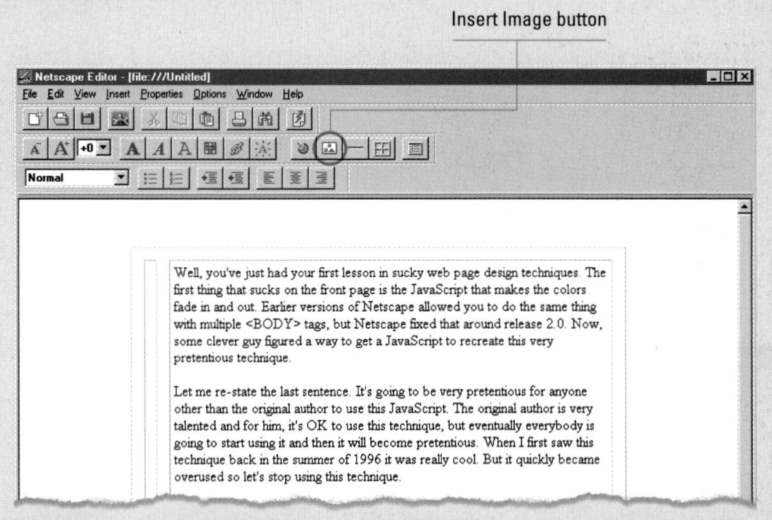

FIGURE 5.11 **The text pasted into the table cell**

FIGURE 5.12 **The Image tab of the Properties dialog box**

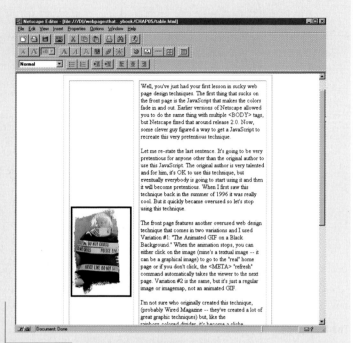

FIGURE 5.13 **Stuck in the middle again**

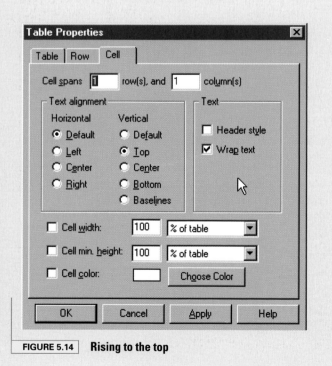

FIGURE 5.14 **Rising to the top**

When you click the OK button, the image is placed in the table cell, as shown in Figure 5.13. However, there's a slight problem—the image is in the middle of the cell. It should be at the top of the cell.

To remedy the situation, select Properties **>** Table to access the Table Properties dialog box. Figure 5.14 shows the correct settings. In the Text Alignment area, you'll find options for setting the horizontal and vertical alignment of the table. For the purposes of this example, set the Horizontal alignment to Default and the Vertical alignment to Top.

Continue the same process for the rest of the images, the links, and the text. Then save the document and open your regular HTML editor to copy the HTML code used in the table (starting at the `<TABLE>` tag and ending with the `</TABLE>` tag).

Figure 5.15 shows what the page looks like after all the editing has been completed (I've left the border on so you can see the columns).

Tables are the best way to limit the width of a Web page, but there are two other ways to move text and graphics around the page: `<MULTICOL>` and `<BLOCKQUOTE>`. These techniques don't necessarily work as well as tables, but you'll see them used on different Web pages.

Netscape's <MULTICOL> = MULTI-PROBLEMS

God bless those Netscape folks. They realize that not everyone can grasp the concept of building tables so they tried to find a way for the average Joe to create what I call "Quick Tables." The tag Netscape came up with is the <MULTICOL> tag, and while the concept is good, the execution leaves a lot to be desired. Figure 5.16 shows what the original WebPagesThatSuck.com page looks like when using the <MULTICOL> tag.

Hey, it's a nice looking page. What's the problem?

1. It's a Netscape-only tag. Microsoft doesn't support it in Internet Explorer.

2. The page is still hard to read. You have to scroll down column one, then back up to the top of column two, and then down to the end of column three.

3. You can't center the multiple columns on a page.

Here's the bottom line: learn how to use the <TABLE> tag.

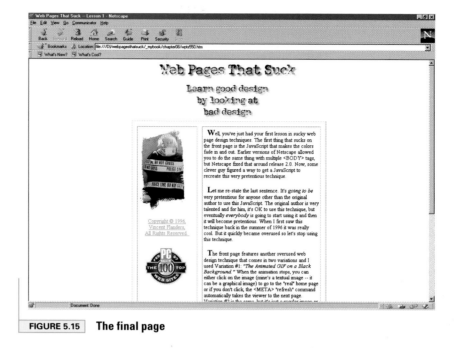

FIGURE 5.15   **The final page**

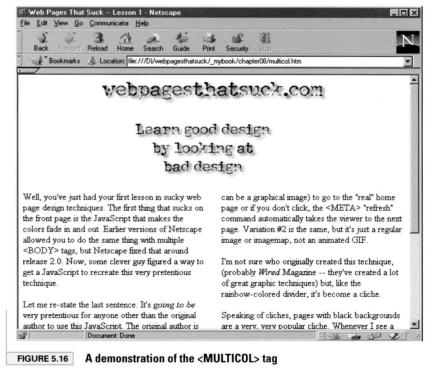

FIGURE 5.16   **A demonstration of the <MULTICOL> tag**

The `<BLOCKQUOTE>` Tag

If you HTML purists weren't choking over the discussion of the `<MULTICOL>` tag, you will be now because we're going to talk about a well-known kludge—using multiple `<BLOCKQUOTE>` tags to create text margins. The purists have a point. With certain browsers, text enclosed by `<BLOCKQUOTE>` tags shows up in *italic* or even stranger renderings, such as font color or face changes. The reason people use the `<BLOCKQUOTE>` tag is because it's easier than creating tables. (Although tables are not as hard as they used to be.) Figure 5.17 shows what the WebPagesThatSuck .com page looks like on a 640x480 screen using three `<BLOCKQUOTE>` tags.

FIGURE 5.17 **Using the `<BLOCKQUOTE>` tag**

So how do you use `<BLOCKQUOTE>` to get the "indented" margins? Like this:

```
<BLOCKQUOTE><BLOCKQUOTE><BLOCKQUOTE>
Here's your text</BLOCKQUOTE></BLOCK
QUOTE></BLOCKQUOTE>
```

Like most tags dealing with text elements, `<BLOCKQUOTE>` is a container tag—you have to tell it where to start and where to stop, essentially "blockquoting" a section. To get the results shown in Figure 5.17, I placed three `<BLOCKQUOTE>` tags in front and three `</BLOCKQUOTE>` tags at the end of the text. There's nothing magical about the number three other than it is the equivalent of approximately three tabs in most browsers.

Remember, you must have the same number of ending tags as you do starting tags.

Microsoft's Solution

Of course Microsoft has it's own proprietary solution— the `LEFTMARGIN` and `RIGHTMARGIN` arguments, which are attached to the `<BODY>` tag, as shown in red in the following example:

```
<body leftmargin=100 rightmargin=100
text="#000000" bgcolor="#FFFFFF"
link="#0000FF" vlink="#E40000"
alink="#FF00FF">
```

This argument basically tells the Internet Explorer browser to make a right and left margin of 100 pixels. As of the writing of this book, Netscape doesn't support these arguments; however, Michael and I think they should—it would solve a lot of problems. It's highly unlikely that margin attributes to the body tag will be incorporated in upcoming HTML specifications. And while Cascading Style Sheets deal with margins, CSS is so screwed up that it will be 1999 before everybody gets to level 1. Go to `http://style.webreview.com/` to learn more about the whole problem.

GENERAL TEXT PROBLEMS

There are a lot of ways to ruin the text on your pages. In the following sections, we'll discuss a few of the more common mechanisms for textual abuse.

<FONT> You

I could make this a really short section by just telling you not to use the `<FONT>` tag, but I won't. The `<FONT>` tag and its `COLOR`, `SIZE`, and `FACE` attributes make many assumptions about your visitors. For example:

Are they using the browser default values?

Are there any physical limitations such as vision impairment, color blindness, and so on?

Which fonts reside on their system?

Let me elaborate:

1. Poor `COLOR` choice on your part may mean a color-blind person can't see your text. Some color-blind surfers set their browser to display the background color as yellow and the text color as black. If you use `COLOR="YELLOW"` or, more correctly, `COLOR="#ffff00"` to emphasize some important text on your site—such as "Warning! Don't touch the nitroglycerin until after the next step!"—a color-blind person won't see the warning and the results could literally be explosive. If you really want to mess with a color-blind person, use the primary colors red and green next to each other.

2. The `SIZE` argument may interfere with the way vision-impaired visitors see your site. They've already set the font size larger than normal. If you increase or decrease the size of the fonts, your site will be hard to read. The same font on a Windows system is larger than on a Mac system. Increasing or decreasing the font size will have, needless-to-say, unpredictable results.

3. The `FACE` argument assumes all visitors have the same fonts on their system as you have on your system. This is highly unlikely given the wide divergence of computer systems (Mac, Windows, UNIX, and so on).

4. Netscape is supporting something called *dynamic fonts*. These fonts are "embedded" in your HTML documents and downloaded just like Java applets to reside temporarily on your hard disk. Just what we need. More bandwidth congestion.

5. Not every browser supports the `<FONT>` tag. However, at the risk of alienating someone, here it goes: "All browsers that count support the `<FONT>` tag."

<FONT> You—Losing *FACE*

There are a lot of things I don't understand: atomic theory, Existentialism, how Bill Buckner let that ground ball bounce through his legs in the bottom of the 10th inning in game six of the 1986 World Series, and why Web designers use the `<FONT>` tag and `FACE` argument to create unreadable pages. I took an old version of the WebPagesThatSuck.com main page and added the following line of code just before the text started.

```
<font face="Brush Script MT">
```

Take a look at Figure 5.18 to see the results.

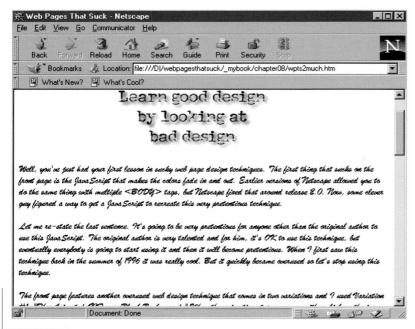

FIGURE 5.18   **Gee, looks like a wedding invitation**

Granted, I'm 49 years old and have bad eyesight but still, folks...if the text is too hard for the average person to read, they're going to hit the Back button faster than Larry King gets married.

<FONT> You—Color Is Stupid

Like most Web page designers, Michael and I have yet to figure out why people use multiple text colors on a page. Almost without exception, using multiple colors of text on the same page simply does not work. You wouldn't give your boss a monthly report where the text had three or more colors on a page would you? I don't know, would you?

<BASEFONT>

The `<BASEFONT>` tag tells the browser how large to display the default font size. If no `<BASEFONT>` tag is used, the default value is three. Both Netscape and Microsoft support this tag.

Where I went wrong on my redesign is I forgot that `<BASEFONT>` doesn't affect text inside tables. Because there wasn't any text outside the table, the `<BASEFONT>` tag was totally useless, and I had to use the `<FONT SIZE=+1>` tag in each paragraph. I need to be disciplined!

Before moving on to text attributes, let's take a quick look at the other `<FONT>` issues.

Don't *<FONT>* Yourself

Be extremely careful if you use the `<FONT>` tag. If visitor's can't read your page, they definitely won't stay. Michael and I make the following recommendations:

1. Let the default browser font take over— it's real cool to basically do nothing.

2. Wait until Netscape and Microsoft agree on a single Cascading Style Sheet specification if you really must try to exert typographical control over your work. (We'll talk about Style Sheets in Chapter 7.) Some designers think they're the future of the Web.

3. Avoid using the `<FONT>` and `<BASEFONT>` tags unless there's no other choice.

INDIVIDUAL TEXT ATTRIBUTES

In Figure 5.19, also shown at the beginning of the chapter in Figure 5.1, Michael and I put every possible bad text idea onto one page—bold, italic, underlined text, and so on. Even if you don't use them in large quantities, they can be difficult to execute well.

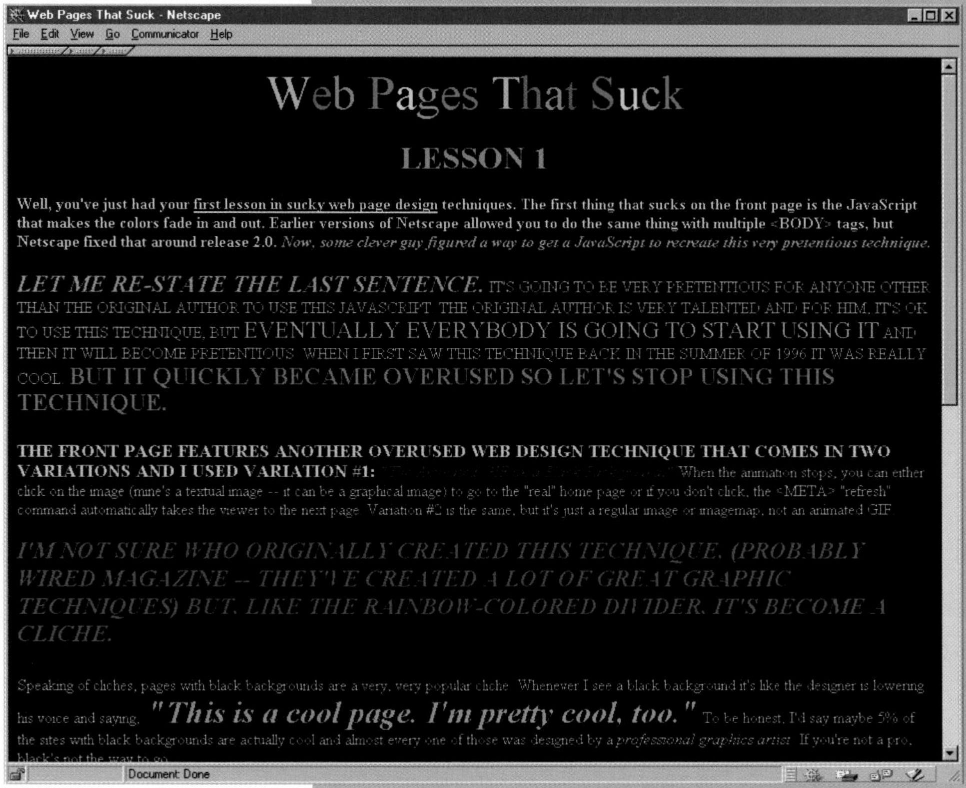

One of my favorite rock bands, the Byrds, recorded a beautiful song years ago called "Turn, Turn, Turn." One of the lines is, "There is a season and a time for every purpose under heaven." It's the same for most of your text-based tags—`<B>`old, `<I>`talic, `<BIG>`, `<SMALL>`, ALL CAPS, and `<U>`nderlined text. There's a time and a season to use them—and not to use them—so be careful. Let's look at how to correctly use individual text attributes to avoid the chaos in Figure 5.19.

Em`<B>`oldened

Let's say we decide to emphasize certain words in the first paragraph of the WebPagesThatSuck.com site, as shown here:

Well, you've just had your first lesson in **sucky Web page design** techniques. The first thing that sucks on the front page is the **JavaScript** that makes the colors **fade in and out**. Earlier versions of Netscape allowed you to do the same thing with multiple `<BODY>` tags, but Netscape

FIGURE 5.19 The only thing missing here is the kitchen sink.

TOO COOL

BE <B>OLD?

The <B> old tag is for emphasis with gusto. Is what you're emphasizing really important?

Use the <B> tag sparingly. When overused, <B> loses its power.

Have a third party (preferably a disinterested third party) look over the page to decide if the emphasis is needed.

fixed that around release 2. Now, some clever guy figured a way to get a JavaScript to recreate this very **pretentious** technique.

Ask yourself this question: "Does the text I'm bolding need the added emphasis?" If the answer is "Yes," hey, go right ahead. Because the eyes go directly toward the bold text, what your brain picks up is:

sucky Web page design…JavaScript…fade in and out…pretentious

This makes sense. On the other hand, you can go overboard:

Well, you've just had **your first lesson** in sucky Web page design techniques. The first thing that **sucks** on the front page is the **JavaScript** that makes the colors fade in and out. **Earlier versions** of Netscape allowed you to do the same thing with multiple <BODY> tags, but Netscape fixed that around **release 2**. Now, some clever guy figured a way to get a JavaScript to recreate **this very pretentious technique**.

Scan the emphasized text; bet you won't get the point of the paragraph.

<I>TALIC

Italic text, like bold, is used for emphasis—in fact, it's the "preferred" means of emphasis in literature and magazines.

The problem is simple. Italic type is hard to read on computer screens, and it's even more difficult to read on laptop computer screens. For this reason, some designers prefer to use bold, rather than italic, when emphasizing text in an HTML document. If you use the <I> tag, use it sparingly.

When it comes to <I>talic, remember <B>old will probably show up better on computer monitors.

ALL CAPS TEXT

TYPING IN ALL CAPS IS FROWNED ON IN E-MAIL AND NEWS-GROUPS BECAUSE IT'S CONSIDERED SHOUTING. IT'S ALSO VERY DARN HARD TO READ, SO DON'T USE IT!!

ALL CAPS TEXT SUCKS LIKE A DUST BUSTER. TEXT IN ALL CAPS IS NOT A GOOD IDEA. ASK YOURSELF, WHEN WAS THE LAST TIME YOU READ A BOOK THAT WAS TYPESET IN ALL CAPS?

There's a possible exception. Sometimes it's okay to use ALL CAPS in a heading if there are fewer than seven words—and the text fits on one line of the screen. For example:

TODAY'S SPECIAL

Don't Use All Initial Caps Either Because It's Also Difficult To Read Text When The Initial Character Is Always Capitalized. Your Eyes Go Up And Down. You'll Most Often See Initial Caps When You're Using A Heading Level 1 Or 2 Tag.

`<U>`nderlined Text

There's a serious problem with using underlined text—it looks exactly like linked text so the tendency is for the viewer to try to click on the text, thinking it will take them somewhere else.

Underlined text is confusing. Not to mention that it has been deprecated (it no longer exists) in HTML 4. Find another way to indicate emphasis.

~~`<STRIKE>`through text~~

The `<STRIKE>`through tag is a specialized tag and should only be used in situations where its meaning is understood. Two possibilities include legal contracts where you want to show that one word, multiple words, or sections have been eliminated, or documents where you want to show that something has changed.

OTHER TEXT PROBLEMS

Not every text problem is related to HTML tags. There are many ways for your text to cause problems. We'll discuss a few of them in this section.

Avoid Jargon

Not everybody speaks English as a first language—even here in the United States. Yes, English is the *lingua franca*—uh, hmm—of the Internet, but you'll do yourself, and your site, an enormous service if you use terms everyone understands.

Toward this end, eradicate slang, Americanisms, and anything else you think your visitors won't understand. Not only are you being courteous, but also you're helping make your site more readable. Speaking of jargon, earlier in this chapter, I used the jargonesque phrase "how Bill Buckner let that ground ball bounce through his legs…" Most people can figure out I'm referring to a sporting event where a player made a mistake. (Readers in Boston are now screaming: "It was more than a mistake!") Throughout the book and in the WebPagesThatSuck.com site, I also reference people and events some readers might not know about. I risk losing the reader at times, but that's part of my persona—the wild, untamed designer from Bakersfield, California. If that's not your persona, avoid jargon.

Tpyos

The fastest way to chase people away from your site is to have a Web page full of typographical mistakes, especially if the page is for a business or nonprofit organization. When people see typos on these pages, they automatically think, "These people are not professionals." Logically, the next thought is, "If they make these simple mistakes on their page, what will they do in their business?"

What makes typos so horrible is the fact that most HTML editors and Web page programs have spelling checkers included. Typos are bad, bad, bad.

FIGURE 5.20 | **Microsoft Pubilsher?**

The worst kind of typo is the kind a spelling checker misses. When I worked in a steno pool at an insurance company I had to type the job description for the Manager of the Data Processing Department. Here's what I typed:

Requirements: Must keep a breast of current developments in the data-processing industry.

It's "keep abreast" not "keep a breast." Spelling checkers can't help you with this kind of mistake nor can they help you with grammar.

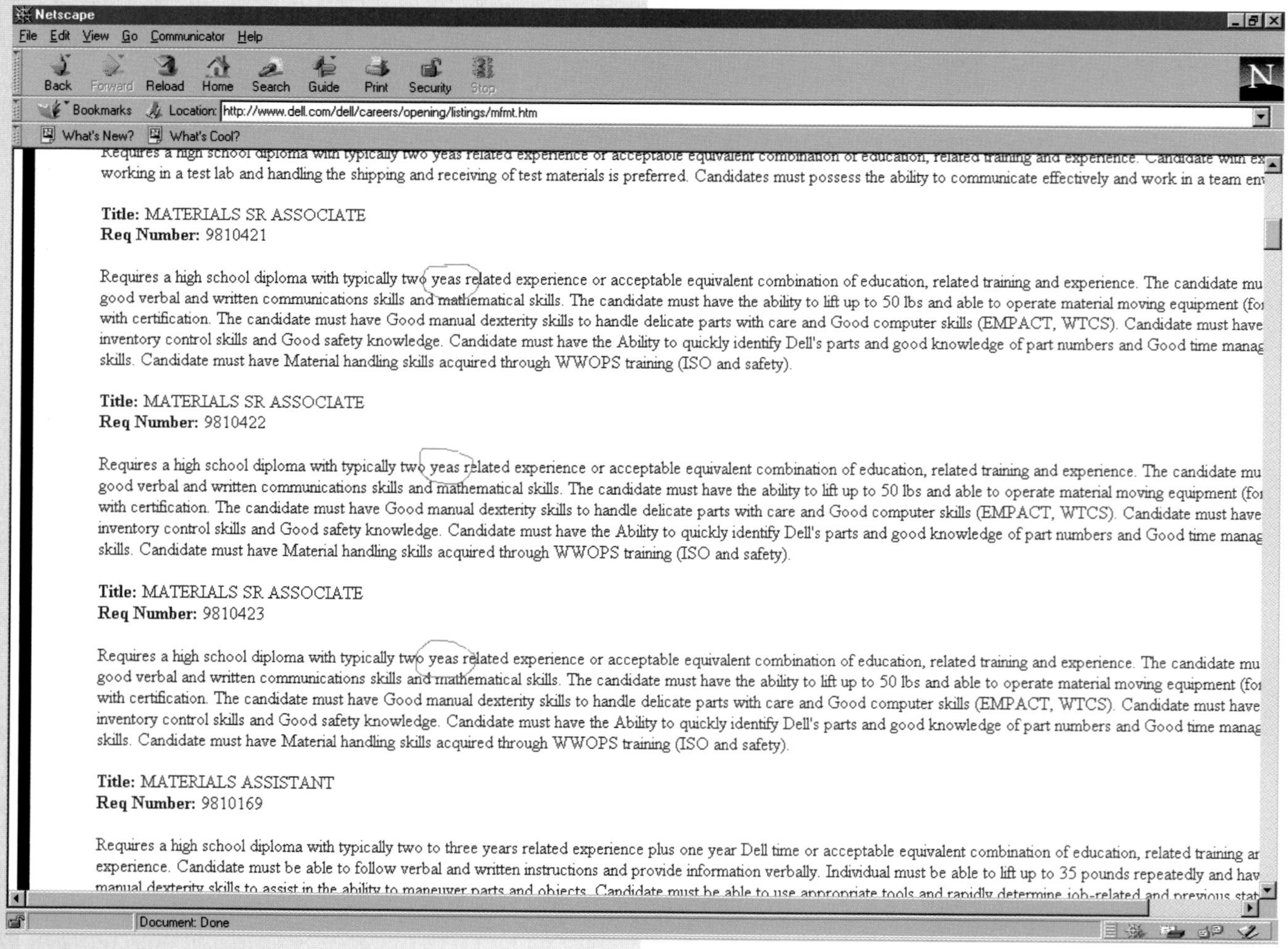

FIGURE 5.21 | **Yeas of experience**

This reminds me of a story a friend told me. When she was a teenager, she worked on a fishing dock with lots of tough guys. One day they were ordering pizza and she wrote down *Cesarean* for the kind, instead of *Sicilian*. She's never lived that down.

Don't think typos are limited to small sites. Even the big boys make them. Figure 5.20 shows you an error on the front page of the Microsoft site.

Figure 5.21 shows you a cut and paste error I found on the Dell Computer site. Cut and paste errors are insidious. You make a mistake and then repeat it by cutting and pasting the text. I guess zero "yeas" of related experience is required.

I remember when the same silly cut and paste mistake happened to me. I was adding some links for my company's "Site of the Day" page for April 13, 1996, and I added a link to the Ronald Reagan Home Page (my ex-company had its fair share of Republicans; that's an interesting phrase—it implies that somehow there's an unfair share). To compensate, I made the April 14, 1996, "Site of the Day" the National Coalition for the Homeless. I copied all the text (including HTML) from the link to the Reagan page, *but I forgot to change the URL!*

When someone clicked on the National Coalition for the Homeless link, they were sent to the Ronald Reagan Home Page. Interesting mistake.

By the way, the word *Tpyos* at the beginning of this section is not a typo.

The `<SPACER>` Tag

The `<SPACER>` tag arrived on the scene at the same time Netscape introduced the `<MULTICOL>` tag. It was a well-meaning gesture, but since Microsoft's Internet Explorer doesn't support the tag, it's relegated to the back alleys of the Internet.

`<SPACER>` simply allocates whatever invisible horizontal or vertical space you choose. For example:

```
<SPACER TYPE=BLOCK WIDTH=10>Here's some text.<P>
```

moves the phrase "Here's some text" 10 pixels to the right, as the example shows:

Here's some text.

Don't use it. It's a Netscape-only tag.

TOO COOL

HIRE AN EDITOR OR PROFESSIONAL PROOFREADER TO LOOK OVER YOUR PAGES

It's especially important to have editorial help before you launch your site. If you can't hire an editor, have two or three people who haven't worked on the site go through it. Besides catching spelling and grammar errors, a good editor will stop you from including the phrase, "My mission in life is to facilitate teams of people to accomplish exciting things."

FIGURE 5.22 Ooh, I'm centered.

The *<CENTER>* Tag

Normally, you don't think of `<CENTER>` as a text tag, but as a block tag—it works on blocks of text and/or graphics. However, I'm noticing a frightening trend on the Internet—whole blocks of `<CENTER>`ed text on a page. Figure 5.22 is a perfect example of this bad tendency.

What gives? While this isn't as bad as a lot of pages on the Internet, it's simply not acceptable. Why not? Because it's become a cliché. It's perfectly acceptable to `<CENTER>` the logo, but not the whole page. Speaking of bad pages on the Internet, Figure 5.23 shows a page where centering is overdone—as is the choice of graphics, multiple text colors, multiple animated GIFs, background choice (the clichéd "stars"), and so on.

Don't `<CENTER>` everything on your page. Use the `<CENTER>` tag judiciously and only where it's needed.

FIGURE 5.23 **Wow! Dynamic Recording Studios**
(http://www.dynrec.com/index1.html)

HOW DO YOU SAY "SUCK" IN MALAYSIA?

The repeating background screams "Suck!" It repeats darn near where their big 8-inch logo finishes, which, by the way, didn't fit on the page when I tried to print it on my Apple LaserWriter Select. (Keep in mind widths of over 550 pixels won't print out on your typical laser printer.)

The low visitor count can't be much of an ego boost, and it's really not a great idea to draw attention to the low count by animating the counter and placing it at the top of the page.

The animated mail going into the slot doesn't do anything for me either. And check this out:

"Best viewed with Microsoft Internet Explorer."

Uh huh. Were they worried it would suck even more in other browsers?

Once again, however, the Americans have aced their international rival in suckiness.

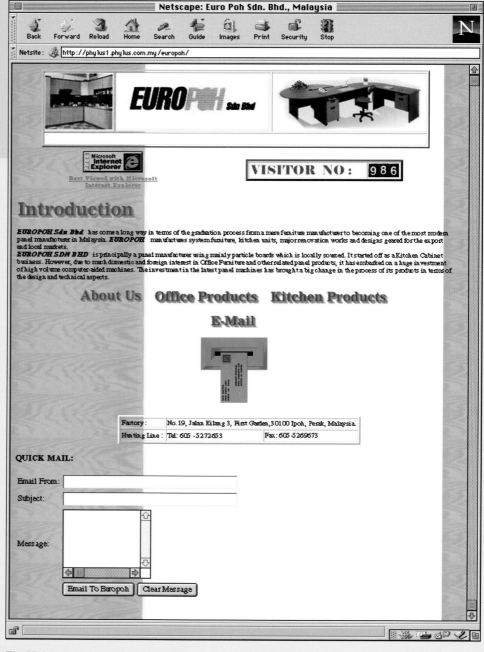

The Malaysian furniture site
(`http://phylus1.phylus.com.my/europoh`)

The U.S. furniture site
(http://nuttmeg.com)

Since I have no life, I like staring at my monitor with drool coming out of my mouth waiting for the page to finish loading. Note the warning though:

"Please wait, this may take a little while to download."

An understatement if there ever was one.

All the text on the page is centered; come to think of it, so are all the images and borders. Speaking of borders, the animated yellow roses have got to go. What possesses people to animate everything? The "Free" burst, the goofy-looking door, the gigantic "Thanks for visiting," the recycled sign, and the lame hammer-hitting-the-nail graphic are also animated. I especially like the copyright disclaimer in regards to all the animations.

Perhaps the recycled logo indicates that all these graphics came from somewhere else and they're just "recycling" them.

And last but not least, the gigabyte worth of banner ads. You can't see all of them because they extend off to the left for about a mile. I counted 14 in all. My first question is "Why"? Is it insecurity that makes people want visitors to leave as quickly as they came? It can't be greed that drives them. I can't believe there's much money in putting all those banner ads on their page. I think the top banner ad sums up this page well, however:

"Ho, Ho, Hum."

Next, we'll cover links and frames. Links are pretty straightforward; however frames…well, let's just say everyone has an opinion about them. Some people love them; others hate them. You'll soon see where we fall on that spectrum.

Flanders & Willis's Reality Check

Few issues about Web design inflame people or are as controversial as the issue of frames. First of all, frames cut up already small screen real estate into even smaller segments. Frames cause the pages to load slower. Many search engines have problems indexing sites with frames. Neither Netscape Communicator nor Internet Explorer 3 will let you print a framed page. It begs the question: Why does anyone use frames? Think before you frame.

Frames and Links

IN THIS CHAPTER

we're going to talk about frames

and links, specifically we're

going to talk about what not to

do. Remember when we talked

about bevelmania in Chapter 4—

well the same thing applies to

frames: "Wow, I just learned how

to make frames and by golly, I'm

going to frame the world!" Stop!

Now I'm not saying that you

should never use frames (other-

wise, there would be no reason

for writing this chapter). As with

all good things, there is a time

and a place for using frames.

But links should be straightforward, right? Wrong. I've seen more vague and mysterious links than I care to remember. Just as with bevels and frames, links can be overdone too. I'm going to show you a site, later in the chapter, with 41 e-mail links. Come on folks, there *is* a limit. Let's explore its outer edge by first looking at a site, shown in Figure 6.1, with a grand total of thirteen frames.

WHY PEOPLE HATE PEOPLE WHO USE FRAMES

In preparing for this chapter, I sat down at my computer on December 7, 1997, and searched my e-mail messages for the word *frame.* The first message in my file was dated August 12, 1996. Eight hours later, my search brought me all the way up to March 11, 1997. I think it's safe to say that a lot of people feel strongly enough about frames to write me. Here's just an itty-bitty sample that catches the general feeling of the messages.

"All pages with frames suck. Plus, they tend to make my browser crash at unpredictable times."

"I hate frames. Your site uses frames. I hate your site."

"[WebPagesThatSuck.com] is absolutely the best use of Frames— which I usually hate."

Why Does
This Page Suck?

**Looking at this site you
understand why people hate
people who use frames.**

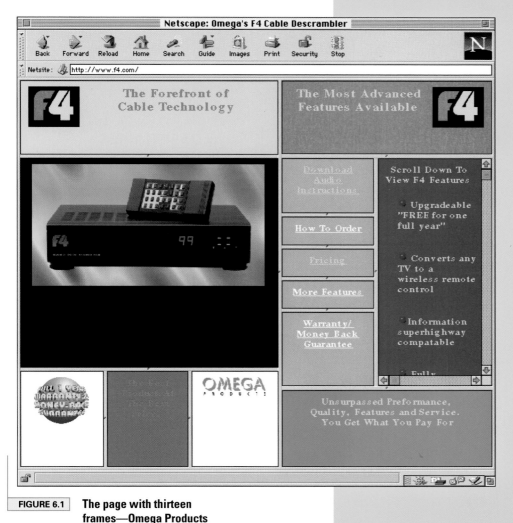

FIGURE 6.1 **The page with thirteen
frames—Omega Products**
(http://www.f4.com/)

Normally, upon viewing
this page, I'd just say
something cute: "If you
have to ask why this page
sucks, you'll never understand." That's true here,
but I'm kinda stunned.

Frames are a navigational
aid. The designer of the
site in Figure 6.1 over-
looked this important fact.
Instead of using frames
as navigational aids, the
designer used frames as
little billboards to block
off sections of text and
graphics for the viewer
to see.

**The designer forgot to
ask the all-important
question: "Would frames
make the navigation
of the site easier for
the visitor?"**

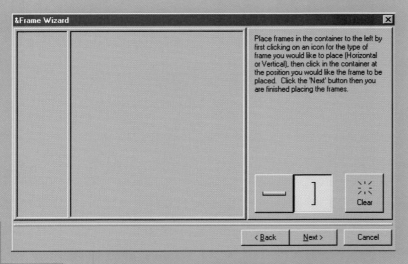

FIGURE 6.2 **The default frame setup shown in WebEdit Pro's Frame Wizard Utility**

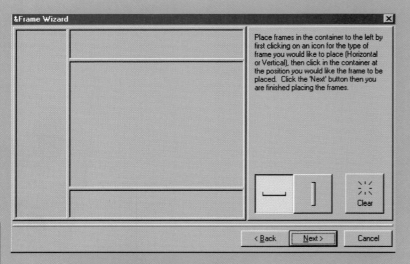

FIGURE 6.3 **Four frame setup, the first version**

Few issues about Web design inflame people or are as controversial as the issue of frames. First of all, frames cut up already small screen real estate into even smaller segments. Frames cause the pages to load slower—which is just what everyone has been asking for, "Yes, Vincent, I want my pages to load even slower than they have been loading." Many search engines have problems indexing sites with frames. Neither Netscape Communicator nor Internet Explorer 3 will let you print a framed page. (You *can,* however, select individual frames for printing.) With all the problems, why did the site shown in Figure 6.1 use so many frames? More importantly, why does anyone use frames?

I think it's safe to say all thirteen frames could have been reduced to two using the default frame setup in WebEdit Pro's Frame Wizard Utility (`http://www.luckman.com`), as shown in Figure 6.2. I'll talk more about WebEdit Pro in the section "Not Knowing How to Create Frames."

In this setup, the navigational links would be in the left frame and all the other material would be in the right frame.

If you really wanted to go to the furthest extreme, you could have a page with a grand total of four frames. Figure 6.3 shows you an example where the navigation bar on the left takes up the complete left side of the screen. If you were to take Figure 6.1

and redesign it using this setup, the top frame would consist of what's currently in the top two frames; the bottom frame would consist of what's currently in the bottom four frames; the left frame would hold the orange navigational links; and everything else would go in the middle-right frame.

There's another way to arrange the four frames. Instead of having the navigational frame take up the complete left side of the screen, you could place it directly under the top and bottom frames, as shown in Figure 6.4.

Any way you slice it, you're getting rid of at least nine frames—possibly eleven. I'd say that's an improvement.

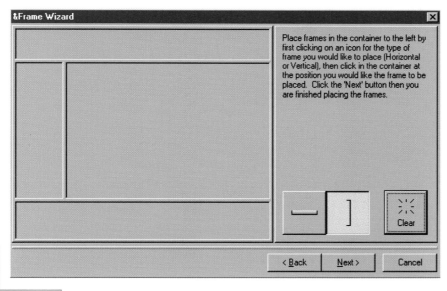

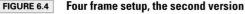

FIGURE 6.4   **Four frame setup, the second version**

Use Tables instead of Frames

In addition to reducing the number of frames, you can use tables to handle the problem of too many frames. Figure 6.5 shows one of Michael's more humorous creations—a cellular phone company called Weasel Cellular Communications. The page shown here is the "Meet the Weasels" page. Weasel has created a little portrait gallery of all the Weasels, and because pictures are framed, they used frames for their portraits. Logical thinking, but still wrong.

FRAME TOOLS

There are HTML editors that can quickly generate frame-based pages, and there are also frame-generating programs that are a godsend to those of us who don't create frames enough to remember the technique.

Many HTML editors, such as HomeSite 3, HotDog Pro, and WYSIWYG editors like Macromedia Dreamweaver, Microsoft Front-Page, and NetObjects Fusion, come with frame-building wizards built in. There are also standalone programs. You can find a listing of frame-based programs at Dave Central at http://www.davecentral .com/htmlframe.html.

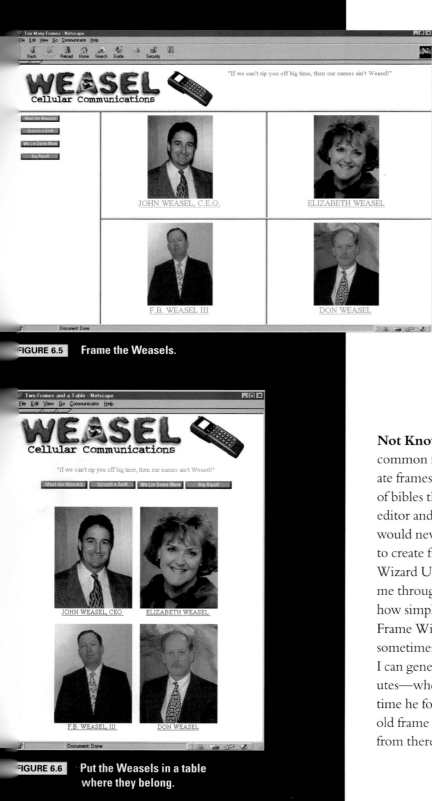

FIGURE 6.5 **Frame the Weasels.**

FIGURE 6.6 **Put the Weasels in a table where they belong.**

The logical solution to eliminating most of the frames is to put the pictures into a table so you can reduce the number of frames from six down to two, as shown in Figure 6.6. This setup is much more logical—the logo, slogan, and button are in a frame that never changes. If you click any of the buttons, the page is loaded into the bottom frame leaving the top frame stationary.

Common Frame Problems

We're going to talk about the four most common problems with frames:

1. Not knowing how to create frames
2. Not using a high-resolution graphics card
3. Vertical scrolling
4. Horizontal scrolling

Not Knowing How to Create Frames The most common frame problem is not knowing how to create frames in the first place. I swear to you on a stack of bibles that if I had to sit down with an ASCII text editor and create a frame-based page all by myself, it would never get created. I can never remember how to create frames so I rely on WebEdit Pro's Frame Wizard Utility (`http://www.luckman.com`) to walk me through the steps. Figures 6.2 through 6.4 show how simple it is to create frames using WebEdit's Frame Wizard. When Michael creates frames, he sometimes calls me on the phone because he knows I can generate a frame outline in less than two minutes—when I'm using WebEdit Pro. The rest of the time he follows one of Vincent's best tips: copy your old frame document into a new document and go from there.

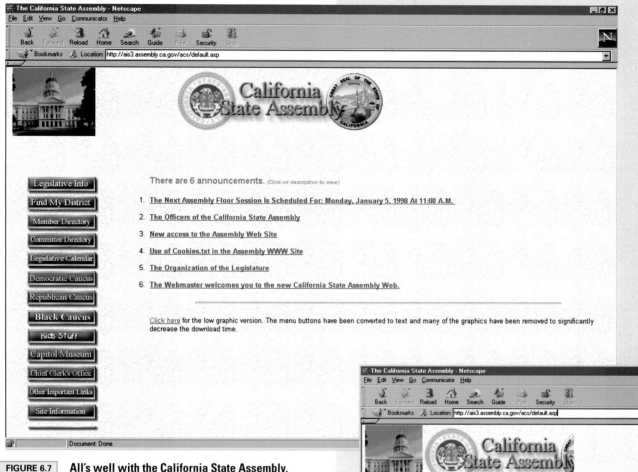

FIGURE 6.7 **All's well with the California State Assembly.**
(http://ais3.assembly.ca.gov/acs/default.asp)

If you want to learn how to create frames without
using frame generators or frame wizards, Joe Barta has
an excellent tutorial called Frames Tutor (http://
junior.apk.net/~jbarta/tutor/frames/).

Not Using a High-Resolution Graphics Card

Figure 6.7 shows the California State Assembly home
page as viewed on a monitor with a graphics card that
supports a resolution of 1150×864 pixels, and Figure 6.8 shows what this same page looks like on a
monitor with a graphics card that supports a resolution
of 640×480 pixels.

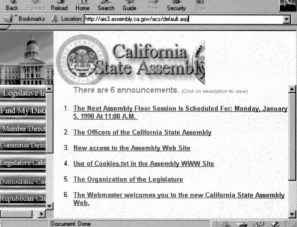

FIGURE 6.8 **All's not well with the California State
Assembly when you're viewing their site
with a low-resolution monitor.**

As you can see, all's well with the world when you own a high-resolution graphics card. The only problem is not all of the world is lucky enough to have this kind of resolution. While it also looks fine at 800x600 pixels, as you learned in Chapter 4, most people have a graphics card that only supports 640x480 pixels. Figure 6.8 gives an approximation of what this page looks like in their world.

The California State Assembly logo is cut off, but even worse, so are all the buttons in the left-hand navigation frame.

What causes this problem? One line of code. (Note: this isn't the exact line of code, but it represents the problem.)

```
<frameset cols="20%,*">
```

Okay, what's wrong? First of all, what the code is saying is let the first column take 20 percent of the screen and the second column take whatever remains (that's what the asterisk means). Everything is fine when you're viewing the page with a high-resolution graphics card because 20 percent of the screen space is larger than the widest image in the left column. Unfortunately, that isn't true when you view the page with a graphics card that has a resolution of 640x480.

For example, if the first column gets 20 percent of the screen space and if there's an image in the left frame that's bigger than 128 pixels, it will be cut off on screens with a screen width of 640 pixels (see Table 6.1).

Total Width of Screen	Number of Pixels Allocated to Left Frame*
640	128
800	180
1280	256

*Please note the number is actually less because the browser takes up a certain amount of screen space.

TABLE 6.1 **Number of Pixels Allocated If the First Column Gets 20 Percent of Screen Space**

What's the solution? Instead of using percentages, use *absolute pixel width*. For example:

```
<frameset cols="140,*">
```

which makes the first column 140-pixels wide. Then give the second column the rest of the space. Table 6.2 is based on the left column being a 140-pixels wide.

Total Width of Screen	Number of Pixels Allocated to Left Frame
640	140
800	140
1280	140

TABLE 6.2 **Number of Pixels Allocated If the Left Column Is 140-Pixels Wide**

Vertical Scrolling Let's face it. Scroll bars on frames are *really* ugly and take up precious screen real estate, as you can see in Figure 6.9.

Designers try to avoid them by using the `scrolling="no"` frame parameter. Figure 6.10 shows you how the first lesson page at WebPagesThatSuck.com looks with the frame parameter `scrolling=` set to "no".

Looks great, except for one problem—*you can't access most of the links in the left-hand navigation frame*. The navigation bar continues past the screen—unless you have a monitor that supports a height of 3,553 pixels. Not too many of those floating around.

Obviously, it doesn't do you any good if your visitors can't navigate your site. The solution is to use `scrolling="auto"` in the frame tag. This lets the frame present a scroll bar if it's necessary; otherwise, it won't. Figure 6.11 shows how `scrolling="auto"` works.

It's okay to set `scrolling="no"` on frames you know will fit in everyone's screen. Generally, you'll see scrolling turned off for short menus that should fit in everyone's browser. Of course, there's always the chance it won't fit, so it's up to you to decide.

Horizontal Scrolling Actually, this issue reared its ugly little head in Figure 6.8, the California State Assembly home page. One of the problems that occurs when you don't specify the absolute width of a frame is that your visitor will have to scroll horizontally if the images are wider than the frame. People just *hate* that because they have to scroll back and forth to read each line, not just scroll down after they're done reading an entire screen. The reason I'm so aware of this problem is because it occurred on an early version of WebPagesThatSuck.com. Believe me, people let me know what they thought about this issue. Figure 6.12 shows another example of the same problem, this time at LiveConcerts.com.

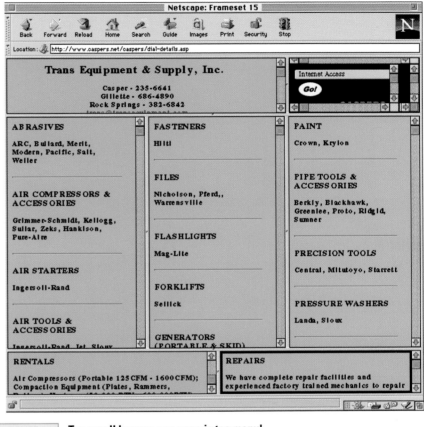

FIGURE 6.9 **Ten scroll bars on one page is too many!**
(`http://www.caspers.net/caspers/dial-details.asp`)

The two outer frames don't scroll, but the middle frame scrolls both vertically and horizontally—this sucks because you have to scroll down a screen and then scroll over to read what's there for each and every line. I know this sounds lazy to those who haven't experienced it, but this is a frequent complaint in my e-mail. It spoils an otherwise very nice looking page.

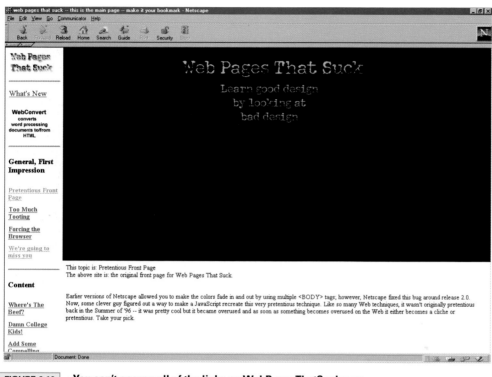

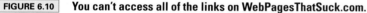

FIGURE 6.10   **You can't access all of the links on WebPagesThatSuck.com.**

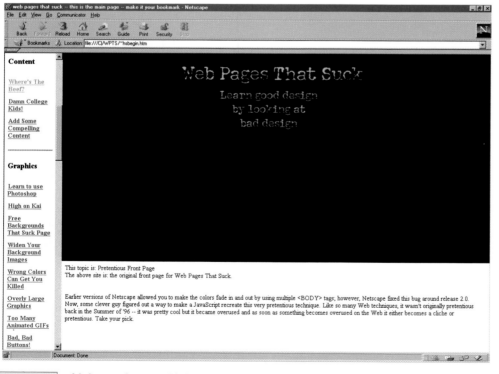

FIGURE 6.11   **It's longer than you think—WebPagesThatSuck.com.**

Click One Frame, Load Two Frames

While we're not going to get into the nitty-gritty of how to write frames, we're going to have to wade a little ways into the water. There's nothing more boring than a step-by-step book; however, there's an important topic we need to talk about: clicking one frame and loading two new frames.

WebPagesThat Suck.com is based on this premise. In early incarnations, every time you clicked on a topic in the left-hand frame, not only would the example and commentary frame load new material, but the navigational bar would also reload—all three frames would reload. This annoyed visitors because every time it happened, they would end up at the top of the navigation frame—even if they had clicked a link at the bottom of the frame. To get to the next topic, they would have to scroll back down the navigational bar. I received a lot of complaints; however, an anonymous gentleman wrote me about how to solve the problem.

I've seen solutions that use JavaScript, but there's no reason to use JavaScript when you can just use frames. This is going to be ugly to demonstrate, but it's going to be worthwhile to learn.

Figure 6.13 shows the most common layout for WebPagesThatSuck.com. We'll use this as a reference point.

The first lesson is loaded by BEGIN .HTM. The frame code for this document is as follows:

```
<FRAMESET COLS="140,*"
frameborder="no"
framespacing="0"
border="0">
  <FRAME
SRC="NAVBAR.HTM"
NAME="left"
scrolling="auto">
  <FRAME
SRC="TOPIC1.HTM"
NAME="right"
scrolling="auto">
</FRAMESET>
```

The HTML in red tells us the important details: A document called NAVBAR.HTM loads in the left frame, and a document called TOPIC1.HTM loads in the frame on the right. For the browser to know which frame is which, you have to assign a NAME value to the frame. I always like to assign logical names, so the frame on the left is assigned NAME="left" and the frame on the right is assigned NAME="right".

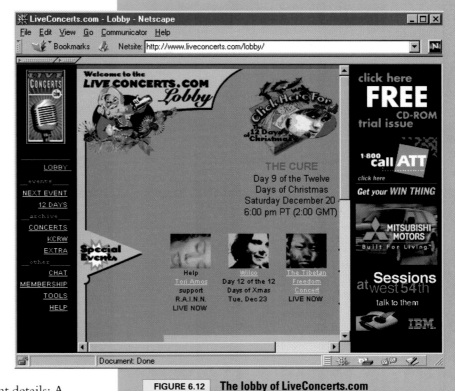

FIGURE 6.12   **The lobby of LiveConcerts.com**
(`http://www.liveconcerts.com/lobby/`)

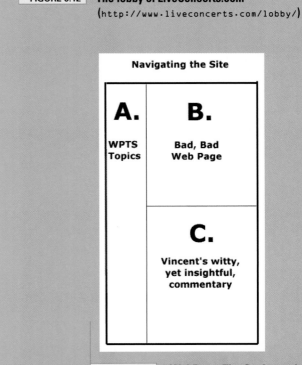

FIGURE 6.13   **WebPagesThatSuck.com layout**

The result is demonstrated in Figure 6.14.

As TOPIC1.HTM loads in the right-hand frame, the following code inside the document is loaded:

```
<FRAMESET ROWS="70%,30%" framebor
der="no" framespacing="0"
border="0">
        <FRAME SRC="PRETENT.HTM"
NAME="topright" scrolling="auto">
        <FRAME SRC="PRETENT2.HTM"
NAME="bottomright" scrolling="auto">
    </FRAMESET>
```

What TOPIC1.HTM is doing is dividing the right frame into two new sections called `"topright"` and `"bottomright"` and loading a document into each of them. The document PRETENT.HTM is loaded into the top-right frame, and the document PRETENT2.HTM is loaded into the bottom-right frame. Figure 6.15 shows the result.

Every time a visitor clicks a topic in the left-hand frame, the steps are repeated.

So I can remember how to arrange my documents, I always use TOPIC*xx* for the new topic I'm covering. For example, the "High on Kai" topic is called TOPIC10.HTM, and it loads KAI3.HTM into the top-right frame and KAI2.HTM into the bottom-right frame.

The navigational bar document, NAVBAR.HTM, never changes. The best way to understand how this works is to play with the document on the CD-ROM to get the feel of how it all works. With a little practice, you can make your own documents where one click loads two new frames.

Frames and Links

If you include links to external sites in your framed pages, then you need to use the `target=_blank` parameter.

```
http://www.webpagesthatsuck.com
target="_blank"
```

Using this parameter opens up a new window for the site. If you don't use this parameter, the new site will load in your current frame, potentially causing some really stupid looking pages.

Before moving on to links, let's take a look at a frame example from Canada.

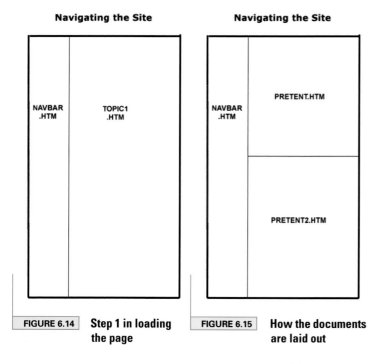

Navigating the Site   **Navigating the Site**

NAVBAR .HTM — TOPIC1 .HTM

NAVBAR .HTM — PRETENT.HTM / PRETENT2.HTM

FIGURE 6.14 **Step 1 in loading the page**

FIGURE 6.15 **How the documents are laid out**

INTERNATIONAL

HOW DO YOU SAY "SUCK" IN CANADA?

Okay, I'll admit when Vincent told me to visit this site—mind you, I speak zero French—I thought it was some kind of dating service. Don't ask me why I thought this. It's not. So having revealed that, let me just say: "This site sucks!"

Frames are the culprit. Seven frames to be exact. And while this is no big deal if you have a 21-inch monitor like we do, it's a real bummer for the average Joe with a 13-inch monitor, as shown in the image below.

Now figure that all those links will load into the little area in the middle and you get an idea of how bad this sucks. Imagine surfing sites and viewing them through a 5"x3" window. Yuck.

I won't get into the ugly graphics and the globe and the stupid animated envelope and the blink tag and the…oh, never mind. Look closely at the little form in the first image shown above. It says *Non-sensible,* which, I'm guessing here, is French for *nonsense,* which is *apropos*—French for *appropriate.*

Another bad thing about frames is that the title never changes. Some search engines use the title in their algorithms. Plus if you bookmark a page with frames, the page you want to view in a particular frame may not appear when you return.

Dude! This is a great sucky site!

Here's what the site looks like on a typical 13–14-inch monitor.

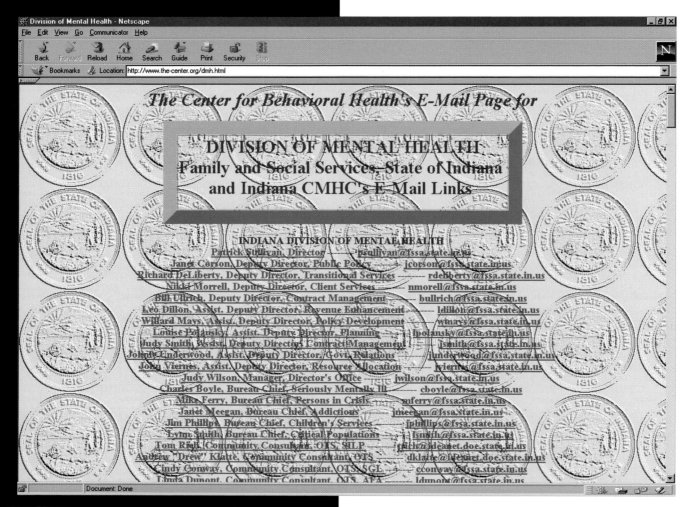

FIGURE 6.16 **The Center for Behavioral Health's E-Mail Page**
(http://www.the-center.org/dmh.html)

THESE LINKS SUCK

Putting links on a Web page should be a straight–forward, logical process. Well, tell that to the folks who designed Figure 6.16. Since we're dealing with a government agency—and we all know government agencies don't speak plain, simple English—we can't say, "This page sucks." We have to say, "This page is aesthetically impaired."

Click Here

Could you possibly use a less descriptive phrase than "click here"? The person viewing the link in Figure 6.17 has no idea where they're going. Assigning text to a link is just the opposite of performing a magic trick. In a magic trick, while the audience is watching you move your right hand and perform the trick with your left hand. On a Web page, you tell people what is going to happen: "When you click this link, you will be taken to WebPagesThatSuck.com."

Figure 6.17 shows a page whose links must be magical.

This figure points out an important fact. When you first look at the page, your eyes are immediately drawn to the blue, underscored link text. Where will you go when you click one of those links?

here

here

this link

good folks

downloading

Boy, is that helpful or what? Basically, the link text tells you nothing. In order to even partially understand where the links lead, you'll have to read the complete text.

By just reading the link, a person should be able to figure out where they will go when they click it.

To make the links more understandable, the page has to be revised and the important words need to be turned into the link text. Figure 6.18 shows the rewritten page.

Why Does
This Page Suck?

I hate to pick on a government agency, but...

I hate to pick on a government agency, but doesn't the page shown in Figure 6.16 look like a bureaucratic page—all cluttered with information in a format you can't really use. I get the feeling everyone is listed by pecking order and no one is left out for fear of offending them.

I've only included the first screen of this page. You might be reading this section at the bookstore, and if you saw the whole page, you'd throw up and then the bookstore would ban you forever from their premises. Not only have I kept you in the good graces of the bookstore, but also I've saved you from great public embarrassment.

Because this section is about links, I'll limit myself to just this topic. Here's what's wrong with the links:

1. The background makes it difficult to read the links.

2. Centering the links makes them difficult to read.

3. The names are not listed alphabetically, making it difficult to find the person you're looking for.

4. There are approximately 41 e-mail links. Lucky for us there aren't 100.

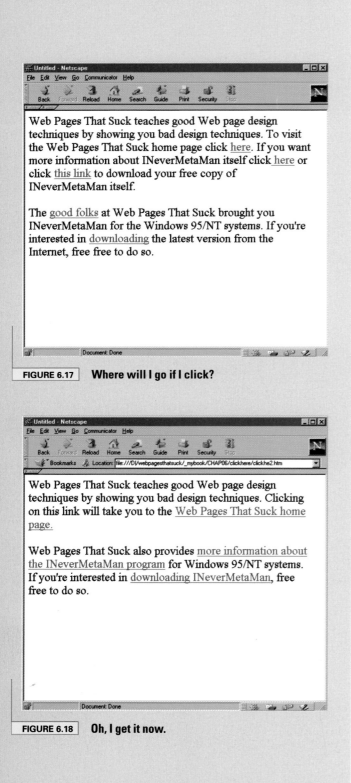

FIGURE 6.17   **Where will I go if I click?**

FIGURE 6.18   **Oh, I get it now.**

This link text tells you that when you click it you will go to:

> Web Pages That Suck home page
>
> more information about the INeverMetaMan program
>
> downloading INeverMetaMan

Gee, that's a lot clearer, isn't it?

Don't Use Form Buttons as Links

Just when you thought links couldn't be made more vague and mysterious, someone decided to use form buttons as links. Figure 6.19 takes us back to the Center for Behavioral Health's E-Mail Page. (I'm sorry, I know I promised I wouldn't show you more of the page.)

First of all, the page is butt ugly. If that weren't grounds enough for dismissal, I should point out that it's difficult to read the buttons, there are too many of them, and if you move your mouse over the button, there's no message in the status bar describing where the button will take you. Of course, those of you who are evil-hearted can have a great deal of fun creating buttons that will take your visitors to places they wouldn't expect to go. For example, you could have a button that said "For Rush Limbaugh Fans," but when they clicked the button, it took them to an anti–Rush Limbaugh page. (Just a thought from your Uncle Vincent.)

Well, so much for the boring edge of Web page design. Let's take a look at the bleeding edge. Everything is a trade-off and so it is with the bleeding edge. On the one hand, it's future technology that could help make your Web site successful. On the other hand, it could waste your time, energy, and money—all of which could be spent making your site better. Let's take a look at some bleeding-edge technologies and see which ones are really useful.

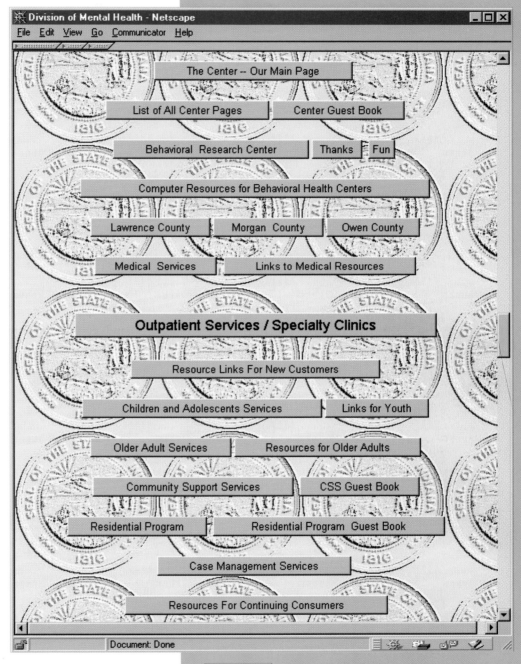

FIGURE 6.19 **Button up—the Center for Behavioral Health's E-Mail Page**
(http://www.the-center.org/dmh.html)

Flanders & Willis's Reality Check

The only sound file anyone on the Internet is interested in hearing is O.J. Simpson confessing. They certainly don't want some random person welcoming them to a home page. Don't use sound files unless they're confessional in nature. If you *do* decide to use sound files, please inform your visitors how large they are by listing the size of the file next to the sound icon.

CHAPTER 7

It's Not Called the Bleeding Edge for Nothing

IN THIS CHAPTER

we're going to look at what passes for the bleeding edge as of today—as you know, today's bleeding edge is tomorrow's fait accompli. That's one of the Internet's most amazing features. Every week there's something new and exciting to add to our Web sites, and like kids with a pocketful of change in a candy store, we want to put everything we can on our pages. Michael and I have spent some time looking at the bleeding edge.

Much to our surprise, some bleeding-edge technologies benefit everyone, and other technologies that we initially dismissed as being stupid actually have some use—generally for larger corporations. We'll start off the chapter by discussing the technologies that will affect everyone (plug-ins and WYSIWYG editors) and then move on to the more advanced technologies (Dynamic HTML and Cascading Style Sheets). We'll also look at some "older" technologies, such as good old sound files, and discuss the pros and cons of using them on intranets versus the World Wide Web.

PLUG-INS

Plug-ins are programs that add functions to your browser that the browser-makers didn't think were important enough to include themselves.

Many plug-ins are specialized for *vertical niche markets* that aren't of concern to the average surfer (for example, chemical information management, SGML documents, stock market applications, and computer-based training). With few exceptions, if a plug-in isn't included with the major browsers, it faces a hard time gaining acceptance. If it doesn't gain acceptance, it generally dies.

If you're looking for the definitive listing of browser plug-ins, go to the

BrowserWatch Plug-in Plaza at `http://browserwatch.internet.com/plug-in.html` for a complete listing of plug-ins available on the Web.

Let's take a close look at one of the more promising plug-ins: Macromedia's Flash.

Macromedia's Flash Plug-in

One of the most widely used plug-ins is Shockwave Flash from Macromedia. Originally, Macromedia had a product called Shockwave that brought multimedia to the Web. The problem with the Shockwave technology was simple: you had to download the whole file before any multimedia was activated. When it first became available, I looked at Shockwave and thought, "Cute," and then when it started crashing my system, I deleted it from my computer. I don't have a lot of patience with new programs. They either work or they get deleted.

Since I erased it from my system, I haven't kept up with every little nuance of the program's history. I know there were different Shockwave plug-ins that worked with different Macromedia products—a version for Macromedia Director, Macromedia Authorware, and Macromedia Freehand. Then, the plug-ins were sort of combined and a streaming version was introduced. It was very confusing.

To make matters worse, a company called FutureWave Software created a Shockwave-type product called FutureSplash Animator, which basically kicked Shockwave's butt because FutureSplash animated pages with files a fraction of the size of Shockwave. Not being dummies, Macromedia bought the product and renamed it Macromedia Flash. "Classic" Shockwave still exists; however, Macromedia is pushing Flash. This program creates vector-based graphics instead of those draw-them-one-pixel-at-a-time graphics, so the results are displayed much faster.

The bad news is everyone who wishes to view a page using Flash has to install the Flash plug-in for their particular browser. Of course, if you've ever been to the Microsoft Network page (`http://www.msn.com/`), you can't proceed any further in the site unless you download the Flash plug-in, so Flash is included in many browsers.

Like every tool, it can be used for good or for evil. Let's first look at a very sucky use of the program, as shown in Figure 7.1.

The Flesh Eaters

Unfortunately, the one technology that hasn't kept pace with the torrid pace of new Web technology is bandwidth. Yes, more and more bandwidth is becoming available, but it can barely keep up with normal demand for Internet services much less the new cutting-edge technologies—technologies that eat bandwidth like a piranha eats flesh.

Speaking of flesh eaters, many of these new technologies also eat up large amounts of time and/or money. Because these technologies are so new and the pressure to get them out the door is so great, software companies don't have time to thoroughly test them in-house. As one software developer told me, "In-house testing? Hell, we send it out as finished and let our customers test it out for us." That's the price you pay for being on the bleeding edge—it's your blood that ends up on the floor.

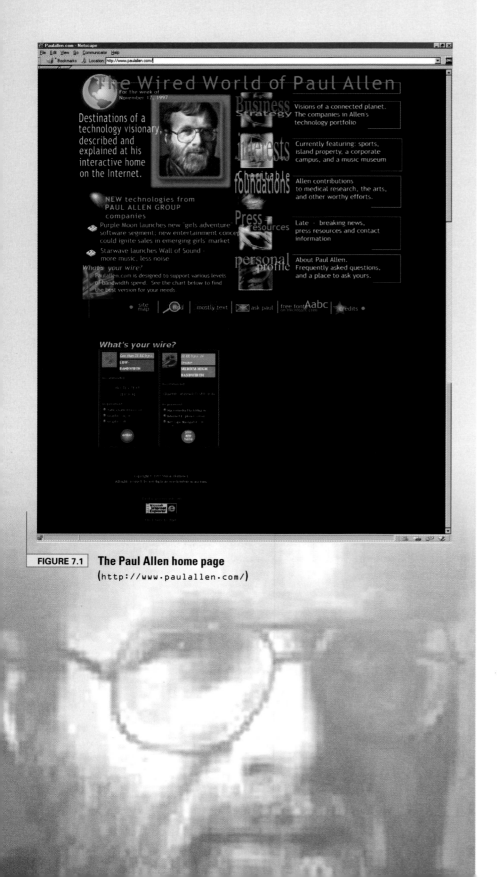

FIGURE 7.1 **The Paul Allen home page**
(http://www.paulallen.com/)

If I'm not mistaken, I haven't discussed anyone's personal page until this particular moment. The reason is simple: personal pages are a form of self-expression that's meaningful only to the author, the author's family, and some of the author's more tolerant friends, but to no one else. As I said back in Chapter 1, a personal page is all about ego and that's fine.

Mr. Allen's page is an exception because he's the cofounder of Microsoft and ought to know better. We all are aware of Bill Gates's relationship to Microsoft, but many of us forget or don't realize he didn't create the Microsoft megapower all by himself. He had some very talented help, and only because of Mr. Allen's illness and subsequent withdrawal from company activity, do we tend to forget the fact that he was a cofounder of Microsoft.

As mentioned in Chapter 2, good Web sites periodically revise their appearance. Also, today's URL is tomorrow's "File Not Found." Many of the sites mentioned and profiled in this book may have changed—hopefully for the better.

However, it isn't fair to dismiss a technology just because someone can't use it correctly. Figure 7.2 shows a site where the designer understands how to use Flash in an effective manner.

If you're artistically inclined, already know Photoshop, and want to get involved in a technology where there appears to be a future, I recommend learning Macromedia Flash.

WYSIWYG EDITORS

If there's one bleeding-edge technology that's going to be successful—and that needs to be successful—it's WYSIWYG (What You See Is What You Get) editors. In early incarnations of WebPagesThatSuck.com, I had a lot of negative things to say about WYSIWYG editors: They were convoluted, the HTML code was noneditable (still true for some programs), the HTML code was nonstandard (still true for some programs), the output looked bad (less true today), and so on. I held on to these beliefs through most of 1997, but the WYSIWYG editors have significantly improved from their Release 1.*x* days. There are more programs to choose from, and there's nothing like competition for improving the quality of software.

WYSIWYG editors let you create Web pages without having to mess with the complexities of the underlying HTML language, and they give you a representation of what your page looks like as you're creating it. There are some non-WYSIWYG HTML editors that have a see-it-as-you-type-it preview mode. As a Windows NT person, my experience with WebEdit Pro and HotDog Pro is that I can

Why Does This Page Suck?

Paul Allen's page demonstrates a bad use of good technology.

1. Mr. Allen's site is animated; however, Figure 7.1 only shows you how it looks when all the animation stops. Feel free to visit his site to see "the real thing." The animation was created using Macromedia Flash.

2. Some people have accused me of liking only boring conservative design and being against all the new technology. Not true. I like *effective* design; however, the site in Figure 7.1 is not effective—it's *effete* (as in *self-indulgent*—not *effeminate*). I also don't dislike new technology; I dislike new technology done poorly.

3. In the old days, the massively rich built ostentatious homes in which to live. Today, the massively rich build ostentatious home pages. Voodoo Chile Paul Allen, who owns whatever Bill Gates doesn't own, has used Macromedia's Flash to build a page that is as garish as anything I've seen. (As an aside, Bill Gates's page is very tasteful (`http://www.microsoft.com/BillGates/default.htm`).)

Paul Allen's page demonstrates a bad use of good technology. In his defense, he doesn't use those silly plopping noises on his images when you move your mouse over them as Macromedia does on their home page (`http://www.macromedia.com/`). While Mr. Allen offers a lower- and low-bandwidth versions of his site, you won't be able to see the links because the Paul Allen page demands that you have the plug-in installed and if you don't (and don't want to download it), you won't see the text at the bottom of the page. In effect, Mr. Allen is saying, "It's my way or the info highway."

TOO COOL

WHY THIS PAGE DOESN'T SUCK

This is the high-bandwidth home page of Amy Grant, former gospel singer turned pop songstress.

Whoever designed her page understands how to use the Macromedia Flash program. It's very tasteful and effective, and it's not overbearing. High-tech glitz with an aesthetic sensibility. Yes, it's 80K, but unlike most sites, it's worth waiting for. Kudos to the designer. When the cursor is moved over a microphone button, the Behind the Scenes bullet is displayed—another great effect that doesn't require JavaScript.

It's worth noting that the "regular" Amy Grant home page (`http://www.myrrh .com/amygrant/`) loads just fine and doesn't use Macromedia Flash. You have the choice of loading the high-bandwidth page or the low-bandwidth page—that's the way it should be done.

code and see my results, but these programs are not as powerful as the WYSIWYG editors on the market. (They do, however, offer you a great deal of control and have useful features—especially HotDog Pro—such as tables, frames, and Dynamic HTML wizards.)

There are any number of WYSIWYG editors on the market. The programs listed here are today's perceived leaders in the WYSIWYG world. While this list of WYSIWYG editors is by no means exhaustive, it's a good starting point. For a complete list of WYSIWYG editors, you'd normally go to Yahoo! but, as of the date this book is being written, they don't offer a listing for the topic. Dave Central offers a section on WYSIWYG editors at `http://www.davecentral.com/htmlwys.html`.

FIGURE 7.2 **Amy Grant's high-bandwidth page**
(`http://www.myrrh.com/amygrant/HIGH/Index.HTML`)

Macromedia Dreamweaver

(`http://www.macromedia.com/software/dreamweaver/index.html`)
For both Windows and Mac platforms. This program's main claims to
fame are its ability to create pages using Dynamic HTML (discussed
later) for both Netscape Navigator and Internet Explorer, its support
for Cascading Style Sheets, and its compatibility with your current
Web pages. Normally, when you edit a document with any WYSIWYG
editor, it radically changes your code.

Microsoft FrontPage 98

(`http://www.microsoft.com/frontpage/`) Basically, this is
Microsoft's idea of a NetObjects Fusion killer. It's loaded with features
(site management and link checking come to mind), but as of mid-
December 1997, it only runs on Windows 95 and NT 4.

NetObjects Fusion

(`http://www.netobjects.com/`) For both Windows and Mac platforms. Its main claim to fame is it allows you to precisely place objects
in an HTML document. The code it generates can really only be
edited by itself, which was great for Web designers when the program
cost $695—their clients were locked into their services. Now that
FrontPage is cutting into Fusion's territory, a price decrease puts
Fusion within the budget of most people. It's one of the first major
tools for building and managing complete sites.

PageMill

(`http://www.adobe.com/prodindex/pagemill/main.html`) For both
Windows and Mac platforms. It's one of the first of the WYSIWYG
editors and pretty amazing for its time.

For most sites over 100 pages (and whose content changes on a regular basis),
Web page design has become too complicated to use regular HTML editors.
Even if you're just designing a site for a Mom and Pop operation, you need to
be able to crank those sites out quickly if you want to survive financially as a
designer. Any tool that can help you generate a site quickly is becoming a
necessity.

Even more important than cranking out regular HTML pages, however, is
the need to crank out pages using Cascading Style Sheets and Dynamic
HTML or, as it's more frequently known, *DHTML*. Since I've brought up
the topic, let's start our discussion.

OH NO

**WHAT REALLY SUCKS
ABOUT FLASH**

While Flash is very cool and
worth learning, I recently noticed
one of its annoying tendencies.
I was visiting c|net and noticed
a banner button that promoted
working for Microsoft. I clicked
the banner and was sent to a
page (`http://www.cnet.com/
Sponsored/PST/`—probably
gone by now) where I was given
the choice of taking a Shockwave or non-Shockwave tour.
Naturally, I went to the Shockwave Flash version.

It was nicely done—even though
I spent some time waiting for the
animation. I then clicked one of
the menu selections and went
to the next page. When I realized
I wasn't interested in this topic, I
hit the Back button instead of
using the navigation buttons. The
whole original Flash animation
started replaying from the beginning. Now this isn't Microsoft's
fault—they did include a navigation bar that I should have clicked,
but it brought up the point that
there's no "finality" to a Shockwave Flash page. That annoys
me. What annoyed me even
more was it crashed Netscape
when I pressed the Back button
to go to the original home page.

WHAT EDITOR(S) DO YOU GUYS USE?

We're using Lee Ann Pickrell and Suzanne Rotondo from Sybex as our editors...wait, you mean HTML editors, not book editors? Oh, that's different.

Michael For reasons even I don't fully understand, I use World Wide Web Weaver 1.1.1—though I have to say that I bought their upgrade and it had more bugs than a RAID commercial. I also use BBEdit 4.5, and Dreamweaver shows great promise.

Vincent I started off with HTML Assistant Pro, moved to WebEdit Pro, and am currently using HomeSite 3 and, to a lesser extent, HotDog Pro. I've messed around with all the WYSIWYG editors mentioned above but am going to put my reconstructed nose to the grindstone and really learn Dreamweaver, which uses HomeSite 3 as an HTML editor, and FrontPage 98.

HTML 4, DYNAMIC HTML, AND CASCADING STYLE SHEETS (CSS) LEVEL 1

Those Web designers who are artistically inclined hate HTML because it's a noninteractive, non-layout-oriented medium. You type in the HTML, the page gets presented by the browser, and the HTML page just sits there sort of dumb and stupid. In "Classic" HTML (HTML 3.2 and earlier), structure was more important than layout. Layout is everything to an artist, and HTML's "start from the top-left corner of the screen and work your way down to the bottom right" approach rubbed their fur the wrong way. To circumvent the lack of native HTML layout tools, designers used tables to set up grids that mimicked the layout they could achieve with PageMaker and other desktop-publishing tools.

Because HTML is a limited language, it is simple to learn, so established graphic art concerns also didn't like the fact that two guys or girls in a garage could put together Web sites and take their Web business away. In the HTML 3.2 days, *anybody* could write HTML pages and put together Web sites that rivaled a Fortune 500 firm's Web site. That was the beauty of the Web—two guys or girls in a garage (or in the case of CDNOW (`http://www.cdnow.com/`), two guys in their parents' basement)—could set up a business that looked as professional as a big conglomerate's.

Now big business and the traditional graphics art community didn't conspire to put the little Web designers and upstart competitors out of business. No, big business decided it needed Web sites that were bigger, better, and more complex than what currently existed—sites with more interactivity, more bells, bigger databases, more electronic commerce, and bigger budgets. The large graphic arts and Web design firms wanted to create those sites. It was a match made in heaven.

The hidden agenda behind the new HTML developments and much of the bleeding-edge technology that's being introduced is to separate the design pros from the amateurs and raise the bar so a Web visitor actually *can* tell the difference between a site for MCA Records and one for Fly-by-Night Records.

Let's take a look at some of the tools being used to put you out of business: HTML 4, Dynamic HTML, and Cascading Style Sheets.

HTML 4

According to the World Wide Web Consortium (better known by the acronym *W3C*), HTML 4 deals, with the following issues:

    Internationalization

    Accessibility

    Tables

    Compound documents

    Style sheets

    Scripting

    Printing

To quote from their document:

"HTML 4 extends HTML with mechanisms for style sheets, scripting, frames, embedding objects, improved support for right to left and mixed direction text, richer tables, and enhancements to forms, offering improved accessibility for people with disabilities."

As it turns out, Dynamic HTML (DHTML) and Cascading Style Sheets (CSS) are really subsets of the HTML 4 specification. Technically, we should all just refer to HTML 4 instead of referring to DHTML and CSS separately, but due to the complexity of those topics, they're always examined separately from HTML 4.

As this book isn't a "how-to-use-HTML manifesto," we'll let those of you interested in learning more of HTML go to `http://www.w3.org/TR/PR-html40/intro/intro.html`.

Dynamic HTML

W3C is in charge of defining the standards for Dynamic HTML (DHTML), and they define it as follows:

"'Dynamic HTML' is a term used by some vendors to describe the combination of HTML, style sheets and scripts that allows documents to be animated."

The goal of DHTML is to create "a platform-and language-neutral interface that will allow programs and scripts to dynamically access and update the content, structure and style of documents." The results are then incorporated and displayed in the page. For more information, go to `http://www.w3.org/pub/WWW/MarkUp/DOM`.

The "some vendors" that W3C refers to are, of course, Microsoft and Netscape. In trying to outdo one another, they created their own versions of DHTML. Netscape gets to claim it's the parent of DHTML because it started the whole mess when it introduced the `<LAYER>` tag. However, Microsoft picked up the kid to make changes and took the lead. The W3C considers the Microsoft and Netscape extensions to be a *Document Object Model,* or *DOM,* which will define how style sheets, JavaScript, and HTML work together to provide interactivity for objects on a Web page. Basically, DOM is a document database that handles every element in the page and how it is used and displayed. Confusing isn't it? The truth is DHTML is a marketing term.

Because DHTML is really a marketing term and because it hasn't been approved by W3C, Microsoft and Netscape are currently mucking up DHTML by

OH NO

DON'T YOU JUST HATE INTERNET MARKETING WEASELS?

When I was recently in the bookstore, I noticed two books that, to the best of my recollection, were titled DHTML for Internet Explorer 4 *and* DHTML for Netscape 4.

That's right—two different DHTML books to choose from because Microsoft and Netscape can't agree to wait for the standards to be established. Obviously, no one in their right mind is going to design two different sites (although Macromedia has a product that does just that), so everybody has to wait for DHTML to be standardized.

proposing different standards. For example, in the area of scripting languages, Microsoft supports VBScript (based on their proprietary Visual Basic language) and JavaScript. Netscape supports JavaScript. However, Microsoft's and Netscape's versions of JavaScript are not totally compatible with each other. (I think they had agreed to agree in some future version.) Doesn't this just suck like a bilge pump?

Figure 7.3 shows Michael's first attempt at writing a page using DHTML. You can also view the latest and greatest version at `http://www.webpagesthatsuck.com/dream/DREAM.HTM`. You should note that the sound files are 200K in size—a little too large for a normal page, but Michael wanted to throw in the kitchen sink and play it too.

Move the mouse over the title logo to hear a screaming sound.

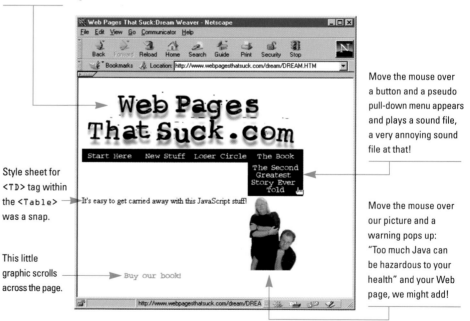

Move the mouse over a button and a pseudo pull-down menu appears and plays a sound file, a very annoying sound file at that!

Style sheet for `<TD>` tag within the `<Table>` was a snap.

This little graphic scrolls across the page.

Move the mouse over our picture and a warning pops up: "Too much Java can be hazardous to your health" and your Web page, we might add!

FIGURE 7.3   **Michael used DHTML to create this version of the WebPagesThatSuck.com home page.**

TOO COOL

MACROMEDIA'S DREAMWEAVER

Vincent turned me on to Dreamweaver—a really cool program for creating Web pages using bleeding-edge technologies. I downloaded their demo software and spent about a day futzing around with it.

Their online documentation is fairly clear—except for the fact that they use terms such as *Behavior inspector*, *Events pane*, and *Events list* without any kind of reference diagram, so it takes awhile to figure out what they're talking about in the instructions. Once I became familiar with the terms, creating mouse-over effects, style sheets, and simple animations was a breeze. (A mouseover effect is when you move your mouse over an image, another image is displayed providing an animation effect. It is most commonly used for menu items.) In fact, it was so easy that it wouldn't be too hard to get carried away with all this JavaScript mania.

The Dreamweaver program is actually a full-featured HTML semi-hemi-demi-WYSIWYG editor that does an excellent job of handling advanced HTML techniques, such as tables and frames, as well as Java/JavaScript applications and forms. It has easy-to-use buttons that create the correct tags to insert Shock-wave, Flash, and ActiveX files.

The style sheet part of this program is really cool! It allows you to call out fonts, sizes, weights, and so on, for your typography. I know what you're thinking. You can already do that using the `<FONT FACE=>` tag. Yeah, but say you're using a lot of tables and you've just finished inserting the `<FONT FACE=>` tag into each of the `<TD>` tags—and your fingers are permanently cramped from all that extra coding—but your art director/client decides that the typeface Arial would look a lot nicer than Scratchy Sans Serif in all of your table data cells. Not good. With Dreamweaver, you can globally edit that tag in two steps. This part of the program is worth the price of admission alone.

If you view the figure shown in Figure 7.3 on the CD or on the Web site, you'll hear the goofy sound files attached to the mouseover buttons. Caution: sound files are large! They take a long time to download. Which means? Anyone? Yes, you guessed it, they suck. They are fun though!

If your pocketbook can afford the $499 price tag, you're a Java/JavaScript junkie, and most importantly, you don't care that pre-4.*x* browsers don't support many of the commands in Dreamweaver, I say, "GO FOR IT!"

Cascading Style Sheets (CSS)

If there's only one bleeding-edge technology that becomes a major force on the Web, it's going to be Cascading Style Sheets (CSS).

Believe it or not, CSS goes back to the stone age of 1994, with the initial draft occurring in May 1995 and final approval being given in December 1996. CSS has now been subsumed under the HTML 4 banner. To quote from the W3C specification for HTML 4 (for a complete description, go to `http://www.w3.org/TR/PR-html40/present/styles.html`):

"Style sheets make it easy to specify the amount of white space between text lines, the amount lines are indented, the colors used for the text and the backgrounds, the font size and style, and a host of other details."

CSS lets you separate document structure from layout (appearance). HTML basically provides the structure for a document—heading and body tags and their associated tags (for example, `<BOLD>` and `<ITALIC>`)—and separates it from the appearance or form of the page. The browser is responsible for displaying the page on your screen, and, if you've ever used more than one browser in your career, you'll know that different browsers may display the page somewhat differently. In fact, Netscape's Navigator displays the page differently depending on whether you're on a Macintosh or a Windows machine.

This inconsistency drives graphic designers crazy because they want to make their Web pages look like print pages—especially magazine pages. If a designer wants a 25-point font—well, that's pretty tough to do using normal HTML. Even the `<FONT>` tag is of no help because it can't deal with point sizes. What's a designer to do?

That's where CSS comes in. If you've ever used PageMaker, Microsoft Word, or the 1986 version of Ventura Publisher, you'll remember the concept of *templates*. In a template, you define *styles* (in Ventura, they're called *tags*) that have certain attributes. For example, a style such as Heading might be 30-point Helvetica bold, indented 3 picas from the left margin. To apply the Heading style, you would type your text, highlight it, and click the Heading tag. Voilà, you're set.

CSS finally gives you template-like control over the appearance of your text on a Web page. Like all technology, CSS can be used correctly or incorrectly and it's *so* easy to use it incorrectly, as Figure 7.4 demonstrates.

The beauty of CSS is that it's incredibly bandwidth friendly. Instead of having to wait for a huge "Oh My God!" graphic to download from the server, all you

FIGURE 7.4 **Great technology run amok—Cascading Style Sheets**

have to wait for are a few lines of ASCII text. The browser does all the work of translating the HTML code and displaying the results on your monitor. Although it's not much to look at, the HTML document shown in Figure 7.4 is a grand total of *721 bytes*, meaning it will take no time at all to download.

There are three ways to create style sheets.

1. You can insert a style sheet inside a document. Only that particular document will be affected by the style sheet.

2. You can create a separate document (ending with the extension .css or something else of your choosing) that defines the elements in the style sheet and then insert a link to the style sheet in the `<HEAD>` tag of each of your documents. This method is the preferred one because it lets you create a "global style sheet" for all the documents in your Web site. Let's say you have 200 different pages in your site and you decide to change all the `<H1>` tags from 26-point Helvetica bold to 30-point Times Roman italic; by creating a global style sheet, you would need to make the change in only one document—sure beats going through each and every document.

3. The third method allows you to define styles for small sections of text.

While this isn't the place to go into a discussion of how to write code for Cascading Style Sheets, it's worth looking at a small snippet to catch the flavor of CSS. We'll use the first method and create a style sheet inside a document. Here's what the code would look like.

```html
<html>
<head>
<title>CSS</title>
<style type="text/css">
<!--
.yourstyle {
font-family: Fajita Picante;
font-weight: bold;
color: teal;
font-size: 90pt;
background-color: maroon;
text-align: center;
margin: 2pt;
border: 6pt;
border-style: groove;
border-color: purple;
}

.body {
font-family: Times Roman;
font-size: 30pt;
font-weight: medium;
line-height: 40pt;
color: blue}
}
-->
</style>
</head>
<body bgcolor="#cc9900">

<divclass="yourstyle">OH MY
GOD!</div><p>
<div class="body">Stylesheets --
The latest and greatest way to make
ugly pages.</div>

</body>
</html>
```

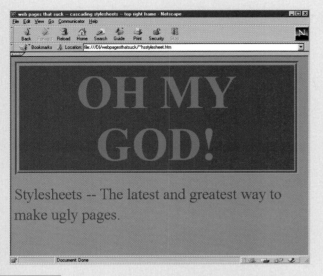

web pages that suck -- cascading stylesheets -- top right frame - Netscape
File Edit View Go Communicator Help
Back Forward Reload Home Search Guide Print Security Stop
Bookmarks Location: file:///D|/webpagesthatsuck/~hsstylesheet.htm

OH MY GOD!

Stylesheets -- The latest and greatest way to make ugly pages.

Document: Done

FIGURE 7.5 **What you see if you don't have the Fajita Picante font on your system**

The sections are color coded to make the discussion easier. The first item to discuss is `<style type="text/css">`. This is the start of the `<STYLE>` tag. It lets the browser know that starting from this point the elements of the style sheet will be defined until the `</STYLE>` tag is reached.

Two different styles are being defined: `.yourstyle` and `.body`. As you can see, the `.body` style, shown in blue, is straightforward: Times Roman 30-point medium weight with a line height of 40 points and a text color of blue. The `.yourstyle` style is Fajita Picante 90-point bold weight with a text color of blue and a background color of maroon. In addition, the text is centered with a 2-point margin, and a 6-point grooved purple border.

In order for the style to take effect, you have to tag the text you want to have that style. Because you can't create your own tags (well, not quite yet), you need to use the `<DIV>`, `<P>`, or `<SPAN>` tags on the text (the green text in the example).

In Figure 7.4, the phrase "Oh My God!" was created using a font called *Fajita Picante.* The screen was captured on a Windows NT system, and because Fajita Picante was on that system, it displayed correctly. However, if the person viewing your style sheet page doesn't have the font you chose, the system replaces the font with one of its own choosing, as shown in Figure 7.5.

As mentioned in Chapter 5, you can never predict what fonts a person will have on their system so it's difficult to choose something artistic. That's just one of the drawbacks to CSS.

The two other main drawbacks to CSS are:

1. Browser support

2. The difficulty in creating style sheets

We'll talk about these next.

Browser Support The first and foremost problem is not every browser supports Cascading Style Sheets. For the most part, Netscape Communicator 4 and higher and Internet Explorer 3 and higher support style sheets (see Figure 7.6); however, that leaves a whole lot of users out in the cold, including people using earlier versions of those browsers. Figure 7.7 shows the same page as shown in Figure 7.4, but in Netscape Gold 3.03, which doesn't support style sheets.

FIGURE 7.6   Internet Explorer 4 on the left; Netscape Communicator 4 on the right

What's really problematic is that there are a lot of discrepancies (as of the date this book is being written) between what each browser supports and how they display style sheets. The CSS specification makes sense, but what the

TOO COOL

LEARNING HOW TO WRITE CASCADING STYLE SHEETS

One of the best places to learn about CSS is c/net's Builder.com site at http://www.cnet.com/Content/Builder/Authoring/CSS/.

Not only do they have a nine-part tutorial, but also they have an excellent reference table (http://www.cnet.com/Content/Builder/Authoring/CSS/table.html).

Web Review offers an excellent style sheet reference guide at http://www.webreview.com/guides/style/.

Finally, Yahoo! has a very good listing of sites that deal with style sheets. You can find it at http://www.yahoo.com/Computers_and_Internet/Information_and_Documentation/Data_Formats/HTML/Cascading_Style_Sheets/.

FIGURE 7.7   Netscape Gold 3.03 displays the page.

browsers display on the screen is totally *FUBAR*. (That's an American acronym that came from the military; it stands for *Fouled Up Beyond All Repair*—or words similar to that.) As Figure 7.6 demonstrates, even our simple example looks different in Internet Explorer 4 and Netscape Communicator 4, both of which support CSS.

As you can see, both displays look about the same except for the color of the box around the background text. If you were to look at the page using Internet Explorer 3, however, the difference would be startling, as Figure 7.8 demonstrates.

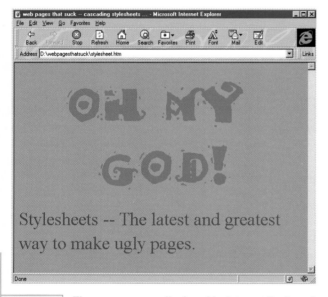

FIGURE 7.8 **The same page as displayed by Internet Explorer 3**

The issue of how well the browsers support CSS is very important. If you go to `http://www.webreview .com/guides/style/mastergrid.html`, you'll see Web Review's Style Sheets Reference Guide. This document lists the different CSS properties and how each browser supports them on each platform. It's pretty darn scary. So scary that while you should get

to know the technology, it's going to take at least a year before the tag situation is sorted out. If you want to start using CSS on your site, visit Web Review's Safe List (`http://www.webreview.com/guides/ style/safegrid.html`) so you'll know which properties are supported by all browsers (a small list), and visit their Danger List (`http://www.webreview.com/ guides/style/unsafegrid.html`) so you'll know which properties to avoid.

The Difficulty in Creating Style Sheets Because of its complexity, CSS is not something the average Web designer codes in by hand. However, because CSS is becoming more important in Web design, many HTML editors are including style sheet creation tools in their packages. I'm a particular fan of HomeSite 3 for Windows 95/NT (`http://www.allaire.com/`) and its Style Sheet Wizard, as shown in Figure 7.9. The Wizard allows you to create style sheets without coding them by hand. If you look at the CSS code earlier in the chapter, you'll realize it's not something you want to do by hand because it's too easy to make a mistake— a simple typo like leaving off a brace can have serious consequences.

If you're not using an HTML editor that has a style sheet wizard and you're running Windows 95/NT and have Navigator 4 or Internet Explorer 3, try CoffeeCup StyleSheet Maker++ (`http://www .coffeecup.com/style/`). This program does the same thing as the HomeSite 3 Wizard. Figure 7.10 shows you StyleSheet Maker++ in action.

Of course, it's the Internet and everyone wants... no, expects...no, demands that software be free. Well, there's actually an amazing free utility from c|net's resident JavaScript god Matt Rotter; it's called, appropriately enough, Style-o-Matic (`http://www.cnet.com/Content/Builder/ Authoring/CSS/ss12.html`).

XML

If there's one important technology that causes my eyes to glaze over it's XML. The short version is it's going to be important—probably when Microsoft's and Netscape's version 5 browsers are released. However, I'm making the bold prediction that Microsoft and Netscape will screw it up by not being compatible with each other and the standard, and we'll have to wait until the year 2000 for order to come from the chaos.

I like to think of *Extensible Markup Language* (XML) as SGML lite. SGML is short for *Standard Generalized Markup Language*—a complex, totally arcane page description language that's been around forever. I remember it from my Wang minicomputer days in the mid-1980s when big-ass companies, such as aircraft manufacturers and other defense contractors, were using it because the government forced it down their throat.

XML lets the user define their own tags, which will let content creators generate more sophisticated Web pages. For example, XML will be used to create order forms for businesses, books, and many database-based pages, such as medical records, encyclopedia entries, technical manuals (the

FIGURE 7.9 HomeSite 3's Style Sheet Wizard (a demo of product is on the CD)

FIGURE 7.10 CoffeeCup StyleSheet Maker++ (a demo is on the CD)

THE `<BOT>` TAG

Speaking of tags I'd like to see created, the first one would be `<BOT></BOT>`.

This tag stands for "Boss Ordered This" and would be used to signify that the material between the beginning and ending tags was ordered by the client over the objections of the designer. If the client was smart enough to view the source and wondered what the tag meant, the designer could say, "It has to do with search engine roBOTs."

SGML influence), and Electronic Data Interchange (EDI).

Look, XML is going to be important and has the potential to make things much simpler on the Web, but you won't need to worry about it for a while. Just keep you eyes open for new developments.

DATABASES

If you want a secure future with lots of money, then learn how to set up electronic commerce (e-commerce) database systems. Putting up a Web site is one thing, but figuring out how to let people securely order by credit card over the Net and then fulfilling their order is another. These issues aren't dealt with in this book, but they are *damn* important. Adding a database system to your site, along with the other e-commerce tools, will jack up the price of your system considerably. Michael and I wish we had the talent to create databases because we'd get out of the HTML/design field and into something that makes *real* money.

If you want to know just how confusing and complex e-commerce is, then read the article "Making Sense of eCommerce" at `http://www.webreview .com/97/12/12/feature/index.html`.

VRML

Back in December 1997, the Virtual Reality Modeling Language 2 specification was adopted by both Microsoft and Netscape. The people who invented the language think it's important. Not many other people seem to care. I don't. Michael cares less. We don't think it's important for anyone, and even if we're wrong, it probably won't make any difference.

THE BLEEDING EDGE FOR INTRANETS

Some of the bleeding-edge technologies are pretty stupid for the average business to be involved in—at least for today. However, if your company has an *intranet* (an internal Internet where you're dealing with serious bandwidth—10 megabits per second), then the following technologies may make a great deal of sense in the right situation. In fact, they could save or make your company a lot of money and may end up as essential business tools.

These technologies are probably most appropriate for large corporations with multiple locations.

Streaming Video and Sound

Streaming video and sound can permit employees who can't physically be present for a meeting to see it in real-time or view it later at their convenience. It isn't uncommon for a corporation to tape an event and then distribute the tapes out to their branches. However, in some cases, it can take up to a month to duplicate, distribute, and view the tape. That's not exactly timely.

Videoconferencing

I'm always amazed at what we, as human beings, will put up with just because it's "high tech." Videoconferencing over the Web and telephone lines initially comes to mind because of the herky-jerky motion, fuzzy pictures, and out-of-sync sound. Of course, on an intranet using a high-end video system with an ISDN or higher connection, you can put together an excellent video-conferencing system that can make people forget they're in a meeting.

Speaking of forgetting you're in a meeting, it isn't uncommon for people to make complete fools of themselves during a videoconference because there's the tendency to think the person on the other end can't see or hear what you're doing.

Digging, picking, and scratching are no-nos. Don't slouch, yawn, giggle, wiggle in your chair, chew gum, doodle on a pad, or let your eyes wander around the room. Focus totally on the task at hand. The best course of action is to think that the people on the other end of the camera can see and hear everything you do—they probably can. Speaking of hearing, get rid of any-thing extraneous that can make a sound—no beepers, pagers, phones, fax machines and, if you're conferencing from home, no kids, no spouse, and no pets. A videoconferencing programmer named Paul Long has put together a whole series of videoconferencing tips that you can find at
`http://www.cmpu.net/public/plong/vctips.html`.

Chat

You're probably wondering how one of the oldest Internet technologies could be on the bleeding edge, especially since Michael and I are chat virgins. At first glance, it seemed dubious that chat had any use other than getting ourselves in trouble with our spouses. As many of you know, chat is when you communicate with others in real time using a protocol called *Internet Relay Chat* (IRC). Originally, most IRC sessions required the user to type in

---

The Bleeding Edge and Resume Building

Resume building occurs when a designer suggests adding a technology to a client's Web site (or to their own company's site) in the hopes of being paid to learn the new technology.

It happens all the time: "Sure, we can install a Netscape/Microsoft/Whatever merchant server system for you," but the truth is they've probably never installed *any* server on *any* system.

I realize the issue of resume building cuts both ways. If you're a consultant, you want to be paid to learn and you're pissed that I've let out one of the dirty little secrets of the trade. If you're a client, you don't want to pay for your designer's learning experience. How do you avoid paying extra? First, look at the designer's home page. While they don't have to use streaming video on every page, they should have used it somewhere on their site if they are recommending streaming video for your site. Think of it this way: while the Pope understands the sanctity of marriage and how sex works, he has no experience. I certainly wouldn't use him as a marriage or sex counselor. I think even Dr. Ruth would be better.

very unintuitive commands, but, like just about everything else related to the Web, improvements have been made. Now you can chat via the Web, and there are newer IRC programs that almost anyone can use (or so we're told).

Chat has received a bad reputation because people use it to talk to others about...hmm...intimate personal details. Then we started hearing interesting stories about schools conducting classes using chat, businesses using chat for customer service—even sales— and we realized that venerable old workhorse was actually on the bleeding edge.

In fact, some of the companies in the chat business are mainly stressing the business aspects of the medium. One company, ichat, Inc. (`http://www.ichat.com/`) stresses "customer service, online sales and dynamic marketing forums" along with "virtual team meetings, message exchanges and searchable knowledge repositories." Sounds completely different from the chat rooms we've all heard so much about.

If you're a large company with a customer service force or are involved in direct marketing, it might be worth checking out this "new" technology.

THE BLEEDING EDGE FOR EVERYONE ELSE

Most of these bleeding-edge technologies don't apply to everyone else. I know…I know you want to play with all the new toys. However, before you start adding that vacation video from your trip to Des Moines or that sound file of your valedictorian speech to your Web site, there are a few things to consider.

Streaming Video and Sound

Before implementing these bleeding-edge technologies, answer the following questions:

> Are you a television station?
>
> Are you a news site?
>
> Are you a movie studio?
>
> Will putting streaming video on your site cause people to write you checks with lots of zeroes in front of the decimal point?
>
> Is there any reason why the world is waiting to see a video you've created?

If you can't answer "Yes" to at least one of these questions, you don't need streaming video or sound on your site. See, it's so simple.

Videoconferencing

Videoconferencing can be useful for the rest of us. If your friends or relatives live long distances away from you and they also happen to have computer systems with videoconferencing hardware and software (it really isn't that expensive), then there's a certain logic to using videoconferencing. That is, if you don't mind the quality. But, let's get real. If you can set up a videoconferencing session with your parents showing them their new grandchild, then no one is going to mind the quality of the images or the connection.

Like every other bleeding-edge technology, you just know that the quality is going to improve and you'll soon be able to have a real-time, full-motion, high-resolution videoconference with your mother-in-law. Wait. Is it to late to stop the advances of technology?

Chat

Chat's probably not a viable option for a small business—you need to have enough customers or employees who would need to use the product. If

OH NO

DON'T USE SOUND FILES

The only sound file anyone on the Internet is interested in hearing is O.J. Simpson confessing.

Well, maybe if you create a sound file that says, "Hi, I'm Fred Jones, and I'm embezzling the company's money and running off to Bora Bora with my secretary (or mailroom boy)," people will be interested. Don't use sound files unless they're confessional in nature. Oh, and if you *do* use sound files, please inform the visitor how large they are by listing the size of the file next to the sound icon. For example, in the original Herbal.com page discussed in Chapter 4 (on the CD-ROM or on the Internet at `http://www .webpagesthatsuck.com/h0/bc1.htm`), Vincent's sound file is 643,588 bytes (628K), while Michael's is 824,106 bytes (804K). Even our mothers wouldn't wait for these files to download.

DON'T USE MUSIC FILES UNLESS YOU'RE A MUSIC SITE

If you load the Herbal.com page and your browser is set up to hear MIDI files, you'll hear a charming piece I recorded back in 1993.

Because I'm not a keyboard player (just a very bad drummer), it's a hodge-podge of garbage. It's also a MIDI file and the quality of the music is related to your sound card. You'll need a very good sound card to hear the true "quality" of my work. The nice part about MIDI files is they're very small. One of the most frequent comments people send to WebPagesThatSuck.com is how much they hate auto-loading music.

COPYRIGHT REVISITED

Back in Chapter 4 we discussed the importance of copyright and clip art. Now let's talk about copyright and music.

Seriously, you can get yourself in a whole lot of trouble by stealing sound files, (even though it's you playing "Stairway to Heaven" on the kazoo, you've still have to pay to use the song). One of the best discussions of this topic is by the law firm of McCutchen, Doyle, Brown & Enersen, LLP. The article is entitled, "Unauthorized Content: Is It Worth the Risk?" and can be found at `http://www.mccutchen.com/ip/ unauth.htm`. The Internet is no longer the domain of weird nerds; it's a business platform, and as soon as money is involved, you know the lawyers will show up. Get used to it.

you're a site devoted to a movie star or rock group (like that damn Hanson my daughter's so hooked on), then it might be applicable. The rest of you can get back to your one-handed typing.

WHEN THE BLEEDING EDGE BECOMES THE BORING EDGE

I know it's hard to believe, but once upon a time the `<TABLE>` tag was on the bleeding edge of Web technology. Now it has become so commonplace that we basically yawn when the topic comes up.

Here are two other former bleeding-edge technologies that are about to make the ranks of yawners.

Java

I know what you're thinking. With all the eruptions that went on and are still going on between Microsoft and Sun Microsystems about Java, how can I say Java isn't on the bleeding edge? Well, these arguments are proof because they're symptomatic of a vendor trying to screw around with an accepted technology—just like what happened to UNIX when a single, unified standard split into a bazillion variations.

My attitude about Java has been well documented on WebPagesThatSuck.com. Comedian Denis Leary has a routine about cocaine that reminds me of my reaction to Java. He says, "Yeah, cocaine makes a lot of sense. I want a drug that makes my nose bleed, sucks all the money out of my bank account, and makes my penis small. Sure." And what do I think of Java? "I want to spend all day waiting for an applet to load that may compromise my system's security and is about as entertaining to watch as a guy making a dog out of balloons. Sure."

Yes, I realize that Java is going to be used to write cross-platform applications, so it's going to be valuable. But let's not forget it's an interpreted language that sits on top of the operating system. We've all heard the phrase about how if you forget the past, you're condemned to repeat it. Well, let me remind you of the past:

USCD Pascal

That should send shivers down the spine of you old-timers. For the rest of you, just replace "Java" with "USCD Pascal" and you'll understand the computing world of the mid-1980s.

Why am I so harsh? Because Java hasn't lived up to its potential—yet. Yes, it may be important, but when it becomes important, you won't notice because it will blend into the landscape. Another history lesson: For years people were talking about "198X will be the Year of the LAN," but when it finally happened, no one noticed because it was accepted. Does anyone remember exactly what year was the year of the CD-ROM? No. It just happened. The same thing will happen to Java.

JavaScript

This former bleeding-edge technology is now a part of the status quo. The most frequent use for the technology is mouseover buttons—the buttons that change appearance when the mouse moves over them. It's become an accepted method for creating navigation buttons. Figure 7.11 shows you the first screen of my personal page.

Normal pictures, but when you move your mouse over the McCauley Culkin–looking kid, you can see what happens in Figure 7.12.

It's important to note that JavaScript is a mainstay in DHTML. That's what makes the animation work, which doesn't mean there aren't some sucky implementations of JavaScript. There are and here are three you should avoid:

1. Scrolling text in the status bar.

2. Backgrounds that fade in and out.

3. Entry-way JavaScripts that make you key in your name before you can enter the site.

Just because you can add a technology to your page doesn't mean you should. Let's use my home page as an example. There's really no reason to use JavaScript because it adds nothing to my site. In the security industry, there's a phrase called "Need to Know," which means if I need to know something, I find out; otherwise, I don't find out. For most Web pages, the operative phrase is "Need to Have"—does adding the JavaScript enhance the page? In my particular case, it doesn't; it's just a needless waste of bandwidth.

That brings me to "Vincent and Michael's Two-Step Recovery Program for Web Designers." It isn't just in the area of bleeding-edge technology that Web designers go wrong. There's a tendency to add graphics, frames, bevels, and so on, to a site because it *can* be added. It's similar to the old joke, "Why do rock and roll stars marry models? Because they can." Unlike most recovery programs where there are 12 steps, Michael and I have pared it down to two simple steps.

Vincent and Michael's Two-Step Recovery Program for Web Designers

1. We admit we are powerless over new Web technologies and our Web sites have become unmanageable.

2. We will only add design elements to a page if they help the site make money or if they are appropriate to the theme of the site.

Before we move on to one of the biggest topics—marketing your site—let's spend the next chapter talking about that always-dreaded, but incredibly important task: site maintenance. Just as periodic maintenance and tuning is important to keep your car running, the same is true about your Web site.

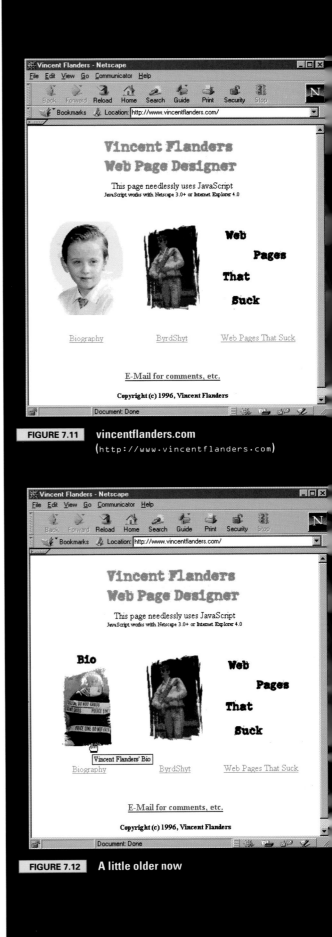

FIGURE 7.11 vincentflanders.com
(`http://www.vincentflanders.com`)

FIGURE 7.12 A little older now

INTERNATIONAL

HOW DO YOU SAY "SUCK" IN IRELAND?

The two sites featured here are small studios, probably with even smaller advertising budgets. But one of the points of this book is that just because you have no budget, doesn't mean your site has to suck!

First, let's look at the Irish Site.

Granted, none of the sites I've created have ever won the much coveted Dora Award, a rating given out by an Irish Internet directory. One Dora equals bad; five Doras equals best. So according to Dora, this site doesn't suck. Much.

Essentially what Temptation Recording Studio has done is put an award for third place at the top of their page. Below that, you see their beveled, button-looking logo, which, of course, isn't a button at all. The site unnecessarily incorporates frames. It's such a small site, why complicate it with frames? Don't forget the handful of gratuitous animated GIFs or the ominous-looking black background. And then comes a rather large and obscure Java applet of what looks to be two people walking down a hallway. The question above reads "Where ARE we going?" Indeed. I'm thinking, "Back to the drawing board."

Temptation Recording Studio—I'm tempted to leave.
(http://www.davidbowie.com/2.0/)

Ziggy Sound Studio—a link to Heaven's Gate
(http://www.cybernet.net/%7Elizerd/ron/ziggy.html)

INTERNATIONAL

Back in the States.

Again, no contest. The U.S. recording studio takes international honors for sucking the most. Where to begin? How about the atrocious black starfield background. Let's see, there are animated CDs (nope), an animated rainbow bar (ick), various animated balls—the animated blue bars are the worst. No, wait, the animated dancing flames definitely suck the most! The broken GIF in the middle is an obscure applet that requires a plug-in, which apparently isn't supported by Navigator. Good. I didn't want to see or hear it anyway. What's really interesting is the dead link (no pun intended) at the bottom of the page to Heavens Gate. Wasn't that the cult (of Web designers) that committed mass suicide in Rancho Sante Fe, California, recently? Hmmmm...

Flanders & Willis's Reality Check

It always amazes us how many people think their job is done once the site is up. Actually, that's when most of the work starts. Think about the sites you visit the most. Is their content static? Let's hope not—otherwise it's like watching reruns of some TV show over and over and over again. Keep your site fresh.

CHAPTER 8

Maintaining Your Site

IN THIS CHAPTER

we're going to talk about the most unglamorous task in the Web page design industry. Is it designing the site? No. Is it creating the content? No. Is it *maintenance*? Absolutely.

Nobody likes dealing with the nitty-gritty issues revolving around making sure the site works. It's no fun. But it's an ugly job that has to be done. A Web site is like a baby—you have to check its health and you have to keep feeding it and changing its "clothes."

BEFORE YOUR SITE OR NEW PAGES ARE PUBLISHED

You can't just throw your pages up on the Web. You have to make sure your visitors can actually see them because, after all, what good is a Web site if your visitors can't *see* your pages? Before your site or new pages are published, you need to

Check for browser support

Validate your HTML

Check links

Checking for Browser Support

One of the more common design mistakes is to assume that because the designer can see the Web page, everyone else can. It's similar to the problem I have when I design Web pages on my 21-inch monitor with an 1152x862–pixel resolution. The pages look great (of course), but when I view them on a smaller monitor with an 640x480 resolution, they don't look so great.

As with everything else in life, pictures explain it best. Figure 8.1 shows the first navigation page at WebPagesThatSuck .com as seen by most browsers.

Right. Fine. No big deal. Figure 8.2 shows you the same page as viewed by the following browsers:

Web TV 1

AOL 2.5 / Windows

AOL 2.7 / Macintosh

Internet Explorer 2

Lynx 2.5

Mosaic 2.11

Netscape 1.1

Browsers compatible with HTML 2 standard (no extensions)

Browsers compatible with HTML 3.2 standard (no extensions)

It's the very same page as the one shown in Figure 8.1. Gee. What a difference! The WebPagesThatSuck.com site had to be created using frames, and because of this, the above browsers can't see the content—they can only see what was put between the <NOFRAMES> and </NOFRAMES> tags. Granted, I should have put a little more information there, but I was lazy.

I know what you're thinking. "Vincent, hardly anyone uses these browsers so your argument is facetious." That's probably true, but there are other Microsoft- and Netscape-specific tags in use that will cause problems for your visitors. If you doubt me, here are words that will cause Web-browsing heartache—*Cascading Style Sheets* and *Dynamic HTML*. We covered these topics in Chapter 7.

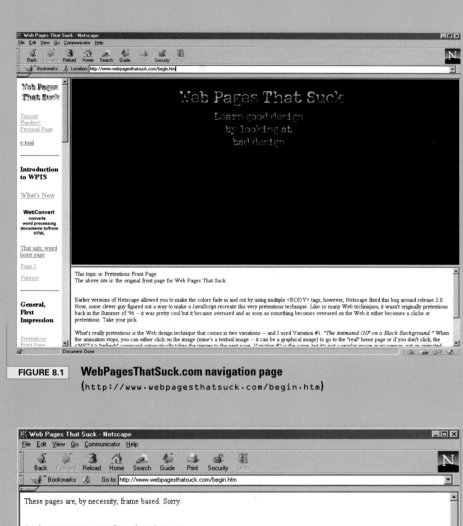

FIGURE 8.1   **WebPagesThatSuck.com navigation page**
(http://www.webpagesthatsuck.com/begin.htm)

FIGURE 8.2   **What people see who use browsers that don't support frames**

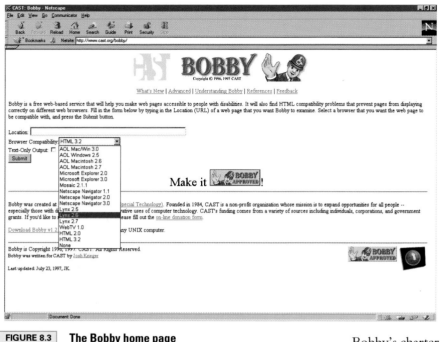

Except for some overdone sites (the Pepsi site, discussed in Chapter 2, comes to mind), most major sites are tending toward the lower common denominator route. This doesn't mean they don't offer some bleeding-edge technology—it's just that they're making it optional.

How can you tell if your site is socially acceptable to the different browsers? To my knowledge, there's no universal testing aid, but there are some sites on the Internet that help and one of them is Bobby (`http://www.cast.org/bobby/`).

FIGURE 8.3   **The Bobby home page**
(`http://www.cast.org/bobby/`)

What are you to do? Like so much of what's happening on the Internet, there are two main schools of thought:

1. Damn the torpedoes—full speed ahead.
This school of thought says use the latest and greatest tags and don't worry about your audience, which is fine if your site exists to stroke your little ego as you saw in Chapter 1. Permission granted.

2. Go for the lower common denominator.
I said *lower,* not *lowest* common denominator. There's a group of HTML Luddites who don't want anybody using any tag that isn't approved. Fine, but at the moment it's pretty much a Microsoft- and Netscape-browser world, so using tags they *both* support—notice the emphasis on the word *both*—is fine.

Bobby's charter is to help Web designers test out their pages to see if they're accessible to those surfers who have visual disabilities. Figure 8.3 shows the different browsers Bobby checks.

While Bobby checks to see if the tags in your document are supported by different browsers, it doesn't show you how your page will actually look on different versions of the same browser—there are differences between how a page looks on the Macintosh version of Netscape and the Windows version. Nevertheless, Bobby will tell you if you're heading toward trouble. The major problem with the program, as of the writing of this book, is it supports neither Netscape Communicator 4 nor Internet Explorer 4 tags. Nevertheless, it is quite helpful in checking your site for browser compatibility.

For those of you who want to ensure compatibility with older browsers, there are two other sites worth checking out: the Web Page Backward Compatibility

Viewer page, shown in Figure 8.4, and the Web Page Purifier, shown in Figure 8.5. What's nice about this site and its companion site is you get to see how your page actually looks using a browser that follows the standards you pick. Very, very cool. Unfortunately, the standards it picks are not up to date.

Validating Your HTML

If you ever get the chance to hang around programmers, you'll eventually hear them cuss at their screen and say something like, "You're doing what I told you to do, not what I want you to do." That's the problem with computers—they're not smart enough to know what you want them to do. It's the same with writing HTML documents—what gets displayed in the browser window is what you tell it to display. Garbage in. Garbage out.

Just as programmers need programs that debug their code, Web designers need programs that check the syntax of their HTML pages. It's even more imperative because a Web designer's work gets displayed on multiple systems, where the average programmer's work is only displayed on one system (the Java programming language is trying to change that, but generally, a programmer only writes for one system). The more platforms you have to deal with, the more room for error.

Debuggers for Web designers are called *HTML validators,* and they should be used on each and every page you write to make sure your code is syntactically correct. (Just because it is correct, doesn't mean it will look good; it just means you're using the HTML code in the proper way.)

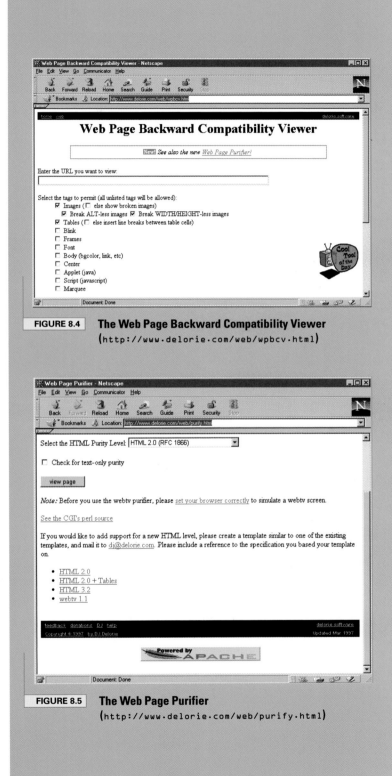

FIGURE 8.4 **The Web Page Backward Compatibility Viewer**
(`http://www.delorie.com/web/wpbcv.html`)

FIGURE 8.5 **The Web Page Purifier**
(`http://www.delorie.com/web/purify.html`)

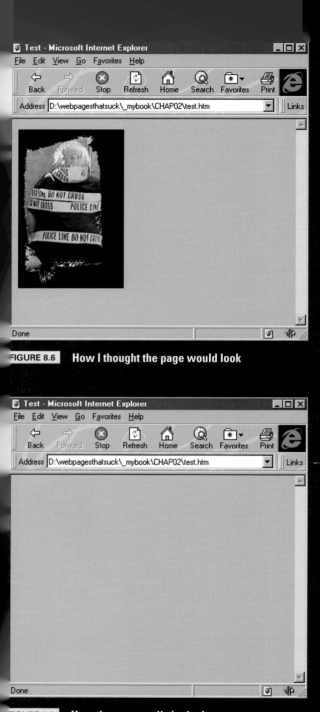

FIGURE 8.6   How I thought the page would look

FIGURE 8.7   How the page really looked

If you write HTML properly, then certain mistakes will be eliminated. For example, Figure 8.6 shows how I thought one of my pages would look using Microsoft's Internet Explorer 3 browser.

Figure 8.7 shows how the page was actually displayed based on the HTML document I created.

I think we have a problem here. Hmm... Because this is a test page, there's very little "code" to "debug" (thankfully). On a normal HTML page that you've written or will write, the situation is much worse, and it would be harder to find the errant code. Here's the code for the page in question. Can you figure out why the image doesn't display?

```
<HTML>
<HEAD>
        <TITLE>Test</TITLE>
</HEAD>

<BODY>
<img src="vince770.jpg
width=160 height=237 border=0>
</BODY>

</HTML>
```

If you're like me, you can't see the mistake, so I ran a Windows-based utility program called HTML PowerAnalyzer from Opposite Software (http://www.opposite.com) on the HTML file. Figure 8.8 gave me the answer.

Oh, yeah. I was missing the ending double quotation mark:

```
<img src="vince770.jpg"
width=160 height=237 border=0>
```

There used to be a time when the browsers weren't so picky and figured out where the ending double quotation mark would go. It doesn't work that way any more. The browsers are ensuring they hold close to the standards.

FIGURE 8.8   **HTML PowerAnalyzer figures out the problem.**

There are two types of HTML validation tools—those on the Internet and those that run locally on your computer. If you want to find them on the Internet, you can always go to Yahoo! at `http://www.yahoo.com/Computers_and_Internet/Information_and_Documentation/Data_Formats/HTML/Validation_and_Checkers/`.

Checking Links

I've included checking links as both a before-you-post-your-pages and an after-you-post-your-pages activity. On small sites, this isn't really much of an issue because you can check your links by hand; however, if your site has a lot of outside links (we discussed whether this is a good idea in Chapter 6), you'll need to use some of the available tools to see if the links on your pages are still valid.

Linkbot and Web Doctor

I tested two link-checking programs: Linkbot ($249.95, `http://www.tetranesoftware.com/linkbot-info.htm`*) and Web Doctor (list price $149.00, but "on sale" at $99.00,* `http://www.bluesky.com/products/bluesky.htm`*). Here's what I discovered:*

LinkBot is definitely the more powerful of the two. I recommend it for checking the links on your *remote Web server* (I didn't like the way it worked on my local files). I thought Web Doctor did a better job of checking local files, but it doesn't check remote files on your Web server.

A number of LinkBot's features are quite important: checking for broken links, missing images, and stale content; finding large pages; and identifying orphan files—which can be important because so many ISPs are lowering the disk storage space available for each client.

If, on the other hand, you don't have two hundred files and aren't constantly updating your site, it isn't worth purchasing either product.

TOO COOL

HTML RENAME!

Vincent and I agree that the best $20 we ever spent on a piece of shareware was for a Macintosh- and Windows-based product called HTML Rename! (http://www.visiontec .com/rename/). *Here's how the company describes their product:*

"HTML Rename!™ eliminates the problems encountered when moving files between DOS/Windows, Macintosh, and UNIX file systems. By changing filenames (case, length, and invalid characters) and fixing links in HTML code, HTML Rename! ensures that your files and Web pages will work on any operating system. Using HTML Rename! before you transfer files (for example, uploading a Web site to a UNIX server) saves you from needing to repair mangled filenames, broken links, and extra or missing carriage return characters in text files."

The reason we needed the product is that an ISP moved files from a Windows NT–based server, which is more forgiving of uppercase and lowercase, to a UNIX system, which wants you to get the case right. It was a nightmare of broken images until we used this product. Bingo! It was done. The product gets our highest recommendations!

Some programs, like FrontPage 98, automatically include the ability to check your links. This ability is being added to more and more editors (HomeSite 3, for example), and, of course, there are standalone utilities that perform the same task. I know what you're thinking—go to Yahoo! to find them. Usually, I'd agree with you, but, at the time of writing this book, Yahoo! actually has a pretty poor listing for link-checking programs. I suggest you go to Dave Central's site at http://www.davecentral.com/urlcheck.html. These programs are Windows-based.

AFTER YOUR SITE OR NEW PAGES ARE PUBLISHED

There are three major site-maintenance activities you need to perform after your site is up and running:

1. Reviewing Web page statistics
2. Checking links
3. Updating and revising your site

Reviewing Web Page Statistics

Unfortunately, not every site has to be concerned with gathering statistics about itself. The reason is simple—some sites don't get enough visitors to make it worth their while to pay additional money for a report. However, some ISPs will automatically generate monthly reports on Web in/activity free of charge. If it's free, be sure to take advantage of the offer.

Although I think you should be getting at least 2,000 hits a month before you start worrying about statistics, there are some other reasons you might feel it's necessary. The following information, shown in Figure 8.9, was taken from the WebTrends site. WebTrends (http://www.webtrends.com) makes a Windows 95/NT–based package that generates Web page statistics. I just bought a copy.

Obviously, the following questions are geared toward WebTrend's strengths, but they're questions every Web page–statistics package should answer:

How can you determine the return on your investment?

How can you measure the traffic on your Web server?

Can you measure both the quality and quantity of visitors to your Web site?

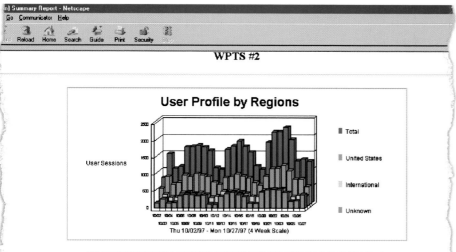

FIGURE 8.9 **Statistics for WebPagesThatSuck.com**

Make Sure Your ISP Includes a

Referrer Log Report

A referrer log report tells you the URL from which your visitor came. If someone searched for "Web Pages That Suck" at AltaVista and clicked the link, the referrer log would tell me the person came from AltaVista.

The reason I'm telling you to make sure they include it is that it isn't always automatically generated. From what I'm told by people who know is that the default value for many Web servers is to not include this log.

How many users visit your site daily? Is that number growing?

What paths do visitors take when they browse your Web site?

From what countries do users connect? What cities? What states?

From what departments do users connect to your intranet servers?

Which is the most active day of the week? The most active hour?

What kind of information is accessed on your server?

Which pages are the most popular?

How many pages are accessed in each directory?

How many users are accessing each directory?

What browsers are used to access your Web server? What operating systems?

Which forms are submitted more than others?

How is your intranet Web server utilized?

There are two spots where you can find different packages. The first is, of course, Yahoo! at `http://www.yahoo.com/Business_and_Economy/Companies/Computers/Software/Internet/World_Wide_Web/Log_Analysis_Tools/Titles/`, and the second is Dave Central at `http://www.davecentral.com/webstat.html`.

Checking Links

I talked about this topic earlier. The only comment that needs to be added is it's very important to periodically check your links to sites outside your site. As we all know, pages get removed, moved, and renamed, and there's nothing that antagonizes your visitors more than dead links.

Updating and Revising Your Site

It always amazes both Michael and me how many people think their job is done once the site is up. Actually, that's when most of the work starts. I don't mean to be discouraging, that's just the way it is. In the next three chapters, I'll talk about the marketing efforts you'll need to undertake. Besides your marketing efforts, however, you're going to need to periodically revise your site. Think about the sites you visit the most. Is their content static? I hope not—otherwise it's like watching reruns of some TV show over and over and over again. Yes, it fills time, but not productively.

I've said it before and I'll say it again: the most effective way to update and revise your site is to add content. Without content, you don't have a Web site—you've got a brochure.

All the good sites modify their look. CDNOW, one of the more popular Web sites and one of the sites people are always using as an example of why the Internet is going to change our lives, has continually honed their site to a fine edge (see Figure 8.10). When it first started, it was much more graphically intense than it is now. I remember the pages taking *forever* to load. They learned, and through learning improved their site—now it's very successful.

Learn from them.

Next, we're going to talk about how to market your site. After all, you might have a great looking site, but if no one knows it's there, then all your work was for naught.

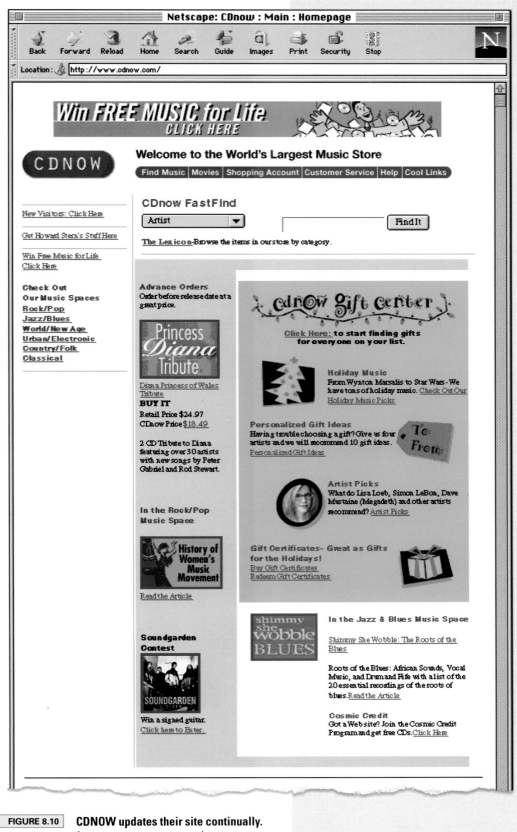

FIGURE 8.10 **CDNOW updates their site continually.**
(http://www.cdnow.com/)

Flanders & Willis's Reality Check

Choose your domain name carefully. When you see analtech.com, you don't immediately think of "precoated plates and equipment for sample preparation and Thin Layer Chromatography," do you? Neither do we. Also, if the domain name you want is available—get it right this minute before somebody grabs it. This is an order!

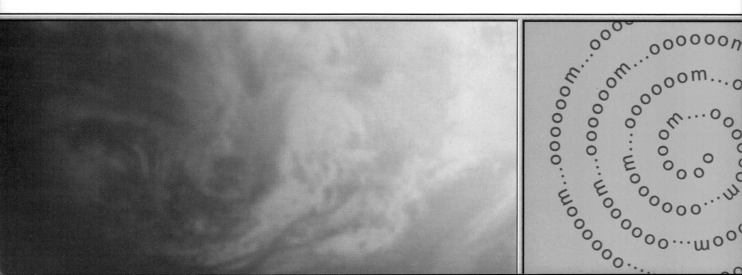

CHAPTER 9

It Takes More Than Luck to Make the Bucks

IF YOU'VE GONE

through the first eight chapters

and followed every suggestion,

you should have a great looking

Web site overflowing with con-

tent. But guess what? That isn't

good enough. The real work is

staring you in the face—you've

got to market the living daylights

out of your site.

This chapter and the next two

chapters are among the most

important ones in the book.

Chapter 9 covers the most important part, and the most elementary part, of your Web-marketing effort—your content and your domain name. Chapter 10 deals with the always amusing, often crazy, and generally bizarre issue of search engines and directories. Chapter 11 covers other ways to market your site. (People often tend to think the Web is the be-all and end-all of the Universe, but it isn't.)

Remember—marketing is about money. We've shown you how to make your site pretty; now we're going to show you how to make it profitable.

WEB MARKETING 101

There are two ways to market your site: First, there are "free" methods, such as site submissions, USENET, and so on; second, there are methods that cost money, such as press releases, advertising, and so on. I'll spend more time discussing the free methods than the paid ones. After all, you've probably become accustomed to thinking of the Internet as "free," haven't you?

Let's start out by taking a look at Herbal.com's home page, shown in Figure 9.1.

Why Does This Page Suck?

Gee, the page looks fine.

FIGURE 9.1 **Only the lonely**

It seems like it's fairly easy to navigate. And judging from this first page, it appears there may even be some content. So what's wrong? The problem is at the bottom of the page.

1. No one has been to the site! Seeing your home page counter register only 132 hits—and most of them have come from you checking to see if anybody has visited your site—sucks more than just about anything that can happen to a site owner.

2. If nobody visits your site, you can't get them to buy anything. If you're an informational site, you've worked yourself to the bone, and no one appreciates your efforts. If you have a personal page and 132 hits, hey...that's pretty good.

What can you do to get more visitors? Marketing. If you want your site to be successful, you're going to have to learn how to market your site to the world.

URL: www.herbal.com

The counter with no count

There are four stages to creating a site on the Internet:

1. Planing and designing the site

2. Gathering and/or creating content

3. Creating the pages

4. Marketing the site

Theoretically, you should spend 25 percent of your time on each of these four stages. The second column in Table 9.1 shows how most people really spend their time. However, if you want to have a successful site ("No Vincent, I want to spend a lot of money creating a failure that'll cost me my job, duh"), the third column shows how you should spend your time.

Stage	Percent of Time People Typically Spend	Percent of Time People Should Spend
1. Planning and designing the site	10 %	50%
2. Gathering and/or creating content	5 %	25%
3. Creating the pages	80 %	25%
4. Marketing the site	5 %	100%
Total	100%	200%

TABLE 9.1 **How Much Time Do You Spend Marketing Your Site?**

Get the point? After planning and designing the site, creating the content, and then creating the pages, marketing your site will take 100 percent of your time and energy.

That said, what steps are involved in marketing your site? Glad you asked. Here they are:

1. Creating significant content

2. Acquiring appropriate domain name(s)

3. Preparing your pages for search engines and directories

4. Submitting your site

5. Marketing on the Web

6. Marketing through other channels

CONTENT, CONTENT, CONTENT

The most important marketing tool you have was discussed in Chapter 3, "Content Is King." I can't stress strongly enough how important it is for your site to have content that will make people want to visit and, more importantly, come back to your site.

Lots of people complain: "I can't get listed by Yahoo!" or "I can't get listed in XYZ." Well, Yahoo! listed WebPagesThatSuck.com two days after it was submitted *and* with a pair of sunglasses signifying it was a cool site and one of the picks of the week. It wasn't because the Web design was electrifying—it was because *the site had significant content.*

Content is king. Content is everything. Content will get you listed in search engines, directories, and magazines faster than any other marketing technique. There's nothing more important.

ACQUIRING APPROPRIATE DOMAIN NAME(S)

Your domain name is one of the most important parts of your marketing plan. The domain name `webpagesthatsuck.com` tells the world that this site is about all that is bad about Web design. The domain name `culinary.com` tells the world the site is about cooking. And `microsoft.com` says you're visiting the Web site of the most powerful software company in the world. Your domain name is your identity on the Internet. The Internet address `http://lsnt7.lightspeed.net/~cwms` doesn't tell you squat— actually, it tells you less than squat. You would have no idea that this URL hosts a site that was just born

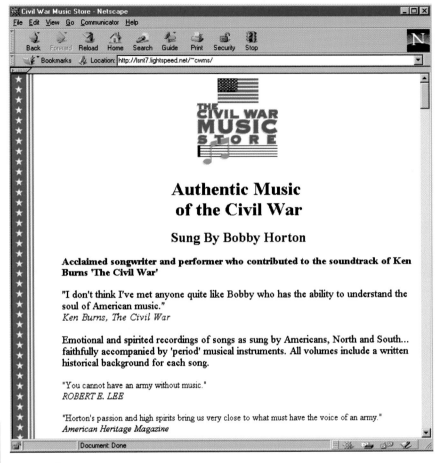

FIGURE 9.2   **A site born to be on the Internet—The Civil War Music Store**

to be on the Internet—the Civil War Music Store, shown in Figure 9.2.

Choosing Your Domain Name

Now that you understand the importance of having a domain name, let's assume the domain name you like is available and you want to grab it before someone else does. If your company is XZZP, Inc. and you can grab XZZP.com, go right ahead and fill out the InterNIC forms or have your ISP do it for you. (For more on registering your domain name, see the section "Get Your Domain Name Now" later in the chapter.)

What's a Domain Name?

Let's clear up a little misconception. For some reason, people seem to think that www.webpagesthatsuck.com *is the domain name. Not true.*

The *www* part is actually the name of the machine where the domain is stored (in this case, the machine set aside as the World Wide Web server). It can be called anything, though the tradition is to name the server for its function. For example, the Civil War Music Store is located on a server called *lsnt7*, which originally stood for "*L*ightspeed *NT* server number *7*." The domain name for WebPagesThatSuck.com is webpagesthatsuck.com.

FIGURE 9.3 analtech.com—the domain name doesn't conjure up images of "precoated plates" and "Thin Layer Chromatography."
(http://www.analtech.com/)

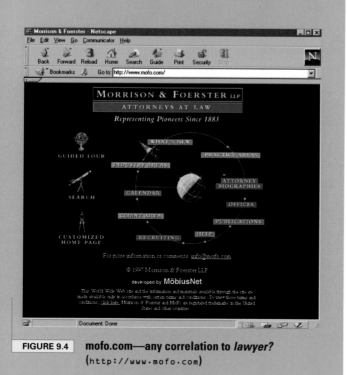

FIGURE 9.4 mofo.com—any correlation to *lawyer*?
(http://www.mofo.com)

Don't be surprised if your choice is taken—especially if you're trying to grab a single word. I mean if diarrhea.com is taken (by Proctor & Gamble no less), what hope is there for your choice? You'll probably have to string two or more words together or hyphenate two words. If you have to use an abbreviation or string some words together, then take a few seconds and ask yourself the following questions.

Is My Domain Name Descriptive? There's a site on the Internet called analtech.com. You're probably thinking "proctology equipment" or something much worse. Actually, this site, shown in Figure 9.3, has given me a whole new perspective on "precoated plates and equipment for sample preparation and Thin Layer Chromatography (TLC)." The name just doesn't describe what the company does.

One of the reasons for the success of WebPagesThat-Suck.com is the URL matches the name of the site— http://www.webpagesthatsuck.com—and, as we know, it's a clever and humorous name that's easy to remember. Actually, the truth is, I should have really called it "Web Pages That Have Something Wrong with Them But Generally Are OK," but the URL would have been www.webpagesthathavesomething wrongwiththembutgenerallyareok.com. First, it's not as clever or as funny. Second, it exceeds the number of characters allowed for a domain name—22. Actually, there are 26 characters allowed, but they count *.com* as four characters, so it's really 22.

Another great example, shown in Figure 9.4, of what seems to be a bad choice of domain names is the one picked by the law firm of Morrison & Foerster— mofo.com. For those of you who are slang-impaired, *mofo* is slang for *motherf**ker.*

If this domain name belonged to a bakery, it wouldn't be as problematic. Most people don't associate *mofos* with bakers. However, I suspect there are people out

FIGURE 9.5 **foodwine.com—all the alternate domain names were taken.**
(http://www.foodwine.com)

there (of course, I'm not one of them) who might find the correlation between *mofo*s and lawyers...well... somewhat appropriate.

When I mentioned my problem with this name on WebPagesThatSuck.com, I received a lot of e-mail explaining the choice. Basically, the law firm knows what it means, and they're proud of their name because they want to have the image of a law firm you don't want to mess with. As long as you're aware of what your domain name means, that's fine.

Are Alternate Versions of the Name Available?
You're probably wondering what this means. Let me explain. There's a really nice site on the Internet called foodwine.com (see Figure 9.5). When I first saw it, I wondered if it wouldn't have been better and easier to have used foodandwine.com for their name. After using InterNICs domain name search facility (http://rs.internic.net/cgi-bin/whois) I discovered an interesting story.

Back on August 24, 1995, a company called Blue Chair Media grabbed foodandwine.com for them-selves; on April 3, 1996, a company called winweb, Inc. grabbed food-wine.com; and on May 7, 1996, a company called Electronic Gourmet Guide registered foodwine.com. As of this writing, only foodwine.com is an active site, but I'm sure they would have loved to own both foodandwine.com and food-wine.com. It's entirely possible those names will become active sites and cause confusion in the marketplace. Of course, if foodwine.com markets itself right, this issue is less likely to pop up. They also have the choice of buying the other two names, but I'm sure it would cost some serious money.

Grab Alternate Versions of Your Main Domain Name

This includes plural and hyphenated versions. I made another huge mistake by not getting herbals.com— *I'm really mad at myself.*

Speaking of alternate versions, some companies are registering names that are similar to the names of their competitors, for example, iagency.com and agency.com. Another example is where a site has the same name as a popular site but uses a different domain. For example, typing in www.whitehouse .gov will take you to the White-house's home page. If you accidentally type in www .whitehouse.com, which I did one day, you'll be sent to a site where... let's just say the only thing the two sites have in common is the President.

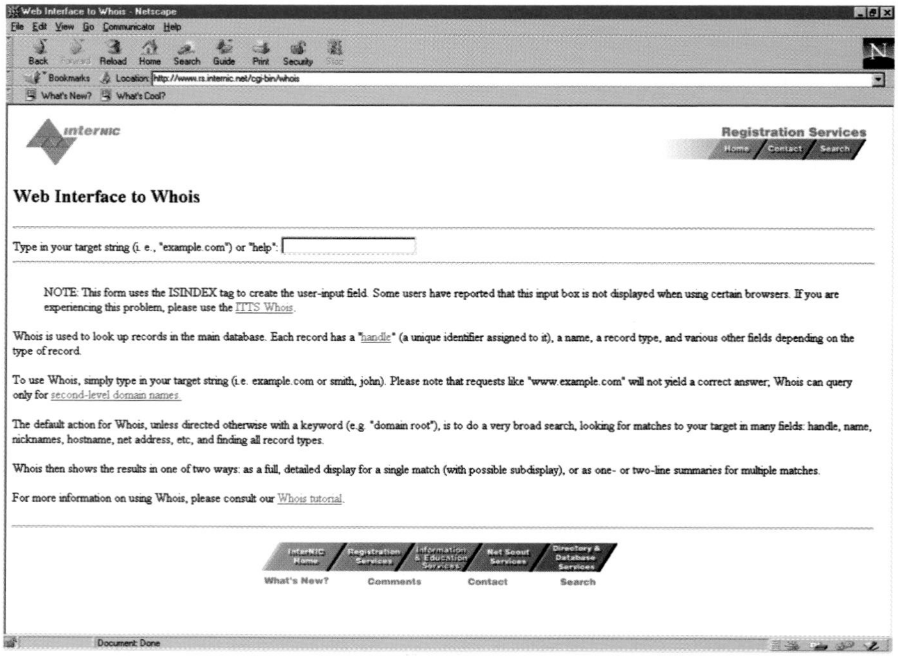

FIGURE 9.6 Go to the InterNIC site to find out if your domain name is taken.

Get Your Domain Name Now!

So how do you find out if that perfect domain name you have chosen is taken?

First, you need to go to the InterNIC site (the organization in charge of reg-istering domain names); the URL is http://rs.internic.net/cgi-bin/whois. Figure 9.6 shows what the site looks like.

In the Type In Your Target String text box, key in the domain name you want to check, press the Enter key, and InterNIC will tell you if someone owns the name.

As this book is being written, there's a horrible controversy about who gets to manage and create domains. Basically, the Internet is running out of good commercial names—the "dot coms" of the world. Because the Internet is running out of good names, the value of a good name goes up.

There's another controversy surrounding domain names. People grab names of large companies and then try to hold these companies hostage by demanding large sums of money to release the domain name. Then there's the situation where companies argue over who really "owns" the domain name. For example, Hasbro, the makers of the game Clue, is suing a company called Clue Computing of Longmont, Colorado. Because Hasbro owns the trademark to the board game version of Clue, they feel this gives them the right to the domain name `clue.com`. Anything having to do with domain names is a very ugly mess.

If you want more details, visit these sites: InterNIC's Registration Services Policy Statements can be found at `http://rs.internic.net/help/policy.html` and the NSI Domain Name Dispute Policy Statement can be found at `http://rs.internic.net/domain-info/internic-domain-b.html`.

Registering Your Domain Name

If the domain name you want is available—get it right this minute before somebody grabs it. This is an order! I jacked around and lost out on `herbs.com` because I didn't grab it when I had the chance. I'm an idiot. The only thing I can say in my defense is I didn't understand how to get domain names—this was back in the dark ages of 1995. Learn from my stupidity. Get your domain name now!

So how do you register a domain name? The methods range from going to the InterNIC site and doing it yourself, to having a third party do all the work. When I first got `herbal.com`, domain names were free but I had to pay a fee of $75 (it might have been $100—I don't remember) to an Internet Service Provider (ISP) to host the DNS. In the old days (1995–1996), people didn't understand what was involved in getting a domain name, and they just went along with whoever was putting their site together. It was an age of "make 'em pay as much as you can," and almost everyone took advantage of the general public's ignorance. Now, most people know how easy it is to get a domain name and the "only" charge is $100 for a two-year license. It's okay for your ISP to make *some* money for registering your site. I certainly wouldn't pay any more than $50 extra for their trouble. Some Web-hosting services will waive any add-on fee (except the InterNIC fee) if you sign up with their service.

No Pain, No Domain

Before you can register a domain name, you'll need several bits of important data from your ISP or system administrator (if that's not you). Here's what you need:

The new domain name that you want to register.

The name and address of the owner of the domain name (you or your company).

The name, address, phone number, and e-mail address of an administrative contact for this domain, generally the owner or their designated representative.

The same details for a technical contact. This should be someone with direct access to the server. If you're using an ISP, they'll provide a technical contact; if you're maintaining your own machines, you can assign this role to your system administrator.

Information for a billing contact, generally your company's accounting department or whoever handles the finances.

The server host name and netaddress for two domain name servers that will maintain domain name service for your account. Your ISP or system administrator will provide this information; it will look something like this:

Host name: NS1 .LIGHTSPEED.NET

Netaddress: 204.216.64.2

If you're maintaining your own servers with a direct connection to the Internet or have established a relationship with a flexible ISP, you can register new domains on your own. The information about the registration process can be found at `http://rs.internic.net/rs-internic.html`. The InterNIC FAQ can be found at `http://rs.internic.net/domain-info/registration-FAQ.html`. It's quite informative; I suggest reading this page first. A word of warning—the InterNIC site is busy and hard to access during normal business hours.

Read the sidebar "No Pain/ No Domain" (on the previous page), for a list of data you'll need to register your site. If you don't want the pain of handling all of this data, let your ISP handle the registration for you, as I do, even if they charge an additional fee. Believe me, the pain your wallet endures will be less than the pain you'll endure if your registration forms are incomplete or incorrect. Your registration will be delayed—during which time the domain name you want is fair game!

Now that you understand some of the subtleties of the domain name business (get similar names, plural versions, and hyphenated versions), we're going to move on to the people who can "Make You or Break You"—search engines and directories. In Chapter 10, you'll learn about techniques that will help get your site noticed.

Before you rush on to the next chapter, grab a beer from the fridge and sit back while we compare a U.S. and Swedish beer site.

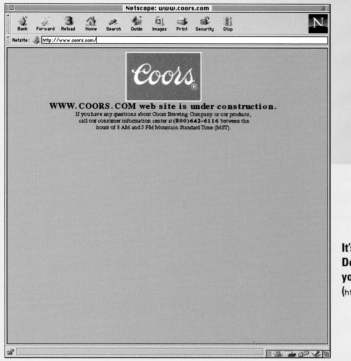

It's December 11, 1997. Do you know where your Web site is?
(http://www.coors.com/)

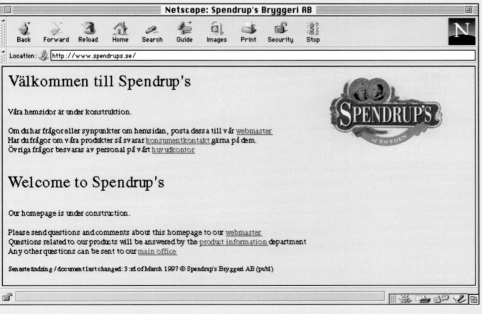

Another page under *konstruktion*
(http://www.spendrups.se/)

INTERNATIONAL

HOW DO YOU SAY "SUCK" IN SWEDEN?

Let's start off with a U.S. beer company site. Coors got the domain name they wanted, coors.com; unfortunately, there's not a lot to say about the site itself since it's "Under Construction." Don't use Under Construction signs— your site should always be under construction. Of course, that means you need to have a site in the first place.

Let's cross the Atlantic to see how the Swedes are doing.

Here we have a Swedish brewery under *konstruktion*. And while being under *konstruktion* doesn't necessarily suck, being under *konstruktion* with no new content for over a year does. Beer gets stale after a year and so do sites with no new content. At least Spendrup's has included links so you can get information on their products, which is more than you can say for Coors.

Flanders & Willis's Reality Check

When indexing a page, some search engines will use only the first *x* number of words or characters. This means you should put your keywords and description as close to the top of the page as you can.

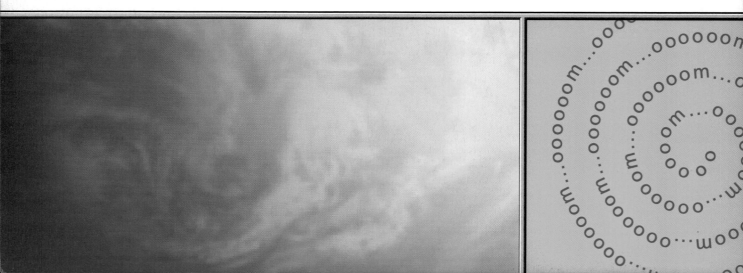

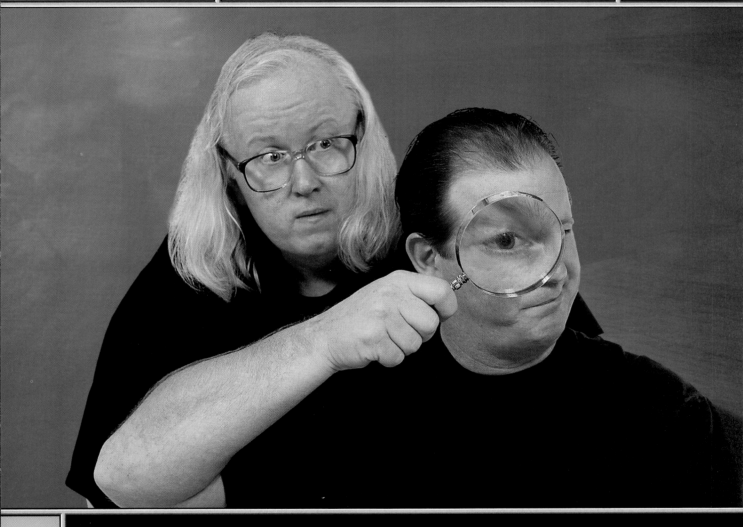

Search Engines and Directories

All search engines and directories are created equal. Some are just more equal than others.

—Vincent Flanders, with apologies to George Orwell

In this chapter, we're going to look at directories and search engines and the right and wrong ways to get your site listed. Registering a site with search engines and directories is one of the most important steps in a Web-marketing campaign. It's also the most cost-effective advertising mechanism out there. However, the process of registering a site can also lead you on a merry chase where you end up wasting a lot of time that could have been better spent adding content to your site.

If you think about it, the Internet is the world's largest highway with no marked exits. Once you're on this highway, you really don't have a clue where you are or where you're going—you're just driving. Directories are great road maps to your destination, but search engines will help you find a place worth visiting.

WHAT'S A DIRECTORY?

A *directory* is a listing of sites grouped into categories. Generally, a directory "knows" a site exists because the directory has provided a mechanism for people to register their sites.

Yahoo!—which is best described as a *searchable directory*, although it's turning itself into a universal home page—has employees who go out and examine submitted sites before they can be listed with Yahoo!. It isn't easy getting listed. I know of a software company that has been trying to get one of their products listed for the past two years but can't because their site doesn't fit in any of Yahoo!'s categories. You need to make sure your site fits in a category that exists on Yahoo!.

You want to be listed on Yahoo!—an entire section has been devoted to it later in the chapter.

FIGURE 10.1 **Magellan lists sites by "acceptability."**
(`http://www.mckinley.com/`)

Speaking of fitting, your URL also needs to fit "accepted standards." The Magellan directory, shown in Figure 10.1, is proof of this fact. I've submitted the URL to WebPagesThatSuck.com (`www.webpagesthatsuck.com`) on several occasions, and it has yet to be listed. I can't prove why it hasn't been listed, but I have a pretty good theory. It's the word *suck* in my URL. I suspect Magellan has a filter that automatically excludes sites with certain words in the URL. Why would they do

this? Well, one reason is Magellan lists sites by "acceptability"; they give red and green lights to sites based on their content, and obviously any site with the word *suck* in the URL *has* to be pornographic.

WHAT'S A SEARCH ENGINE?

A *search engine* uses a software program known as a *spider* that goes out and searches for prey—it feeds on URLs—and when it finds what it's looking for, it indexes page(s) based on its own proprietary and secretive criteria. After your pages are indexed, they can then be searched using keywords. When a person conducts a search, they submit keyword(s) to the search engine, and the search engine looks in its database for matches. When it finds matches, it displays the title of the page and a description or the first *x*-number of words in the site.

Each search engine has its own unique way of rating the importance of URLs. You obviously want your pages to be among the first listed. Different figures have been tossed about, but the general consensus is most people don't look at more than the first 20–40 listed links or the first couple of pages of listed sites. Many people spend a great deal of time trying to figure out how to make the search engines and directories list their site high on a query result list. Later, we'll talk about some good and bad techniques for improving the ranking of your site.

WHERE SHOULD I REGISTER MY SITE?

This is a very good question because there are hundreds of places where you can list your site. This is also a controversial question because the two opposing schools of thought argue rather loudly about the righteousness of their position. One school of thought says, "Register it any place they'll let you register your site." The other school of thought, to which I belong, says, "Register your site with the most important search engines and directories. Later, you can register your site elsewhere."

My reasoning is simple. You've got a limited amount of time; there are too many places to register; and most of the directories and search engines just aren't that important. Sorry guys, but it's true. Register your site with the important search engines and directories first.

On the CD-ROM, Michael and I have created a frames-based HTML document that is worth it's weight in gold! It is shown in Figure 10.2. Notice that we've created links to the important and slightly less important search engines and directories. All you have to do is click the link and fill out the information at the site. The document breaks up the different search engines and directories into two categories:

1. Important Sites

2. The Rest

Let's conduct a search of the pros and cons of several search engines and directories and see what we come up with, shall we?

Which Search Engines and Directories Are Important?

Okay, what determines whether a search engine or directory is important?

Ranking on `http://www.100hot.com`. This site lists the 100 most popular sites on the Internet in a number of different categories. Here's the list from their search engines and

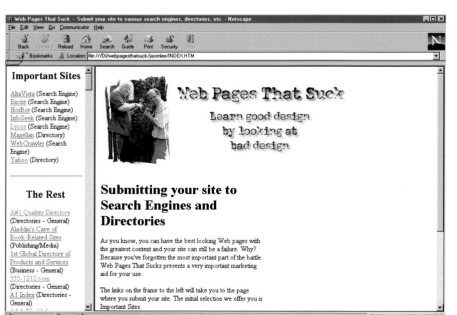

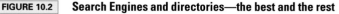

FIGURE 10.2   **Search Engines and directories—the best and the rest**

directories category when I went to the site:

Ranking	Directory/Search Engine
2	Yahoo!
3	Excite, Magellan
6	AltaVista
15	Lycos
20	HotBot
38	Infoseek

Netscape was ranked number one.

Ranking on ViaWEB A company called ViaWEB (`http://www.viaweb.com`) has a product called Live Store, which is a high-end software package with sophisticated tracking facilities. Using this software, companies, such as Rolling Stone, Virgin Interactive, and Frederick's of Hollywood, can see how much money online shoppers have spent and which search engine they came from. The amount of money spent varied by as much as a factor of three. (Table 10.1 gives an overview of some of the results; you can find the research at `http://www.viaweb.com/vw/search.html`.)

The study indicates that Yahoo! generates more sales per visitor than the other sites. More sales means it's more important to you, the Web site owner.

Final Ranking Based on their position in ViaWEB and the Hot100, these are the "Big Eight" search engines and directories, in order of importance:

Ranking	Directory/Search Engine	
1	Yahoo!	(Directory)
2	AltaVista	(Search Engine)
3	Excite	(Search Engine)
4	Magellan	(Directory)
5	Lycos	(Directory)
6	HotBot	(Search Engine)
7	Infoseek	(Directory)
8	WebCrawler	(Search Engine)

These are the search engines and directories where you need to be listed. The others, at best, are second tier—the equivalent of a AAA team in the minor leagues. (Because Yahoo! uses AltaVista, I moved AltaVista up higher in the listing.)

Source	Visitors	Sales	Sales/Visitor
Yahoo!	170,522	$ 53,553	$ .31
AltaVista	164,369	37,067	.23
Lycos	24,895	5,302	.21
HotBot	16,917	2,513	.15
Excite	226,321	26,478	.12
Infoseek	217,448	26,170	.12
WebCrawler	179,551	17,943	.10
Total	1,000,023	$169,026	$ .17

TABLE 10.1 **The Amount of Money Spent by Search Engine**

Inktomi—a company that makes a search engine used by HotBot—has recently signed a deal with Microsoft for the use of their search engine.

Obviously, this will have an effect on future final listings because neither Inktomi nor Microsoft are listed. It's also worth noting that Yahoo! signed a deal with Microsoft that makes them "the exclusive third-party provider of global directory services on the MSN Premier subscription service and on MSN.com, the online service's free Web site." What this all means is the final ranking shown on the previous page is not so final and, like the Internet, is subject to change at less than a moment's notice.

Listing on Netscape's Search Page   Netscape is one of the most visited sites on the Internet. If you've used Netscape, you probably know about the Search button on their toolbar, which, when pressed, brings up the screen shown in Figure 10.3.

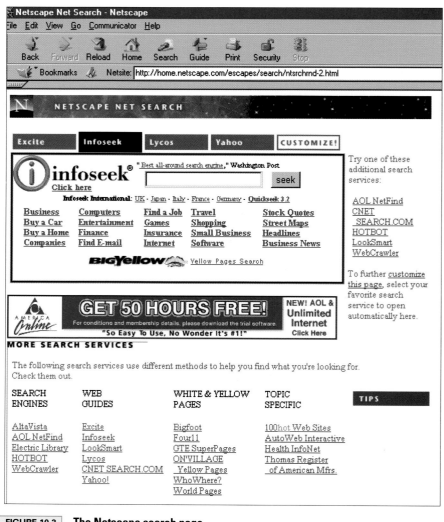

 FIGURE 10.3   **The Netscape search page**

Any site listed in Figure 10.3 is important; however, there are some things you need to take into account:

AOL NetFind is powered by the Excite search engine.

Electric Library is a subscription service that searches different magazines and newspapers in its database.

CNET's SEARCH.COM uses Infoseek.

LookSmart uses AltaVista.

Yahoo! also uses AltaVista in addition to its own directory. When you search on Yahoo! and your topic isn't listed in any of its categories or sites, it goes to AltaVista and sees if it can find anything there.

All the rankings you've seen so far in this section have put Yahoo! at the top of their list. Since Yahoo! is so important, let's continue our search there.

Yahoo!

Yahoo! is in a league by itself. Yahoo! is godlike. To me, it is the first, the best, the most important directory and search engine. Not to mention that without Yahoo!, WebPagesThatSuck.com would have been a bad gas smell in the wind of history. Yahoo! picked WebPagesThatSuck.com as one of their Cool Sites of the Week. With the kind of traffic Yahoo! generates, it was just a matter of time before the site became a cause celebre. Without Yahoo!, this book wouldn't exist. Need I say more?

Unlike AltaVista, who will accept any and every submission, Yahoo! uses real people to check out each submission. This way, a staff member can look at the site and see if it's correctly categorized and worth being listed. There's nothing more important than showing the people at Yahoo! that your site has substance.

Yahoo! differs from most other directories in that you have to place your site in the exact category by starting at the bottom of the pyramid and working your way up. Here's a better explanation: If you're a business site, you would start the listing process by choosing the "Business and Economy" category from Yahoo!'s home page, as shown in Figure 10.4, and then choosing

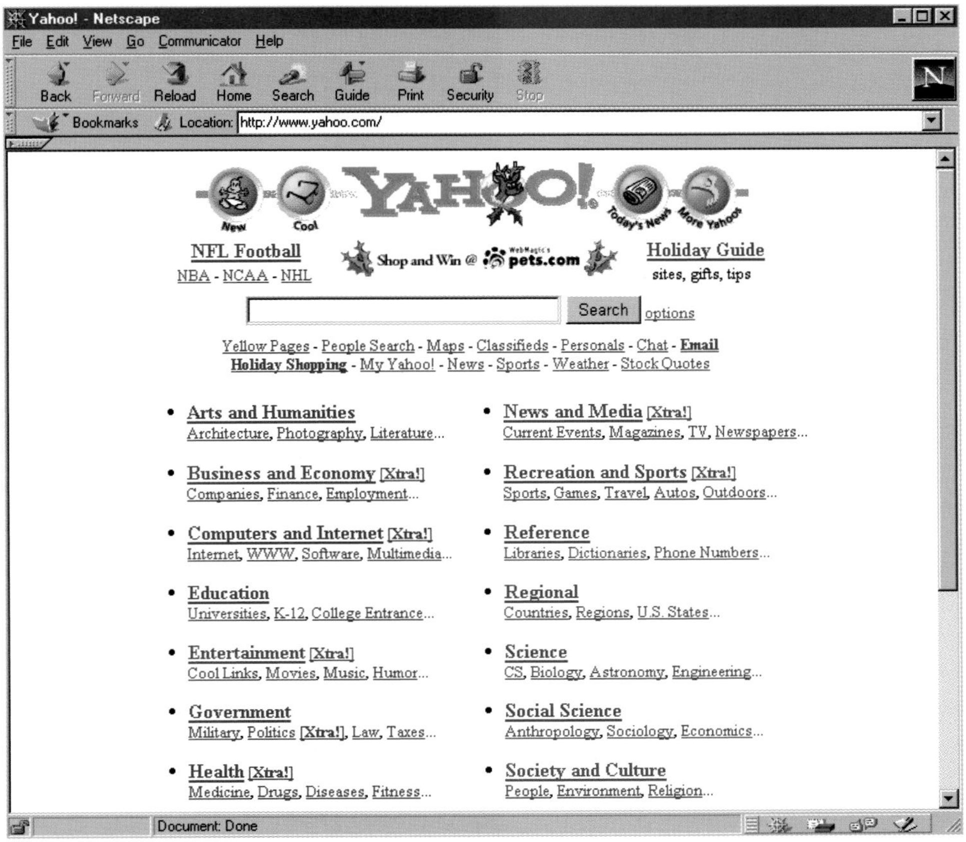

FIGURE 10.4 **Start the listing process from Yahoo!'s home page.**
(http://www.yahoo.com)

Add URL

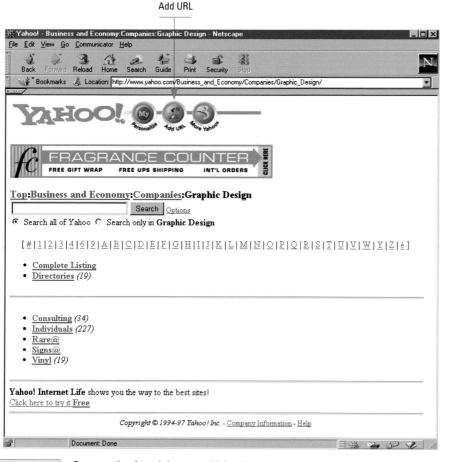

FIGURE 10.5 **Once you've found the exact Yahoo! category where you want to list your site, click the Add URL button.**

up under a *normal query*—that means any query other than the name of your company. Let's use my favorite nontopic *vitamins* as an example.

Under what Yahoo! category should a vitamin product be listed for the best effect? The way to find out is to perform some research by searching for the word *"vitamins"* and seeing what Yahoo! comes up with. You want to list your site in the first or second category that Yahoo! finds. Try it out:

1. Go to the Yahoo! home page (`http://www.yahoo.com`).

2. In the search box, type **"vitamins"**.

3. Press the Enter key. Figure 10.6 shows the results.

one of the topics from the "Business and Economy" category page. Generally, you would choose "Companies," and then you would have to break it down further. For Willis Design, Michael's site, you'd choose "Graphic Design" and—now that you have the exact category—you'd click the Add URL button at the top of the category's page, as shown at the top of Figure 10.5.

Yahoo! wants you to do the categorizing work for them—and you should do it yourself because you don't want a third-party to do this important task for you; however, it is still difficult to have your site pop

Obviously, you would want to list your site under "Business and Economy: Companies: Health: Nutrition: Supplements: Vitamins" because it's the first listing at the top. But if you look down at "Yahoo! Site Matches," you'll see there are three companies listed: Vitamins Network, Health-Smart Vitamins, and Spectrum California Vitamins. How did they get listed? That's easy. Out of the 25 companies listed under the main heading, only these three had the word *vitamins* (plural) in the *title*. I'll let you in on a little secret: the title of your site is very important to many, if not most, search engines and directories.

For example, say you have a mail-order concern where you sell herbs and vitamins, and it's called

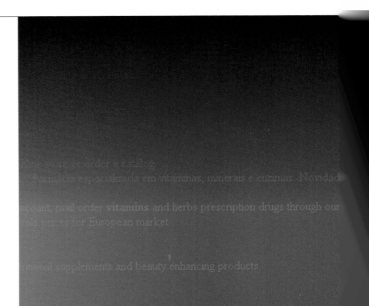

Found **2** Category and **354** Site Matches for **vitamins**.

Yahoo! Category Matches   (1 - 2 of 2)

Business and Economy: Companies: Health: Nutrition: Supplements: **Vitamins**

Business and Economy: Products and Services: Business Opportunities: Multi-Level Marketing: Health: Vitamist Spray **Vitamins**

Yahoo! Site Matches   (1 - 18 of 354)

Business and Economy: Companies: Health: Nutrition: Supplements: **Vitamins**

- **Vitamins** Network - chat rooms, forums, library and stores relating to **vitamins**.
- HealthSmart **Vitamins**
- Spectrum California **Vitamins**

Business and Economy: Companies: Health: Nutrition: Supplements

- Pride **Vitamins** - Take pride in your health. Shop our online store or order a catalog.
- **Vitamins** & Minerals - produtos importados e nacionais. Farmácia especializada em vitaminas, minerais e enzimas. Novidades sobre rejuvenescimento. Melatonina e radicais livres.
- Personal Support **Vitamins** & Health Foods - offers discount, mail order **vitamins** and herbs prescription drugs through our partner PrideMed.
- Atlantis **Vitamins** and Supplements - mail order, wholesale prices for European market.
- Vitamist Spray **Vitamins**
- Cooks Discount **vitamins** and Herbs
- Good Earth **Vitamins** and Health Store - all-natural nutritional supplements and beauty enhancing products.

Health: Nutrition

- **Vitamins** Network UK

Health: Nutrition: Austin Nutritional Research Guides

FIGURE 10.6   **Yahoo!'s search results for the word *vitamins***

Vincent Flanders' Herbal Remedies (it better not be unless your name is *really* Vincent Flanders). If you want to list your site under "Vitamins," it might be a good idea to change the name of your company to Vincent Flanders' Herbal Remedies and Vitamins. We'll talk more about the importance of titles later in the chapter.

There have been rumors about delays in getting sites listed at Yahoo!, but quite frankly, they are under no obligation to list your site. Give serious thought to how you will get your site listed with Yahoo!; it's critical to your success. Really.

TOO COOL

SOURCES FOR PROMOTING YOUR SITE TO PROMOTE YOURSELF

A couple of cottage industries have sprung up around preparing and submitting pages to the search engines and directories:

1. *Site submission.* Companies will sell their services or software to get your site listed by up to 500+ sites.

2. *Site ranking improvement.* Companies will sell you papers or services that will show how to improve your ranking by the search engines and directories.

While you can pay for this information, a lot of these sites (especially the ones that sell submission software) have posted suggestions on their Web pages. These sites realize this information is the kind of content people want to see, and when these sites get lots of hits, they can induce companies to advertise on their pages. That's one way they make their money. The software sites, of course, want to sell you software.

The Yahoo! page shown here is considered part of this chapter for the simple reason that it lists sites that deal with announcing and promoting a site.

You can find this page on the Web at `http://www.Yahoo.com/Computers_and _Internet/Internet/World_Wide_Web /Information_and_Documentation/ Site_Announcement_and_Promotion/`.

These sites should be up to date with the latest information about the whole promotion process. This is an extremely important link. Go there and start surfing.

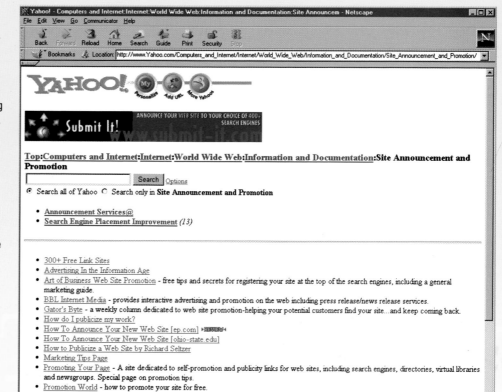

Visit links on this page to learn more about announcing and promoting your site.

What about the Other Search Engines and Directories?

By basically ignoring the 700+ other sites on the Internet, I know I'm going to alienate every company selling information or listing services and what not, but let's face some serious reality here. It's like the wireless telephone marketplace. If you have access to 100 cities (or whatever the real number is—but it's a small number), you'll have a market penetration of 80 percent. Yes, there's still that 20 percent out there, but it's not worth the cost or effort you'll have to make to achieve 100 percent penetration.

PRELIMINARIES TO SUBMITTING YOUR SITE

Even with great content you still have to play the search engine/directory game. How do you get listed? What are the tricks? Which sites are important? I'm going to discuss these issues in detail, but I want to warn you that the rules of the search engine/directory game are constantly changing because the search engines and directories are changing—they're getting smarter. You used to be able to fool them by putting hidden text in your pages. It doesn't work with some of the engines. Today's tricks become tomorrow's jokes.

As you might expect, Yahoo! has a whole category devoted to improving your search engine ranking. Keep this URL in a safe place, and don't share it with anyone—*it's extremely important:* `http://www.Yahoo .com/Computers_and_Internet/Internet/World_ Wide_Web/Information_and_Documentation/Site_ Announcement_and_Promotion/Search_Engine_ Placement_Improvement/`.

Your first stop should be this link; however, I want to point out a few useful links that deal with search engine secrets. Definitely check these out.

Search Engine Secrets `http://www .globalserve.net/~iwb/search/index.html`

Search Engine Placement Pointers `http://www.infoscavenger.com/engine.htm`

Web Ranking Tools `http://www .bruce clay.com/web_rank.htm`

Before you start submitting your site, there are a few things to consider that will save you time in the long run. Don't waste your time trying to trick the search engines; they figure the scams out eventually. Also, don't spend all your time trying to improve your listings in the search engines and directories unless you're a site with little or no content. The rule of thumb is that the amount of time you spend playing the "search engine game" is inversely proportional to the quality of your site.

This doesn't mean that you don't spend any time improving your position. Even the big boys need to play the game, but you only have so much time—spend it wisely.

With that said, let's get on with the process of submitting your site.

THE FOUR STEPS TO PREPARING YOUR SITE FOR SUBMISSION

The four steps involved in preparing your pages for submission to the search engines and directories follow:

1. Create 10 keywords and a sentence that describe your business or site.

2. Use the keywords and description in the `<META>` tags.

3. Use the keywords and description at the beginning of your page(s).

4. Choose the title for your page very carefully.

1. Create 10 Keywords and a Sentence That Describe Your Business or Site

Don't gloss over this step! You *must* spend time deciding what words you're going to use as keywords. When you submit your site to the different search engines and directories, you'll discover that many of them want you to use keywords to help define your site for search queries.

There are several reasons for spending time on this step. When people query a search engine or directory trying to find information about a topic, they have to use keywords—hopefully the same words you chose to describe your site. Keywords also help the various search engines index your site. The HTML tag called `<META>` has several parameters, but two of the more important parameters allow you to define keywords and to create a description so search engines can better index your site. Creating a list of keywords and writing the descriptive sentence will also help you focus on the purpose of your site.

Please note that a keyword is not just a single word—it can be multiple words—*web design* is a keyword just as *web* and *design* are keywords.

What Ten Keywords Best Describe Your Business or Site?

You're probably asking yourself, "Why is this important?" It's quite simple. When a person uses a search engine or directory to conduct a search, they type keywords into the search query that they think are related to the topic they want to find. If the keyword they type matches one of the keywords you submitted, your site *should* (and I want to emphasize the word *should*—or perhaps I should put it this way: there's a chance your site *might...*) pop up in the query results. There are other factors, of course, that determine whether your site will pop up, but keywords are the secret to many of the search engines and directories.

When I said 10 keywords, I was underexaggerating—a rarity for me. Focus on the 10 most important words. Then you should actually create a list of 20–30 keywords. The number of keywords that the search engines and directories will take varies; nevertheless, they're good to have in your back pocket just in case.

Rank Your 10 Keywords with the Most Important One First and the Least Important at the Number Ten Position Because most, if not all, search engines assume keywords at the beginning of the list are the most important, you should put the most important keywords at the beginning of your list.

Know How Many Keywords Each Search Engine Will Accept Like everything to do with search engines, this value changes. The links in Yahoo!'s site promotion category will have the up-to-date information. Check it out.

Which Keywords Should I Use? Well, you know your business better than I ever will. Put yourself in the shoes of someone trying to find your site. What words would that person use? If your competitor is on the Internet, try looking them up. What words did you use to find them? I suspect the same words you used to find a competitor would be the same words used to find your site. You can also ask customers (always make sure they're happy customers) which keywords they would use if they were looking for your site.

Although I don't know your specific business, I can offer some basic guidelines to follow:

> **Brand or trade names** If you own the company that makes Kleenex, use it.
>
> **Company name** One of the most common ways people try to find a company is to use its name.
>
> **Conceptual words** If you're a farmer, use *farming*.

At Herbal.com, the products for sale are herbal greeting cards and dream pillows. With that thought in mind, here are 15 possible keywords:

1. greeting cards

2. herbal greeting cards

3. herbal cards

4. dream pillows

5. herbal pillows

6. herb pillows

7. culinary herbs

8. medicinal herbs

9. herbal cooking

10. cooking herbs

11. herbal gifts

12. herb gifts

13. herbal

14. herb

15. herbs

What One Sentence Best Describes Your Site? For WebPagesThat-Suck.com, the sentence is "Learn good Web design by looking at bad Web design." When you read the sentence, you know what the site is all about. If you're in a business where many people do the same thing, it's a lot tougher. What can you say about vitamins that is catchy and gets the point across? I'm not here to help you figure out your marketing slogan; I'm here to get you to think about creating that one sentence.

Keyword Tips, Tricks, and Techniques Okay, now that you probably more than understand the importance of choosing the right keywords, I'm going to let you in on a few secrets.

1. Use keywords on each main page in your site.

If your site is organized in a top-down fashion, you'll have a home page (entry page) that contains links to the major sections of your site. Each major section will need its own keywords. For example, the main sections of Herbal.com are Greeting Cards, Cooking Herbs, Herbal Info, Medicinal Herbs, Dream Pillows, and Order Desk.

TOO COOL

YOUR KEYWORDS SHOULD SHOW UP IN YOUR ONE SENTENCE DESCRIPTION

"Herbal.com provides herbal greeting cards and dream pillows plus information about different types of herbs." While this one sentence description for Herbal.com seems fine, it would be more effective if I had used some of the important keywords. A new and improved description would be:

"Herbal greeting cards, dream pillows, and information about herbs and herbal topics can be found at Herbal.com."

The lesson: use your keywords throughout your document.

Create Multiple Descriptions

Some search engines will let you submit a 10 word description while others will let you go on forever. To play it safe, create different descriptions with the following word counts:

10	50
20	60
30	75
40	100

This way you won't be caught by surprise when you submit your site to the various search engines and directories.

You'll use a (slightly) different set of keywords for each page. Obviously, there will be a certain "core" set of keywords—for the purposes of this example, *herbs, herb,* and *herbal*—that will be used by all pages. However, you would obviously put *greeting cards* at the top of the keyword list on the Greeting Cards page; *dream pillows* at the top of the Dream Pillows page; and *cooking herbs, herbs and cooking,* and *culinary herbs* at the top of the Cooking Herbs page.

2. Keep your home page short and put keywords at the top of the text.

I'll spend some time discussing this in the section "Use the Keywords and Descriptions at the Beginning of Your Page(s)."

3. Use keywords in your <TITLE>.

This is insanely important. In fact, it's so important, I'll devote a whole section to this topic. See "Choose the Title for Your Page(s) Very Carefully."

4. Use lowercase for keywords.

Using lowercase for keywords is especially important when using <META> tags, but it's equally important in your document. Let's use the AltaVista search engine as an example. Here's a little sample of the difference a case makes:

guitar	164,088 hits
Guitar	59,193
GUITAR	7,184

Search engines like lowercase—well, at least you'll get more choices.

5. Don't forget plural (or singular) versions of your keywords.

Notice that the Herbal.com site uses singular and plural versions of keywords such as *herb* and *herbs.* If your site is about movies, you may have thought of using *film* but forgotten *films.*

6. Check the keywords your competition uses in the <META> tag of their main document.

We'll spend some time talking about the <META> tag in a moment, but, briefly, it's an HTML tag with two parameters that will help certain search engines index your site. The <META> tag is found between the <HEAD> and </HEAD> tags. Here's the <META> tag for a cool film site shown in Figure 10.7 and called, logically enough, Film.com:

```
<META> name="keyword" content="film,
movies, musicals, thrillers, movie
reviews, interviews, directors, actors,
actresses, openings, movie games, humor.">
```

Notice that they've used twelve keywords to describe their site and that it appears, at least to me, that the keywords are in descending order of importance with *film* being first and *humor* being last.

By viewing the source of your competitor's document, you can see what keywords they've used. (Viewing the source code is usually fairly simple. For example, in Navigator 3, select View > Document Source. If you have Netscape Communicator, select View > Page Source. Consult your browser's Help files for more information.)

7. Don't copy your competitor's keywords!

This is just research. For all you know, your competitor is a nitwit and chose words that don't work. Go to a search engine and use the keywords and see what happens. Does your competitor show up?

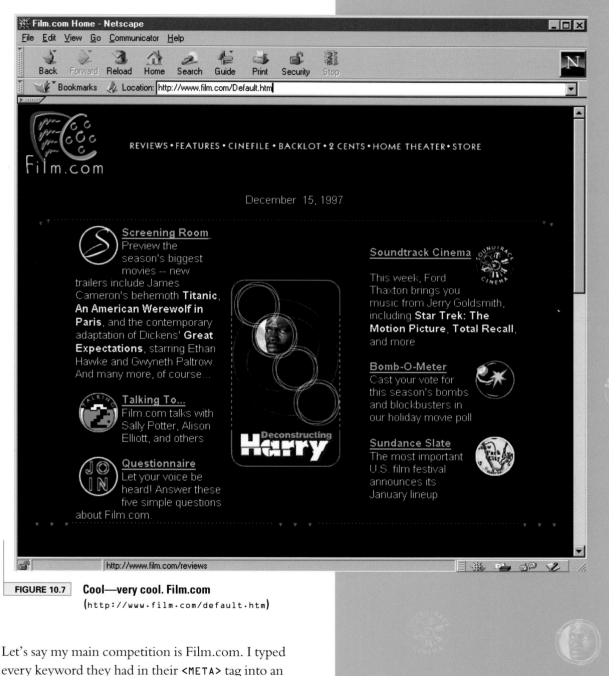

FIGURE 10.7 Cool—very cool. Film.com
(http://www.film.com/default.htm)

Let's say my main competition is Film.com. I typed every keyword they had in their `<META>` tag into an AltaVista query. There were 300,000 documents that matched my search criteria! Here's what I got from

OH NO

DON'T USE COMPETITORS' NAMES AS KEYWORDS IN YOUR `<META>` TAGS

Using your competitors' names as keywords is a popular and very sneaky technique. The reasoning is flawless: you put the name of a more famous company who happens to be your competitor or one of their products in the `<META>` tag keyword parameter. The `<META>` tag is invisible, but it is used by some search engines for indexing purposes. When an unsuspecting soul searches for the name of that company, one of the sites that might turn up would be your site. An unsuspecting person might click your link and you've stolen a customer away.

When the law firm of Oppedahl & Larson found out someone was using their name as a keyword, they sued on the grounds of unfair competition, dilution of trademark, and trademark infringement. At the time this story broke, there appeared to be legal sentiment in favor of Oppedahl & Larson—or so *WebWeek* reported in its August 25, 1997, issue. In a similar case, a court ruled that it was illegal to use the word *playboy* or *playmate* (as in *Playboy* magazine) as a keyword. You can find the complete article at `http://www .news.com/News/Item/ 0,4,14242,00.html`.

the first 10 documents out of about 300,000 matching the query, best matches first:

> **Word count** movie games: about 100; thrillers: 4,605; actresses: 20,860; movie reviews: about 30,000; musicals: 31,122; openings: 118,570; actors: 126,605; interviews: 286,329; humor: 310,643; directors: 534,565; movies: 790,940; film: 1,590,770

However, Film.com did not appear on the first page of my query response. In fact, it didn't show up in the first 10 pages (200 listings).

I then tried a little experiment. I went to several of the important search engines and directories and used Film.com's first four keywords (*film, movies, musicals, thriller*). Here's what I got:

Excite	Not listed on first page.
Lycos	Not listed on first page.
Yahoo!	Not listed on first page.
HotBot	Not listed on first page. As a matter of fact, HotBot had only 70 listings. Film.com didn't appear in any of them.
WebCrawler	Film.com site listed on the first page.
Infoseek	Film.com site listed on the first page.

Listed on two of seven first pages. Hmm. Doesn't seem very good, does it? Why am I so focused on the first page? Simple. *You want your Web site to be listed on the first page of a results query.* In fact, you'd love it to be the very first listing. Most people searching for information don't have time to go through 20 pages of links; they'll look at the first few listings, and if you're lucky, the complete first page before giving up.

8. Use filenames as keywords.

If possible, use a keyword as the name of a link. If you have a link to a page where you're going to talk about shampoo, call the page shampoo.htm. Don't call it shamp.htm or shampoo1.htm—it won't help you.

Keyword No-No's For some reason, people like to play games with keywords in an attempt to improve their ranking by the search engines. I imagine the majority of these people have no content and are desperately trying to get someone—anyone—to visit their site. Here are some keyword no-no's.

1. Don't stuff keywords.

In the dark ages of 1996, there existed a practice called *keyword stuffing* or *keyword spamming* that was thought to improve the odds of getting your pages listed. Some people suspected that search engines used a *relevancy factor* in ranking sites—the more times a keyword was used the more important it was. A page that used the word 50 times was listed higher than a page where the word was used once. Some Web page manglers...I mean..."designers" would put dozens of keywords at the bottom of the page and hide them by making the text match the background color.

Most of search engines are now wise to this trick and they don't like it. They won't like your page or your site and may not list it. However, it appears that, as of the writing of this book, AltaVista does not punish transgressors. I've seen some rules of thumb that say you shouldn't repeat your keyword more than five or six times on a page, but I can't prove this one way or the other.

2. Don't add irrelevant keywords.

Some jerks were loading their pages with words that had no relevance to their site. They were sticking in practically the whole dictionary and lots of crude words that weren't in the dictionary. I think it's safe to say that most of these sites didn't have any content worth visiting and should be sent to the depths of perdition. End of rant.

The search engines also caught on to this trick, and there are rumors that some engines will penalize you for the practice by not listing your site or by shoving you to the back of the listings.

There are a few problems that some Internet cretins just don't seem to understand.

1. Even if the addition of extraneous keywords gets you hits to your site, they're going to be from people who have no interest in the product you're promoting. They're going to be upset.

2. If you stuff your page with sexual keywords, you might get tons of extra hits, which that could cause your ISP's Web server to crash (anyone spamming like this probably doesn't care).

3. If you're using *sex* or other such terms as keywords, the audience you're attracting are hormonally challenged teenage boys who are not only *not* interested in what you have to sell, but also probably do not have any money to spend.

3. Don't use common words as keywords.

When you go to the AltaVista site, shown in Figure 10.8, and enter the query **web**, Figure 10.9 shows what you'll get.

AltaVista found almost 12 million sites with this keyword; they didn't return any documents because that's too many documents to retrieve. Because this

TOO COOL

COMPLAIN ABOUT YOUR EVIL COMPETITOR

If, for some reason, your competitor has used keyword stuffing or has added irrelevant words to their site and is listed fairly high on a query result, complain to the company running the search engine.

Search engine companies hate it when someone tries to take advantage of them. They may even remove the site from their listing—even though the search engine actually ignored the stuffing! Isn't it great? Your competitor tries to finesse the search engine, it doesn't work (although they still got listed high), and then they get kicked off! Is the Internet great or what?

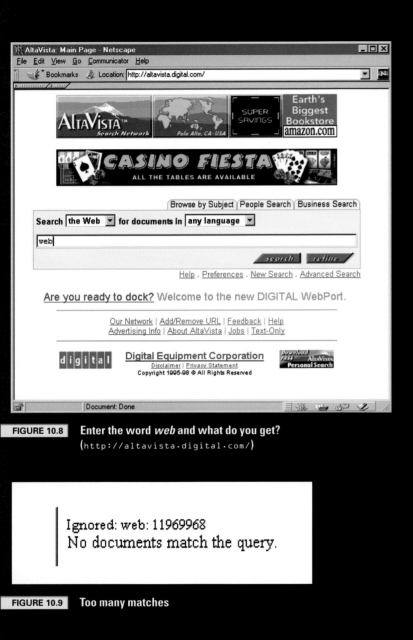

FIGURE 10.8 Enter the word *web* and what do you get?
(http://altavista.digital.com/)

Ignored: web: 11969968
No documents match the query.

FIGURE 10.9 Too many matches

excludes many single words, try using multiple words as keywords. While the word *web* had nearly 12 million hits, the phrase *web page* had "only" 1 million hits. Imagine how difficult it is to be listed on the front page.

Even if you change your keyword phrase to *web page design,* you'll still get 1 million hits. Interestingly, the phrase *web page designer* has only 2,000 hits. Hmm... Before you put together your keyword list, go to AltaVista and see how many documents contain these words. However, you should also consider that AltaVista is one of the search engines that indexes everything. Other search engines don't, so just because AltaVista returns 1 million documents does not mean that another engine will.

4. Don't use JavaScript.

We talked about JavaScript in Chapter 7, "It's Not Called the Bleeding Edge for Nothing," where you learned that, with few exceptions, JavaScript shouldn't be used. There's another problem with using JavaScript on your pages—the code has to be placed at the top of the page and it eats into your word count. Some search engines will index the first 200 words or 1,024 characters or some fairly small arbitrary number, which means the JavaScript will be indexed before the keywords you placed at the top of your page. Some sites suggest that if you're using JavaScript you need to use

TOO COOL

INeverMETAMan's opening screen

META MANAGER AND INEVERMETAMAN

When most people create Web pages, they generally don't put <META> tags in their documents. When Vincent became a Webmaster back in 1995, he hadn't even heard of the tag. By the time its importance was general knowledge, he had over 200 documents without tags. Imagine how he felt about inserting <META> tags in those 200+ documents.

Well, Opposite Software (`http://www.opposite.com/`) has a solution for Windows-based machines. It's called HTML Meta Manager and is part of

Opposite Software's HTML Power Tools collection. The beauty of this product is it will go through all your files and insert <META> tags for the description and keywords. It also lets you change the name of the document's <TITLE>. It's a great product, but it doesn't include some of the other useful parameters, such as:

Author's name

Company name

Date page posted

How to deal with search engine robots

Whether to flush the cache

Refresh to a new URL

To solve this deficiency, Geoff McAvoy and Vincent created INeverMETAMan. (The title is based on Will Rodgers' famous line, "I never met a man I didn't like.") Here's the opening screen.

Geoff, one of those darn wonder boys we can't stand—you know, young, good looking, talented—wrote this program in Visual Basic for Windows 95/NT systems. Besides giving you the opportunity to add keywords and a description, it also lets you fill in the parameters missing in HTML Power Tools.

OH NO

SOME INTERNET SCUM WITH NO CONTENT HAVE SCREWED UP THE `<META>` TAGS

It's obvious that `<META>` tags serve an important indexing function. But like everything good, some Internet scum are screwing it up for the rest of us. Here's a `<META>` tag description that shows you what I mean:

"We provide help for women suffering spousal abuse and who need to solve their problems quickly."

Gee. If a woman were in trouble, this might be the kind of place she might want to contact. The problem is when someone clicks the link it takes them to a gun store. Now, I'm not saying a gun isn't the right solution—it just might not be the solution the person originally had in mind. And in our litigious society, it wouldn't surprise me to see the woman sue the gun store.

If I remember correctly, one of the search engines mentioned this case as the reason they don't use `<META>` tags when indexing a site. Thank you very much, Internet scum.

`<META>` tags—but Excite doesn't recognize `<META>` tags and it's rumored both Lycos and WebCrawler also stopped recognizing them. The result? Picture a Southern sheriff. Imagine him saying, "Ya'll in a heap of trouble, boy."

5. Don't frame me in.

Some search engines ignore pages with frames because they don't know how to follow the links. If you have to use frames on pages you want indexed, then make sure you include some text material in the `<NOFRAMES>` part of the page. Include a couple of paragraphs that describe your site using all your keywords and your sentence, along with links to any of your pages that don't have frames. This will help the search engines find the material you want them to find.

2. Use the Keywords and Description in the `<META>` Tags

Hey, that's one of the reasons I had you create a list of keywords—the `<META>` tag is one of the main places to put your keywords. Several search engines use them to help index your site.

The best description about how the `<META>` tag works is provided by the AltaVista search engine. You can find the reference at `http://altavista.digital.com/av/content/addurl_meta.htm.`

Normally, when a search engine is queried, it will spew out the first two lines inside the document. With AltaVista and other engines that support the `<META>` tag, the contents of the description portion of the `<META>` tag are displayed. For example, the `<META>` tag for the Herbal.com page is:

```
<META>  name="description" content="Herbal greeting
cards, dream pillows, and information about herbs and
herbal topics can be found at herbal.com.">
```

Using this `<META>` tag, the search result would be:

```
Herbal.com
Herbal greeting cards, dream pillows, and information
about herbs and herbal topics can be found at
herbal.com. http://www.herbal.com/ - size 8k - 29 Aug 97
```

3. Use the Keywords and Description at the Beginning of Your Page(s)

When indexing a page, some search engines will use only the first *x* number of words or characters. This means you should put your keywords and description as close to the top of the page as you can.

Let's take a look at the Herbal.com's home page, shown in Figure 10.10.

Although the opening text gives us that nice folksy, herbal feeling, not many keywords are mentioned in the body of the text. Let's see, the only keywords mentioned are *herb* and *dream pillows*. The links will show up, but most of the logical herbal keywords are not there. Looks like I've got some rewriting to do, especially because some search engines, such as Excite, only grab words listed in the body of the page. You can see why it's important to make sure the keywords and key concepts are included in the body of the page for your search engine to find.

As I mentioned earlier, you don't want to keep using the same keywords over and over—just make sure you've got a few in the text and in the `<META>` tags. Then you should be covered.

When search engines compile information— either from your text and/or from the `<META>` tag—the amount of information they compile varies. Infoseek, for example, will grab 200 words.

Figure 10.11 shows the final version of the Herbal.com page. The text in red is the new material that was added. Notice the emphasis on keywords.

The `<META>` tag, however, isn't the only place where you can insert keywords; you can also put them in your ALT arguments.

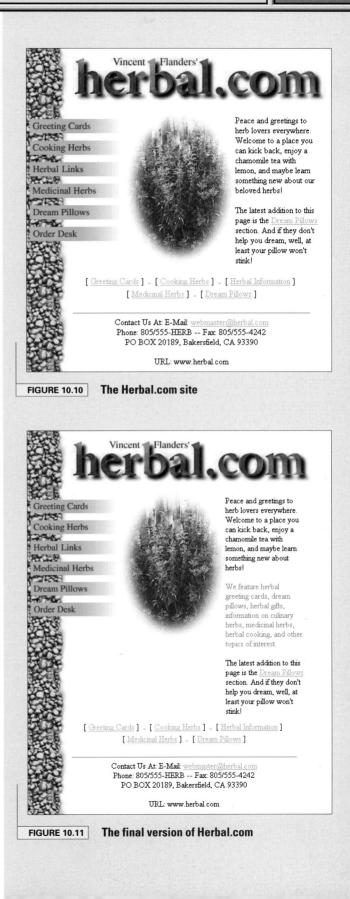

FIGURE 10.10 **The Herbal.com site**

FIGURE 10.11 **The final version of Herbal.com**

Put Keywords in Your ALT Arguments Not only do the keywords in your ALT arguments help those people who are visiting your site with the images turned off know what links to click, but they also give you an additional opportunity to get your keywords inserted in the search engine. (We talked about ALT arguments in Chapter 4.) Infoseek publicly claims it uses text in ALT arguments when indexing a site. I'm sure others do, too. Figure 10.12 shows the Herbal Links button.

Herbal Links

FIGURE 10.12   **The Herbal Links button**

The composition of the tag is as follows:

```
<IMG WIDTH=180 HEIGHT=27 BORDER=0
vspace=7 ALT="Herbal Links"
SRC="butinfo2.gif">
```

The ALT argument is totally wasted. When someone moves their mouse over the image, they'll see the phrase *Herbal Links*. That doesn't tell them squat.

The ALT parameter needs to be changed to read:

```
ALT="Herbal Links by herbal.com
your source for greeting cards,
herbal greeting cards, and info
on herbs, herb growing, culinary
herbs and the herb world"
```

To avoid repeating your keywords over and over (remember: you might get penalized by the search engines for trying to stuff keywords), divide them among the different images.

4. Choose the Title for Your Page(s) Very Carefully

Depending on the search engine, the title you choose can significantly affect your site's ranking.

Yeah, I know. I sound like the guy on TV who says, "Eating XXX cereal has been shown under some circumstances to reduce the likelihood you might suffer and die from a bad disease." Like everything else concerning search engines and directories, "it depends" and everything "is subject to change without notice." *Caveat emptor*—there's no caviar for the emperor.

For example, AltaVista takes the title of your page very, very seriously. I used two different search criteria:

1. A two-word search—*web graphics*

2. A single-word search—*herbs*

Every site listed on the first page of the results query had those words listed in the title.

Also, the closer the words are to the front of the title, the better the ranking; the title "Web Graphics for the Professional" would be listed higher than the title "We Are an Auto Body Repair Shop and We Also Create Web Graphics."

On the other hand, Excite, shown in Figure 10.13, could care less about your title—if you are conducting a two-word search. Only one of the ten titles listed had *web graphics* in the title. When I took *web* and *graphics* individually, the total went up to five out of ten. Not very convincing. What really seems to count with Excite is the number of times the word appears on the page.

Let's see what a single-word search using the word *herb*s found: four out of ten titles listed had this word in the title—significantly better than *web graphics*

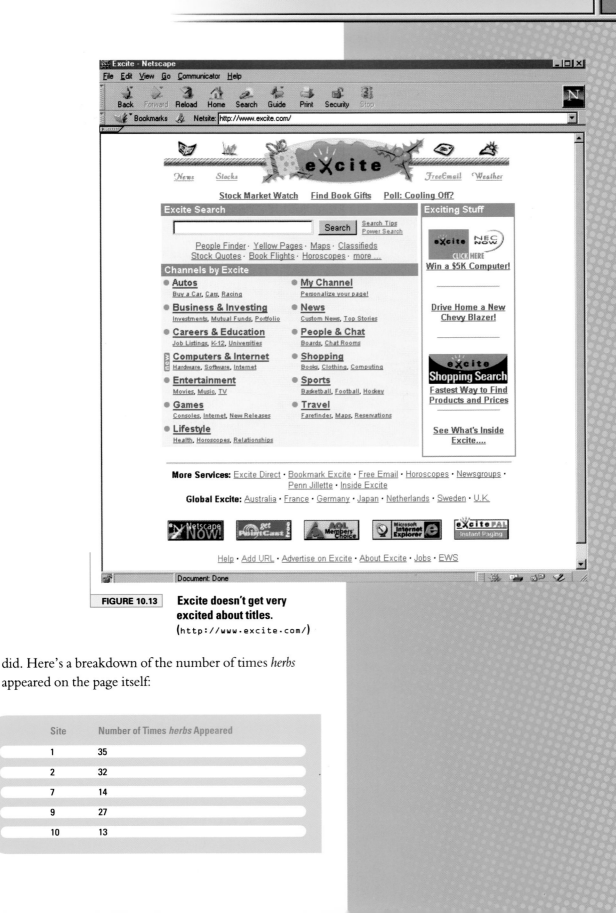

FIGURE 10.13 **Excite doesn't get very excited about titles.**
(http://www.excite.com/)

did. Here's a breakdown of the number of times *herbs* appeared on the page itself:

Site	Number of Times *herbs* Appeared
1	35
2	32
7	14
9	27
10	13

Site 9 is just another page from Site 1. Obviously, Excite doesn't seem to punish people for repeating words. You should note, however, that the words were not stuffed one after the other, but interspersed throughout the page.

Table 10.2 shows the results of a two-word and one-word search using different search engines.

Search Engine	Two-Word Search: Number of Times Words Appeared in Title	One-Word Search: Number of Times Word Appeared in Title
AltaVista	10/10 or 100 percent	10/10 or 100 percent
WebCrawler	7/25 or 28 percent	10/25 or 40 percent
Excite	1/10 or 10 percent	5/10 or 50 percent
Infoseek	4/10 or 40 percent	3/10 or 30 percent
Yahoo!	20/20 or 100 percent	20/20 or 100 percent
HotBot	0/25 or 0 percent	22/25 or 88 percent

TABLE 10.2   **How Do the Search Engines Compare?**

When it comes to searching, HotBot seems to be quite schizophrenic. It scored zippo on a two-word search, but a quite respectable 88 percent on a one-word search. At this time, it would appear the HotBot engine needs some fine-tuning.

Which search engine is best? Obviously, the search engine that's best is the one that lists your site highest. On the other hand, *PC Computing* magazine held a contest to see which search engine was better at finding information. According to a press release issued by the magazine on May 9, 1997, HotBot, shown in Figure 10.14, was the winner (check out the whole press release at `http://www4.zdnet.com/pccomp/searchpr.html`).

Speaking of search engines, I'm always amazed at what people will try to sell. The Cobb Group has created a newsletter called "Power Searching with AltaVista" and is selling a 12-issue subscription for $59 ($49 for the e-mail version). Who says you can't make money off the Internet?

SUBMITTING YOUR SITE

You've got your page primed with keywords; you've got your <META> tags in shape; you've applied to your page every tip, trick, and technique mentioned in this chapter—now you're ready to actually submit your site to the various search engines and directories. The question is: Do you want to submit your site yourself or do you want someone else to do it for you? Actually, there's another alternative. You can sit and wait and hope one of the search engines finds your site, but the chance of that happening is close to nil. You need to get off your…and do something.

Here are the pros and cons of having someone else submit your site.

First, the pro:

> **Pro** You're not doing it. You think you'll be able to spend your time on other productive activities, but see **Con 1**.

And then the cons:

> **Con 1** You're actually going to end up doing most of the work yourself. Do you think for one minute that another company is going to know what keywords are important to *your* business? They're going to have to ask *you* for the keywords. Since they have to ask you for all the information, you might as well do it yourself.

> **Con 2** Whoever submits your site wants to get paid for their effort. That's how it works under the capitalist system.

> **Con 3** It's been my experience that search engines and directories want the site owner to

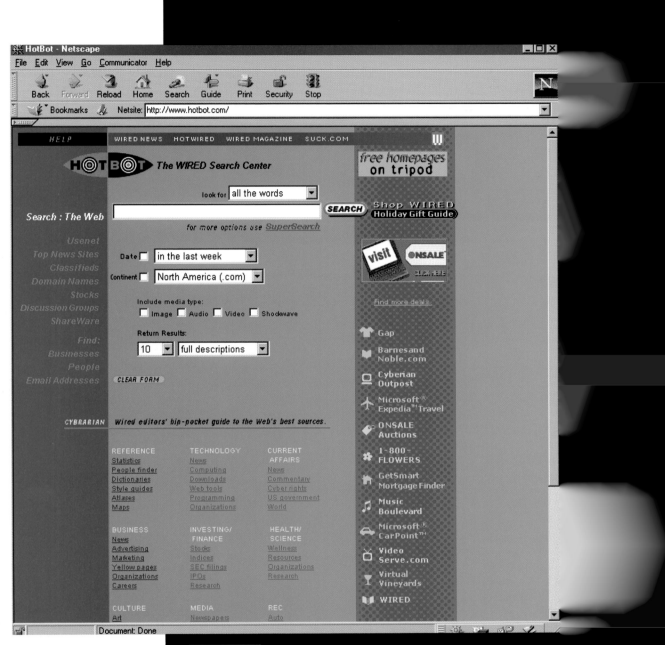

HotBot won *PC Computing*'s contest to see which search engine was better at finding information. Hmm...

(http://www.hotbot.com/)

**DON'T SUBMIT BEFORE
YOUR SITE IS READY**

It's like going to the prom without your jacket. Yeah, you can do it, but the results won't be what you were hoping for. If the spiders go to your site and don't find a main page, they may not come back for a long, long time. Don't antagonize anyone.

**DON'T DUPLICATE PAGES
AND SUBMIT DIFFERENT URLS**

At least one search engine checks for this tacky technique (Infoseek), and I trust the others are equally aware. The goal of this technique is to submit the same page multiple times thereby boosting the relevance scores and, hopefully, getting pages listed more frequently or higher in any search query. Don't do it. Spend your time adding content; don't spend it trying to be tricky.

actually submit the site. It's like me asking Sharon Stone's manager if Sharon wants to go out with me. It would be better if I asked directly.

Now let's examine the pro and con of doing it yourself.

First the pro:

> **Pro** Nobody knows your site better than you do. Nobody cares about your site like you do. Nobody else will put in the time needed to do it right.

And then the con:

> **Con** Man, oh, man. It's a lot of work.

Submission Software

No, it isn't some sort of S&M software, if that's what you're thinking. There's a lot of software on the market (much of it shareware) that will help you automate the process of submitting your site to the various search engines and directories.

Neither Michael nor I have tried any of these packages (I bought one, but haven't used it yet). I think the concept of using a software package as a one-stop way to submit your site is great—but so are the concepts of eating right and exercising. Hmm... The nicest part about some of these packages is they offer updates on a fairly frequent basis.

If you're looking for a list of promotion software, Dave Central Software Archive has a list of Windows products (sorry Mac folks) at `http://www`
`.davecentral.com/webpro.html`.

FOLLOW-UP

Just when you think you're done, you're not. Just because you submit a site to a search engine or directory doesn't mean they're going to list it. You may have submitted the site incorrectly. Some typical boo-boos include:

Typos in the URL (*very* common).

Your host server was down when the search engine visited (another reason it's important to have a good web-hosting service).

You submitted it too many times.

Violation of standard accepted practices (for example, keyword stuffing).

Some—maybe all—of the services want the full URL and you left off the http:// part of your URL.

Keep track of whether you're listed with the search engines and directories. To make sure you actually get listed, you'll need to perform the following steps:

1. Keep a log of each place you submit your site and the date you submit the site. Use the log shown in Table 10.3 as a guide. You also need to list when you checked the site and what its ranking was.

2. Check to see if your site is listed. If it isn't, resubmit.

Site	Date Submitted	Date Checked/ Ranking	Date Checked/ Ranking	Date Checked Ranking
Yahoo!				
AltaVista				
Excite				
Magellan				
Lycos				
HotBot				
Infoseek				
WebCrawler				

TABLE 10.3 **Submission and Ranking Log**

Now you see why you don't want to mess with an outside service and why I'm against initially submitting to anything more than the most popular search engines and directories. The process of submitting your site is not trivial. Neither are the other promotion methods. Surely, you didn't think you would get off the hook that easy—as you'll see in the next chapter, where we're going to be looking at non-Web-based marketing concepts to promote your Web site.

Flanders & Willis's Reality Check

If you own your own domain name, put your URL on everything you can—letterheads, business cards, anything you give away as a promotional item, any advertising, billboards, and so on.

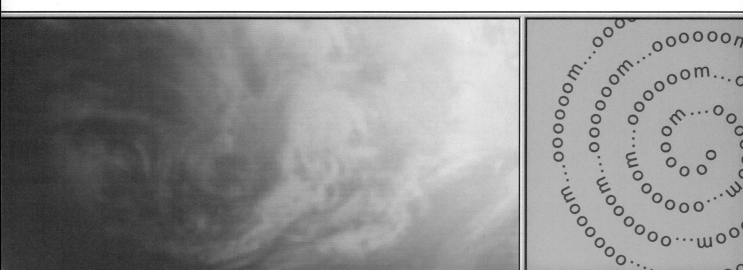

CHAPTER 11

Other Ways to Market Your Site

IN THIS CHAPTER

we're going to look at some of the other ways to market your site. Besides search engines and directories, there are at least a dozen or so other ways to market your site on the Internet. You can break these methods into two major categories: the *free* methods and the *cost* methods.

Since your ears probably perked up at the word *free,* I'll talk about these methods first.

But (and there always is one) while *free* does mean there should be little, if any, dollar outlay on your part, it doesn't mean you won't spend valuable time using these methods—because you will. After covering the free methods, I'll devote much of the chapter to the cost methods. However, *cost* doesn't just mean money; besides implying a dollar outlay, the word *cost* may also mean significant time will be spent.

As I've said before, your work is never done. You should always be marketing your site. I'm going to finish up the chapter by giving you some ideas that will help you market your site. Some stuff might seem obvious—checking out the competition—but you might not have thought of periodically resubmitting your site to search engines or of subscribing to your competition's mailing list. I'll discuss these tips, tricks, and techniques, plus some others, at the end of the chapter.

MARKETING YOUR SITE FOR FREE

Everything on the Internet is free, right? Well, it isn't, but you wouldn't know it from talking to people. They think the Internet is a world of free content, free software, free bandwidth, free everything. Well, while much on the Web isn't actually all that free, there *are* some free ways to market your site.

These methods are the ones worth focusing on:

- Bookmarks
- Reciprocal links
- Link exchanges and banner ads
- Web rings
- USENET
- Press releases and publicity

Ask Visitors to Bookmark Your Site

This technique is the simplest one for getting people to come back to your site. Not everyone will purchase something or inquire about your services the first time they visit. You need to get visitors to come back, so you might as well ask them to bookmark your site. It costs nothing. It's easy. Of course, it always helps if you have some content on your pages so your visitors will *want* to come back. One of the nicer graphics I've seen asking you to bookmark a site is shown in Figure 11.1 and can be found at `http://www.wilsonweb.com/webmarket/`. This is also a wonderful site for Internet marketing and promotion material. Figure 11.2 shows a bookmark image that appears on the CD. Use this image as a reminder to your visitors to bookmark your page. You can, of course, also create your own image.

Reciprocal Links

The premise of a reciprocal link is this: "I'll provide a link on my page to your page if you provide a link on your page to my page." Some search engines check to see how many links there are to a site—the more links there are, the more important the site must be, so they might rank the site higher.

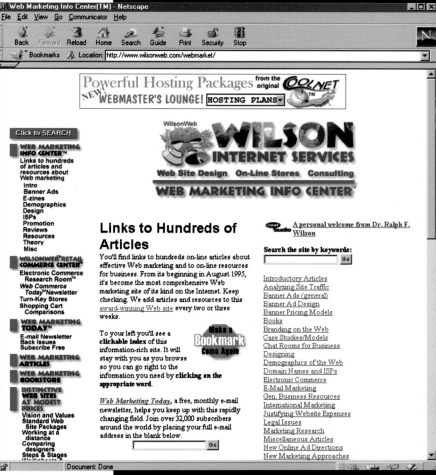

FIGURE 11.1 Bookmark this site—lots of Web marketing info. Wilson Internet Services
(`http://www.wilsonweb.com/webmarket/`)

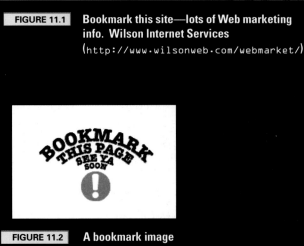

FIGURE 11.2 A bookmark image

You'll find a lot of people who say you need to spend time trying to get as many reciprocal links as you possibly can. I personally don't like the concept of reciprocal links because it never seems like a win-win situation. Usually, one of the sites is "more important" than the other and so it becomes an uneven trade. Spend your time developing content. When you have content, people will want to link to your site and you don't have to offer anything in return.

Link Exchanges and Banner Ads

I haven't spent a lot of time trying to understand the subtleties of how link exchanges operate. It looks to me like a link exchange is where unsuccessful or marginally successful sites put up banner ads for other unsuccessful or marginally successful sites in an attempt to increase traffic. Most banner spaces worth anything at all cost money. So, while you shouldn't necessarily turn down free banners, be aware of the fact that they may not exactly be prime real estate.

Web Rings

Some readers may not be familiar with the concept of a Web ring so I'll quote from the source itself—Webring (`http://www.webring.org`). Figure 11.3 shows their home page.

FIGURE 11.3 **Webring offers a way to link sites together.** (`http://www.webring.org`)

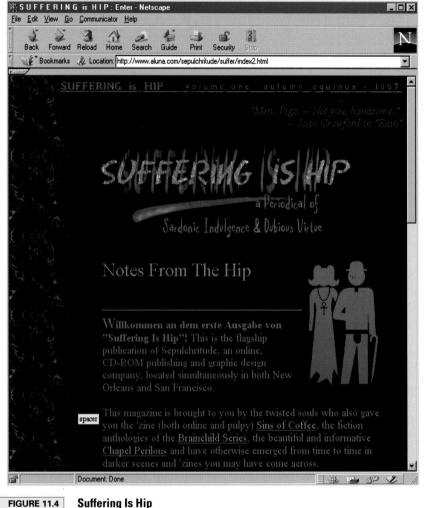

FIGURE 11.4 **Suffering Is Hip**
(`http://www.aluna.com/sepulchritude/suffer/`)

"The Webring is a way to group together sites with similar content by linking them together in a ... ring.... you can click on a 'Next' or 'Previous' link to go to adjacent sites in the ring and—if you do it long enough—end up where you started."

Figure 11.4 shows just one of the many sites you can access on Webring. This one was in the Small Press 'Zines ring.

Interestingly, the concept is catching on and may actually generate money—for Webring. Their spiel to advertisers is they are a new version of the search engine. For example, instead of using a search engine to find sites on computer graphics, you can just go to one of the graphics rings and then proceed as if on an Internet tour. Webring wants to sell advertising (who doesn't), and it's possible they might.

I'm not sure if this is a workable concept for your site or not. As much as I'm tempted to dismiss the concept as another bad idea, I'm not going to fall into that trap. I'm not afraid to admit that I don't know—and I don't.

USENET

USENET is comprised of the 30,000+ newsgroups on the Internet. It's like a great big bulletin board where you can post your own messages and read messages others have posted. On the down side, USENET is where you find most of the pornography, left- and right-wing wackos, conspiracy theorists, people without a life, and so on. On the plus side, it contains newsgroups on serious topics, such as AIDS and mental health. Almost every topic imaginable and unimaginable is on USENET.

USENET is also where you'll see *spam* messages about how to get rich quick, fill out chain letters, and other multilevel marketing malarkey. *USENET spamming* is the posting of one article to a large number of inappropriate groups.

Some people think USENET can be used to market your site *if* you are subtle about what you're doing. When someone asks about the value of the herb Valerian as a sleeping aid, you don't post a message saying, "I sell a sleeping compound made out of Valerian." What you're supposed to do is respond about how good/bad Valerian is and then insert the plug in your signature line:

```
Vincent Flanders,
http://www.herbal.com
Herbs that won't kill you
```

The readers of the newsgroup posting will see your signature line and put two and two together: "Ah, he sells herbs. Valerian is an herb. He must sell Valerian."

Every so often a story appears about how somebody posts messages to a USENET group, gets new customers, and through word-of-mouth builds up a successful business. Yes, it's possible. But what is always overlooked in these articles is the business in question is a very, very nice vertical market and the main reason the site is a success is because the business stresses customer service as its number one priority. If the company had lousy customer service, this story would *never* make it into print.

Yes, you *can* post to USENET and become a success story, but posting to USENET won't make you a success. Here's my take on using USENET to promote yourself or your business: *Don't post messages to USENET.* Why? People are easily annoyed if you post something that they don't feel is acceptable on that particular day, and then you set into motion a whole series of correspondence that isn't very nice. Personally, I stay away from USENET—except to see what's happening in the alt.music.byrds newsgroup.

Press Releases and Publicity

Most publications don't give a left-handed flying farkle about a new Internet site—unless it has killer content—so sending out a press release about your Web site is a waste of time. However, *specific* publications may be interested in your new products. Don't send e-mail or a press release about your vitamin business to a heavy machinery publication. They just don't care. What's worse is when they get your material they're going to be so mad that they're going to send out evil thoughts—thoughts so evil you could wind up on permanent bed rest! (Hey, I have the right to try and scare you. It's for everyone's good.)

I've listed this topic as a "free" method, but it isn't necessarily free. If you use the mail to send your press release, there's postage and printing expenses…

Lists of Newspapers and Magazines You're going to need a list of newspapers and magazines for any publicity campaign.

For newspapers, I suggest N-NET (`http://www.n-net.com/`). It's a wonderful listing of all the newspapers in the United States. It might be a little too wonderful; it includes magazines and a lot of papers you probably won't be interested in using.

For magazines, I suggest Yahoo! (`http://www.yahoo.com/Business_and_Economy/Companies/News_and_Media/Magazines/`), which has a good listing (broken down by categories) of the different magazines that have Web sites. I haven't found an all-inclusive magazine list, but I'm still looking.

TOO COOL

IT'S A SECRET

Don't spread the word about these sites—most of them aren't that well known. It's to your advantage to not let your competition know about them.

MediaFinder from Oxbridge Communications, Inc.

(http://www.mediafinder.com/) This site bills itself as follows: "For subscription, advertising and mailing list rates & info for 90,000 US & International Print Media & Catalogs." What is of interest to you is MediaFinder provides directories of magazines, newspapers, newsletters, and periodicals that include phone numbers and the name of certain members of the editorial staff. No addresses are given. It will, however, help you target your promo materials with a rifle shot rather than a scatter gun approach.

Public Relations Online Resources and Organizations

(http://www.impulse-research.com/impulse/resource.html) Very good list of links that you have to wade through.

Direct Contact Publishing's Comprehensive Media Guide to More Than 3,000 Magazines, Professional Journals, Trade & Consumer Publications!

(http://www.owt.com/dircon/mediajum.htm) Provides the URLs for magazine Web sites ranging from Woodshop News to Textile World. Once you find the category where your product fits, visit the site to find the e-mail address for the editorial department.

e-mail MEDIA (Peter Gugerell)

(http://www.ping.at/gugerell/media/) This is a list of worldwide e-mail addresses for media companies ranging from Accountants on Line to Women's Wear Daily. The list is rather old and, hence, somewhat suspect. But it is nevertheless interesting.

E-mail Press Release Services Comparison (http://www.urlwire.com/email-releases.html)

You can also pay to have your press release sent by e-mail to different organizations. This article reviews these different services.

Some other valuable links you should check out include:

The Care and Feeding of the Press

(http://www.netpress.org/careandfeeding.html) Although it's oriented toward reviewing software, this is another great inside look at what editors want and don't want to see. Remember: you do not want to piss off people who buy ink by the barrel.

A Publicity Primer (http://lamar.colostate.edu/~hallahan/hpubty.htm)

Includes "Ideas for Generating News about Your Organization," "Publicity Materials Checklist," "4 Keys to Success," and "3 Ways to Generate Publicity Coverage."

Press Releases

(http://www.msn.fullfeed.com/~djournal/press.html) The Wisconsin Desktop Journal provides some very helpful instructions on how to write and send press releases.

14 Tips for Sending Effective Press Releases (http://www.azstarnet.com:80/~poewar/writer/press.html)

The title says it all.

Organizing a Press Release

(http://www.custard.co.uk/prguide/organise.html) Just what it says.

If you have a product for the computer industry, perhaps the most insightful look into the editorial process is provided by Andrew Kantor, editor-in-chief of Internet Shopper magazine. As a former associate editor at a computer magazine, I wish I had had this list to send to the vendors in the marketplace I was covering. (You can also find these tips at `http://marketing.tenagra.com/releases.html`.*)*

PRESS RELEASE TIPS FOR PR PEOPLE

by Andrew Kantor, Editor-in-Chief, *Internet Shopper*

Published with permission.

I get a gadzillion press releases every day. I also get half a gadzillion phone calls, many about those very press releases. Most of the mail ends up in the garbage (or the trashcan, depending), and many of the phone calls aren't returned.

In a seemingly unending effort to help public relations people get the hang of giving me—and, I believe, other press people—information we can use, here are my Tips for Getting Your Press Release Read and Mentioned. There are only eight; I'd like to expand it to ten eventually.

1. Know who you're writing to and what we want. I get a lot of releases that we never use (promotions, new hires, non-Internet products), and a look at an issue or two would make that obvious. Yes, I know you've simply pulled me from your database as "computer-magazine editor," but those databases are sophisticated enough nowadays that you can filter on the type of release you sent.

2. Think whether it's something we'd cover. Again, if you read the magazine, you'll see that we rarely if ever mention new Web sites unless there's something very special about them. Still, I get calls and letters about such-and-such a company's new Web site. For an Internet magazine, that's not news, guys—everybody's on the Net.

3. Know my lead time. Monthly magazines typically have lead times of 2 to 4 months. Calling me on August 1 to say "I hear you're covering Net publishing in your September issue" doesn't make much sense. (This also applies if you're releasing a product in six months; refusing to tell me about it for secrecy reasons just means I won't write about it until a few months after it's available. That's bad for us both. Ask me; I sign NDAs.)

4. Don't annoy me with follow-ups. Trust the mail. Trust the Internet. Trust my fax machine. If you sent it, I got it. If I have questions, I'll call. (Sorry about the tone on this one. It's a pet peeve.)

5. Keep your database up to date. Press releases sent to editors who are no longer with us end up on my desk, and I almost always toss them. If you can't bother to check the masthead twice a year...

6. Remember that I'm an editor on deadline. Setting up a half-hour conference call with your president to tell me about your new product—when a press release would have given me all the relevant information—just wastes your time and annoys the editor. Like #4 says: If I'm interested, I'll call you with questions. Really!

7. Get my name right. It's not hard to spell. (And try to get the title right, too: "Andrew Kantor, Editor-in-Chief.")

8. Don't be familiar. I don't have a nickname in my signature. I don't use one in real life. If you use one in a press release (for example, "Andy"), I get cross and throw it out. (The same goes for a voice mail message—as soon as I hear "Hi, Andy," I hit the Erase Message button. I'm not joking.) You wouldn't call Rich Santilesa "Dick," would you? So, unless you know me, don't use a nickname.

MARKETING THAT COSTS MONEY

Although you can get a lot of mileage out of "free" resources to publicize your site, there's nothing like spending cash. The trick is not to spend it all promoting a Web site.

Don't get suckered into spending large sums of money on promoting your Web site on the Web.

Let's get real. If magazine ads, television, direct mail, or any other activity is what's generating sales, don't neglect these avenues just because there's this new medium called "The Web." Here are the cost methods we'll be talking about in this section:

- URL everything
- Direct mail
- Advertising in your normal media
- Banner advertising
- Paid services
- Software

URL Everything

If you own your own domain name (for instance, I own `herbal.com`), put your URL on everything you can—letterheads, business cards, anything you give away as a promotional item, any advertising, billboards, and so on. Figure 11.5 shows one of my favorite examples of clever URL placement:

FIGURE 11.5   **Trader Joe's supermarket bag**

Don't Use Your URL Unless It's a Domain Name   Virtual paths don't count. If your URL is *www.zzzzzzzz.net/~mycompany*, don't use it. Why? I know of an example where the Internet Service Provider moved a company from one machine to another. The URL changed from ***www**.zzzzzzzz.net/~mycompany* to ***www2**.zzzzzzzz.net/~mycompany*, effectively making obsolete every promotional piece the company created. This is another reason you should own your own domain name.

Direct Mail

You don't necessarily need direct mail to announce to the world that you've got a new Web site, but let me tell you this, direct mail should be an incredibly important part of your regular marketing program. If you want to see how important direct mail can be, see the sidebar "Direct Mail Marketing—Keep It a Secret" for some magazines that will help you understand the ins and outs of direct marketing.

Advertising in Your Typical Media

Unless you've created a purely Web-based business, you've been advertising in newspapers, on radio, on television, through direct mail, and so on. Don't stop advertising in these media.

Your Web budget should be *in addition to* your regular media budget—it does not *become* your media budget. Don't rob Peter to pay Paul.

Banner Advertising

A banner ad is an advertisement that is placed on a Web page, and that uses animation, cute jingles, and other enticements to get the viewers to click the ad and go to the sponsor's site where they'll hopefully buy

something. Originally, the term *banner ad* signified a horizontally oriented ad at the top of the page, but it's been bastardized to be just about any ad located anywhere on a page.

If you're thinking about paying to take out a banner ad on another site, you've probably got the kind of money where you can afford to hire a media-savvy advertising agency to help you plan your marketing strategies. It's a good idea to do both.

Paid Services

There are truckloads of companies out there who will be glad to take your money. I haven't tried any of them, and I suggest you at least try doing it yourself before you spring for the money. If you need a list of companies that specialize in this service, try `http://www.yahoo.com/Business_and_ Economy/Companies/Internet_Services/Web_Services/Promotion/`.

Software

Although I've purchased one product to assist me in my marketing efforts, I've never had the time to test it out. Like most products, I'm sure some people swear by it while others swear at it. For a list of software (Windows-based) try Dave Central at `http://www.davecentral.com/webpro.html` or Windows95.com at `http://www.windows95.com/apps/webauth-promote.html`.

MORE MARKETING TIPS, TRICKS, AND TECHNIQUES

In this section, I'm first going to point you toward some of the marketing resources on the Internet, where you can learn everything you've ever wanted to know and more about marketing. Then I've got a few tricks up my sleeve to show you.

TOO COOL

MARKETING SITES ON THE INTERNET

These are some of the cool sites I've discovered that cover a wide range of topics. I think they're valuable. Check them out.

Yahoo! (http://www.yahoo.com/ Business_and_Economy/Marketing/) Start off at Yahoo's marketing site. The next site is Yahoo's marketing magazine site.

Yahoo! (http://www.yahoo.com/ Business_and_Economy/Magazines/ Marketing/) The place to start for magazines about the topic of marketing.

Web Marketing Info Center

(http://www.wilsonweb.com/ webmarket/) One of the best resources on the Internet that deals with marketing. You could and should spend days here. What Dr. Ralph F. Wilson has done is something everyone should be doing— providing content. The main business at the Web Marketing Info Center (WIS) is Web design, online stores, and consulting, but Dr. Wilson realized that no one really cares to visit another Web page designer's site, so he created a marketing information site that attracts customers. He also offers an e-mail newsletter on marketing.

NetMarketing

(http://www.netb2b.com/) This site is an adjunct to *Advertising Age* magazine, one of the most well-known marketing magazines in the business. It's quite good; spend time at this site.

Internet World

(http://www.webweek.com/) God, I love these folks. Without them, we wouldn't be writing this book. Besides the usual sections on news and design, they have an excellent section on Marketing & Commerce. Check it out.

American Demographics / Marketing Tools

(http://www.demographics.com/index .html) What can I say? Great sites, great info that goes beyond the Web. Remember folks, marketing existed long before the Web did.

Guerrilla Marketing Tactics

(http://www.gmarketing.com/ tactics/weekly.htm) An off-beat, yet accurate look at Web marketing.

The Mining Company

(http://marketing.miningco.com/) Another excellent site.

NetProfit

(http://www.netprofitmag.com/index.htm) Great site with a heavy emphasis on Web marketing.

Advertising World

(http://advweb.cocomm.utexas.edu/world/) Bills itself as the Ultimate Marketing Communications Directory.

Periodically Resubmit Your Site to the Search Engines

The search engines come back and revisit sites at different intervals, so it is especially important to resubmit your site after you've made major changes—for instance, after implementing the suggestions in this book (adding content, limiting the size of your files, creating useful site navigation, and so on).

Check Out Your Competition

This is pretty elementary, but you'd be surprised how many people fail to check out their competition. Check out your competition's Web sites. You'll be surprised at what they put up there. Because Internet time is so much faster then press time (the lead time for a magazine ad or article ranges from 2–3 months in advance), there's a chance you'll find out what the competition is up to and be able to react faster than if you found out about it in the trade press.

Keep Checking Your Competitors' Sites

It's not uncommon to check out your competitors when you're first putting up a Web site. That's fine, but if your competitors are smart—and never underestimate your competition—they'll be updating their site. A big mistake you'll probably make is to stop checking their site. I understand your logic. You've got to spend 200 percent of your time building, updating, and marketing your site. Nevertheless, you *must* check your competitors out at least once a week to see what's new on their site. Why? Because an Internet site can go up immediately while a print campaign won't show up for 2–3 months. Your competition might put its new marketing plan up on the Net before it rolls out in print.

Put "checking the competition" on your list of things to do Monday afternoon after you've gone to all the Monday morning meetings.

Be sure to bookmark your competition.

Get an Additional Internet Account at a Major ISP

I'm not suggesting you abandon your local ISP, but you want anonymity when you're visiting your competition. You never want the competition to know you've been visiting them, so if you have your own server (like most major corporations) or you're with a regional ISP that your competition could easily identify, you need an account with a major ISP. Why? Because almost all Web servers keep log accounts of visitors. Using Herbal.com as an example, let's say I visit a competitor's site that sells herbs. They're reviewing their log record and see that a visitor from `herbal.com` or `lightspeed.net` (my local ISP in Bakersfield, California) has been to their site; they might get suspicious. If they see a visitor from `earthlink.net`, they wouldn't be as suspicious. Just for the record, I have nothing to do with Earthlink—they were just the first name that popped into my head. I could have just as easily said AT&T.

Subscribe to Your Competition's Mailing Lists

Make sure your e-mail name is nonidentifiable—like `b49a@earthlink.net`. Also put a bogus name in the Real Name field. You should use a bogus name anyway because some forms can grab your name from the e-mail field or if you're requesting a mailto: link. If your competitor asks visitors to join an e-mail mailing list to get the latest information, you'll be able to sign up without them suspecting anything.

Don't Put Anything on Your Web Page You Don't Want the Whole World to Know

If you've read the preceding material, there's a chance your competition has also read it. And if you're smart enough to be checking your competitor's site, then they're smart enough to be checking your site. They might even be reading this book right now.

In the next section, Michael and I ask an all-important question.

CODA

"Hey, what did we learn today?"

That's how the ending segment on a comedy news program called *The Daily Show* starts.

Ask yourself the same question.

Your initial response is probably "How to keep your Web pages from sucking like a bilge pump," but that's not the "right" answer. Yes, there is a right answer to this question.

Here's the right answer: "How to improve your Web pages so people write you checks with lots of zeros in front of the decimal point." *Web Pages That Suck*—the book and the site—is about making money.

When Web designers bring up the subject of money, they also have to bring up the dreaded subject of "The Client."

The relationship between artist and client is extremely delicate. What the client brings to the relationship is money and, generally, a complete lack of taste about art, design—hell, just about everything. The designer brings to the relationship taste, talent, and an awareness of what works in each medium—a fact that's extremely critical in Web design. A designer can create a print ad that takes up 100Mb of disk

space because disk space is irrelevant. You can't have a Web page that's even 100K.

Hopefully, the client will defer to the designer's vision—but then again, we all hope for world peace. More often than not, the client wants Rome built on their desk yesterday for $20 and they're not loathe to shove their weight around because they know the designer "has to take it." What does a designer do?

Well, if you're a successful designer—meaning that you've been in business for at least one year—you already know the answer. You have to take it. When the client says, "I think this first sentence on the front page of my Web site should be bigger and in red and the second sentence should be even bigger and in blue," you should try to persuade them of the error of their ways. But—the client is always right. Well, let me amend this statement. The client is always right when the check clears.

With the information we've provided in these last three chapters, you should be well on your way to putting together a successful Web-based marketing effort. Get started right now!

ABOUT THE CD

The CD included with this book is full of useful stuff. First, it contains all of the images we created, plus links to all the sites mentioned in the book. We've also included Software That Doesn't Suck. We've chosen products that meet two important criteria: 1) They serve an important function for people designing for the Web; 2) They stand out among the other tools for one reason or another. We recommend you check them out as you design your pages—they could make your life a lot easier or more interesting.

You can also link to WebPagesThatSuck .com, where you can access any updated information to the book, which will only be available to the purchasers of this book. You can access these links directly from the CD.

NOTE FOR WINDOWS 95/NT USERS

To install the software from the CD, either use the CD's installation interface or install the software directly from the CD. To access the CD's installation interface, double-click on ClickMe.exe.

To access the images, HTML pages, and links mentioned in the book, click the Authors' HTML by Chapter button in the CD's installation interface.

NOTE FOR MACINTOSH USERS

To install the software from the CD, select the executable file in each programs folder.

To access the images, HTML pages, and links mentioned in the book, select the Index.htm file in the HTML folder.

STUFF FROM THE BOOK

The images, HTML pages, and links are organized by chapter, as shown in the Figure A.1. Let's say you want to take a look at some of the sites critiqued in Chapter 2. To get to these links, click the Chapter 2 link in the left-hand frame. Figure A.2 shows the Chapter 2 page.

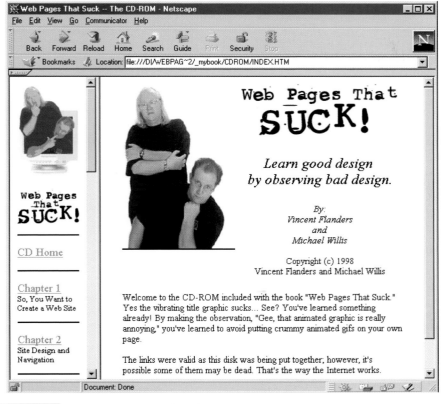

I've organized the sites into various categories: Informational Sites and Sites Critiqued and/or Mentioned in This Chapter. To obtain updates on Chapter 2, click the "Chapter 2 Updates…" link.

The links to outside sites were valid as this disk was being put together; however, it's possible some of them have since changed or are simply dead. That's the way the Internet works. Check out the Web site for updates.

SOFTWARE THAT DOESN'T SUCK

The following demos/shareware programs are included on the CD-ROM. These are the programs that we think don't suck. It should be noted that not every program we like is on the disk. Many programs we like and use every day are not available for inclusion on a CD-ROM. Some companies didn't want to sign our authorization form and instead had their own 1,000 page form—it became too complicated for us to deal with.

For more software that we like, please notice the programs we mention throughout the book. We've tried to include all of the best products or product review resources available on each topic. Additionally, as new software is added to the list, you can find those updates on WebPagesThatSuck.com under "Software That Doesn't Suck Updates…." Please note that these updates are only for purchasers of the book. For specific installation instructions, please consult the CD's Readme.txt file as well as the Readme.txt file included with each program. (Windows 95/NT users click the CD Info button in the CD's installation interface to access the CD's Readme.txt file.)

BoxTop Software's GIFmation Demo (for Windows 95/NT and Mac)

BoxTop Software's GIFmation (`http://www.boxtopsoft.com`) is a program that creates and optimizes animated GIFs for cross-platform animation application. It offers a lot of features like preview controls, small file sizes, and cool effects like onion skinning.

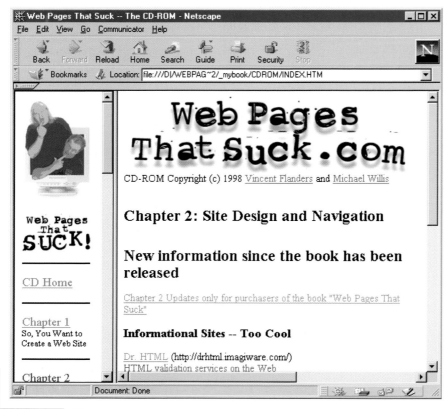

Chapter 2, "Site Design and Navigation"

DeBabelizer Pro Demo
(for Windows 95/NT and the Mac)

This tool, from Equilibrium (http://www.equilibrium.com), is a cross–platform, automated graphics, animation, and digital processor for Web and desktop-publishing productions. It allows you to apply filter effects, color corrections, and text overlay to images with scripting.

Eye Candy 3 Demo
(for Windows 95/NT and the Mac)

Check out Alien Skin's (http://www.alienskin.com) Eye Candy 3. It has 21 filters for paint programs that support Photoshop APIs. The 19 additional effects include texture, distortion, and production filters, as well as specialized effects.

BoxTop Software's PhotoGIF 1 Filter Demo
(for Windows 95/NT and the Mac)

BoxTop Software's (http://www.boxtopsoft.com/) PhotoGIF Filter is a program that optimizes GIF images.

CoffeeCup StyleSheet Maker ++ Shareware
(for Windows 95/NT)

CoffeeCup StyleSheet Maker ++ (http://www.coffeecup.com/) lets you quickly create compelling Style Sheets.

GIFBuilder Demo
(for the Mac)

GIFBuilder (http://www.gifbuilder.com/) is a scriptable utility to create animated GIF files on the Macintosh.

GIF Movie Gear 2 Demo
(for Windows 95/NT)

GIF Movie Gear (http://www .gamani.com/) by gamani productions is a program that creates and optimizes animated GIFs. Its preview-window picture show allows you to try it out before it goes on your Web page.

HomeSite 3 Evaluation Version
(for Windows 95/NT)

Allaire's (`http://www.allaire.com`) HomeSite 3 is a pure HTML editor. You simply put your cursor on a page where you want tags to appear, and then click a button or select a menu item and voilà—it's all there for you.

HTML Power Tools Test Drive Demo
(for Windows 95/NT)

HTML Power Tools (`http://www.opposite.com/`) will aid you in the Web design process. Utilities include HTML Meta Manager, HTML PowerSearch, HTML PowerAnalyzer, plus more.

HTML Rename! Shareware
(for Windows 95/NT and the Mac)

HTML Rename! (`http://www.visiontec.com/`) renames files so they run on different operating systems.

HVS ColorGIF 2 Demo
(for Windows 95/NT and the Mac)

HVS ColorGIF 2 (`http://www.digfrontiers.com`) is a plug-in that, among other things, reduces the size of a GIF image. This software works with paint programs that support the Photoshop APIs.

INeverMETAMan

This free program helps create META tags, which are used by search engines to index your site according to the keywords and descriptions you use. It also includes other META functions such as page refresh.

Paint Shop Pro 4.14 Shareware
(for Windows 95/NT)

JASC Software's Paint Shop Pro (`http://www.jasc.com/`) is an image viewing, editing, and conversion program.

Ulead's GIF Animator 2 Trial Version
(for Windows 95/NT)

GIF Animator (`http://www.ulead.com`) helps you create and optimize animated GIFs.

Ulead's SmartSaver 3 Trial Version
(for Windows 95/NT)

SmartSaver 3 (`http://www.ulead.com/`) optimizes your image files.

Ulead's WebRazor Trial Version
(for Windows 95/NT)

WebRazor (`http://www.ulead.com`) is for Web imaging and animation; it's designed for use with Photoshop and FrontPage.

WebGraphics Optimizer 2.04
(for Windows 95/NT)

Web Graphics Optimizer (`http://www.webopt.com`) is a great tool for optimizing and compressing images for your Web pages.

WinZip 6.3 Shareware Evaluation Version
(for Windows 95/NT)

WinZip (`http://www.winzip.com`) compresses files into archives used for distributing and storing files.

C

SOFTWARE THAT DOESN'T SUCK AND MORE

The CD contains the made-up sites and many of the images we created in the book, plus links to the sites we mention and to WebPagesThatSuck.com, where you can access any updated information to the book.

The CD is also packed with Software That Doesn't Suck, which you should check out as you're designing Web pages on Windows 95/NT and Macintosh. This software could make your life a lot easier. For more information on these products and the platforms they run on, see the Appendix.

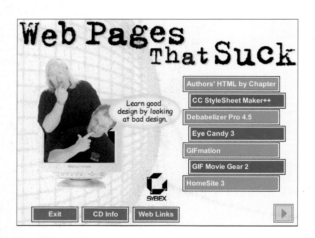

BoxTop Software's GIFmation Demo
creates and optimizes animated GIFs for cross-platform animation application.

BoxTop Software's PhotoGIF 1 Filter Demo
optimizes your GIF images.

CoffeeCup StyleSheet Maker ++ Shareware
lets you quickly create compelling Style Sheets.

DeBabelizer Pro 4.5 Demo for Windows 95/NT and DeBabelizer Pro Lite LE Demos for the Mac
apply filter effects, color corrections, and text overlay to images with scripting.

Eye Candy 3 Demo contains 21 filters for paint programs that support Photoshop APIs.

GIFBuilder Demo creates animated GIF files.

GIF Movie Gear 2 Demo
creates and optimizes animated GIFs.

HomeSite 3 Evaluation Version
is a pure HTML editor.

HTML Power Tools Test Drive Demo
aids you in the Web design process.

HTML Rename! Shareware
renames files so they run on different operating systems.

HVS ColorGIF 2 Demo
reduces the size of a GIF image.

INeverMETAMan
helps create META tags, which are used by search engines to index your site.

Paint Shop Pro 4.14 Shareware
lets you view, edit, and convert images.

Ulead's GIF Animator 2 Trial Version
helps you create and optimize animated GIFs.

Ulead's SmartSaver 3 Trial Version
optimizes your image files.

Ulead's WebRazor Trial Version
is for Web imaging and animation.

WebGraphics Optimizer 2.04
optimizes and compresses images for your Web pages.

WinZip 6.3 Shareware Evaluation Version
compresses files into archives used for distributing and storing files.